W9-BWI-461

TH3RD PARTY

VOL. II
STRANGE BEDFELLOWS

ENJOY THE STORY
ENVISION THE POSSIBILITIES !

STEVEN NEMEROVSKI

Wasteland Press

www.wastelandpress.net
Shelbyville, KY USA

Third Party:
Volume II: Strange Bedfellows
by Steven Nemerovski

Copyright © 2016 Steven Nemerovski
ALL RIGHTS RESERVED

First Printing – August 2016
Paperback ISBN: 978-1-68111-128-5
Hardback ISBN: 978-1-68111-129-2
Cover artwork is derived from original oil painting "Eagle" by Marcel
Kahhak (2009), Kahhak Fine Arts & School, Carbondale CO,
Phone: 970-963-5901, Web: www.mkahhak.com

This novel is a work of fiction. Names, descriptions, entities, characters, places and incidents included in the story are either products of the author's imagination or are used fictitiously. Any resemblance to actual persons, business establishments, products, events and entities is entirely coincidental.

NO PART OF THIS BOOK MAY BE REPRODUCED IN ANY FORM, BY PHOTOCOPYING OR BY ANY ELECTRONIC OR MECHANICAL MEANS, INCLUDING INFORMATION STORAGE OR RETRIEVAL SYSTEMS, WITHOUT PERMISSION IN WRITING FROM THE COPYRIGHT OWNER/AUTHOR

Printed in the U.S.A.

0   1   2   3   4   5   6   7   8

FOR MY GIRLS
NANCY, LISA, LAUREN & ELIZABETH
ILYMTTWW

ACKNOWLEDGEMENTS

I knew that writing Volume II of the *Third Party* novel series would be more challenging than Volume I. The story and plot are more complex and I decided that Volume II had to stand on its own. That required weaving sufficient background from the Volume I plot and characters into the early passages and striking a delicate balance. It also meant that I had to lean more heavily on my support team, particularly with respect to editing.

Barb, Tom, Dave, Ed and Guy got the short straws and fought their way through the early manuscripts. Heidi found missing ingredients, particularly when it came to character development and what I call "flavor." Susan stepped up again regarding punctuation and syntax. As with Volume I, Nancy gave the final blessing before I handed the final manuscript off to Tim at Wasteland Publishing.

I would like to give special recognition to Andy for assistance with Illinois election law, to Rye for the cover design and layout and to Dawn for her usual excellent typing support.

I am grateful to everyone for their help in making Volume II the best it could be.

CHAPTER ONE

Writer's block? This can't be happening!

By his own calculations, Nat Carson had written over ten thousand columns. At least half were under the *Chicago Tribune's* banner and the rest for his Springfield-based rag *The Back Bench*. The topics of his long-ago past as a beat writer fresh out of Northwestern's Medill School of Journalism covering the city's West Side—scintillating debutante sightings, riveting amateur sports team results, frightening man-bites-dog reports—had, to his great relief, fallen away quickly, allowing him to cover education. Ultimately he'd found his true professional love: lampooning the sleaze of City Hall. How he'd transitioned to Springfield politics remained a bit of a blur, but it had led to the creation of his own mini daily and blog. In the end, that was all that mattered.

Writing *The Back Bench* meant freedom from the editors who always knew better, from the meaningless deadlines and, most important, from the constant need to feed the bureaucracy with his whereabouts and schedule. It didn't hurt that his income had more than tripled over the years, either.

So why, so many thousands of articles later, was he in this shroud of mental impotence? It should be a snap to enlighten the world to the crazy, upside-down results of the preceding day's election with wit and accuracy; a slam dunk to best the *Trib*, *Sun-Times*, and *Daily Herald*. The political reading world was chomping to get another taste of Nat Carson's spin. Well, maybe not chomping, but at least waiting expectantly for the insight that had separated *The Back Bench* wheat from the rest of the chaff for over fifteen years.

Nat pushed back from his desk. The laptop cursor throbbed at him like his headache, but with a lot more guilt attached. Most days Nat could go from his notes to pushing the print button before you could say *Meet the Press.* As recently as Monday, on the eve of the election, he had spun half a dozen stories about the candidates and their concluding maneuvers along with pieces paraphrasing last-minute trash talk the Democrat and Republican PR whores had thrown at him. And, to even the score, some fluffier crap from the upstart E Party.

So what was up with this fucking writer's block?

It was the most stunning upset in the history of Illinois politics. E Party candidate Tom Robinson Jr. had been elected, in no particular order, the state's first Black governor, the state's first third party governor, and the state's first Baseball Hall of Famer-turned-governor. Yet, suddenly and inexplicably, for the first time since that goofy freshman year class on existentialism, Nat was suffering from erectile dysfunction of the brain.

Just start typing, asshole. Get over it.

Nat stared at his fingers hung poised over the keyboard, willing them to hit the keys.

The E Party was only in its second election cycle, but had already endured a tsunami of negative attacks from both the Democrats and Republicans in attempting to become the country's only effective, competitive third party. In its short two-year existence, it had faced every dirty trick in its opponents' playbook of slanderous personal attacks and Election Day mayhem, constantly vilified by the talking heads on the right at *Fox News* and on the left at *MSNBC.* In the most insidious and clever assault, its leaders, Alex "Atlas" Stein and Gen. Samuel Huntington Smith, had been indicted in the matter of *U.S. v. Stein* on bogus, politically induced tax fraud charges resulting in the freezing of all of their personal accounts as well as the E Party political funds.

Miraculously, E Party candidates for lieutenant governor, comptroller, and treasurer had also won, and the party had increased its presence in the Illinois legislature from fourteen representatives to twenty-five, and eight senators to fourteen. Moreover, its first slates of legislative candidates in Pennsylvania, Iowa, and Indiana had all managed to disrupt the majorities held by Democrats or Republicans in those states.

Recount? You bet your ass! That was Nat's prediction, anyway. The Republicans would spare no expense to prove that their candidate for governor had not lost by less than one tenth of one percent of the vote from over four million cast.

This is your fifteen minutes of fame, buddy, Nat reminded himself. *Fire up the damn laptop and get going.* Or better yet, it couldn't hurt to catch forty winks, maybe 'til 5 a.m. or so. Get a fresh start. He could still crank out an edition by six. He'd done some of his best writing in the wee hours, hadn't he?

For once, it wouldn't be at the end of an all-night binge.

* * * * * * *

As Nat Carson was self-diagnosing his brain cramp and considering a quick snooze, the assembled E Party celebrants at the Sheraton Grand Chicago were inventing new adjectives to describe the moment. Governor-elect Thomas "Jackie Jr." Robinson, the celebrated baseball superstar, was thinking about how different this experience felt from, and yet was reminiscent of, winning the division championship. To his right, Atlas, the E Party's founding father, was feeling a gamut of emotions centered around a lifelong career in resolving large-scale episodes of post-traumatic stress—a career that had allowed him to save literally thousands of lives. Tonight, he sat reflecting on how far they'd come on this unpredictable, impossibly arduous, yet wonderfully uplifting journey. Across the room, Atlas's partner-in-crime, General Smith, a highly decorated veteran responsible for all E Party ground troops, was feeling the letdown of exultation born of the cessation of hostilities. At his side, Julie "K.C." Covington-Stein, Atlas's bride and long-ago staffer on the winning side of Kennedy beats Nixon, was finally giving into the pent-up, complex range of emotions she'd been carrying with her like a constant companion.

Nothing in their collective psyche could ever have anticipated the emotional high of the E Party's victory in the Illinois governor's race, the remarkable culmination of a three-year journey to demonstrate to the entire country the potential benefits a third party could bring to an empty, dysfunctional political system.

The final vote tallies had not been confirmed until just short of 3 a.m. It was now approaching sunrise. Champagne, e-mails, texts, calls, tweets, and the outpouring of emotions had been flowing non-stop for hours.

* * * * * *

When the final tally for governor was tabulated at Cook County Democratic Headquarters, the remaining diehards and staffers still assembled held a collective pregnant pause with the same thought: Was it a win or a loss?

For the second consecutive biennial campaign, the party's grip on the Illinois General Assembly had loosened. Prior to the advent of the E Party, they had held unassailable majorities in both the House of Representatives and in the Senate for over a generation. They were now reduced to numbers formerly attributed to the lowly Republicans: 25 out of 59 seats in the Senate and 54 out of 118 seats in the House. It seemed an eternity since those numbers were 33 and 67, but in actuality, such dominating totals were only a few years in the rearview mirror.

Heading into election night, the Democrats held all six statewide offices. Within seven hours of the polls closing, they had barely hung onto attorney general. The E Party now boasted four out of six, and the Republicans had, inexplicably and tragically, captured the patronage-rich secretary of state slot. No one in the room could recall a time when the Democratic Party of Illinois had held only one statewide office.

Heading into the weekend before the election, the polls had shown their candidate for governor running second to the Republican in a tight three-way race. Surely, the prowess of the Democrats' Election Day machinery would make the difference. But, under the category of "ours is not to reason why," their party chairman—the all-powerful Speaker of the House, David Kennedy—had orchestrated a last minute, seventy-two hour, no-holds-barred campaign to elect the E Party candidates for governor and lieutenant governor.

Their local political leader, Cook County Democratic Party Executive Director Danny Ryan, had deployed every available resource, human and financial, in an attempt to honor the Speaker's unorthodox demands. And though it might not have been his to reason why, Ryan couldn't help but wonder what the hell had just happened.

The question on everyone's lips at headquarters remained: Was it a win or a loss?

* * * * * * *

While Democrats throughout the Land of Lincoln were playing mental seesaw and the E Party was embracing the still reverberating thrill of victory, the Republicans were adamantly refusing to acknowledge the agony of defeat. They were in possession of the same vote tallies as the entire Internet-connected world. They could add them backward, forward, and sideways. And as long as two plus two equaled four, Robert Allen, their candidate for governor, would have 3,582 fewer votes than Tom Robinson.

Elizabeth DiMaggio, their leader and mastermind, had bet the ranch, the enchiladas, and her party's unborn children on an Allen victory. Every penny and every second had been dedicated to ensuring a Republican would take up residence in the governor's mansion for the next four years.

Scott Grusin, their national party chair, had similarly committed untold resources. For five consecutive presidential campaigns, Illinois had been as blue as the Mediterranean. Grusin had viewed Robert Allen as a critical link to twenty electoral votes in the next contest for the White House.

Three thousand five hundred eighty-two votes, DiMaggio kept repeating to herself. Less than one-third of a vote per precinct and too many decimal points to the left to correctly pronounce. On the worst election morning-after of Elizabeth DiMaggio's political life, she could not begin to contemplate raising the five million or more it would take to challenge the results. She had no clue as to why or how, but Speaker Kennedy had stolen, had *hijacked*, another election. One way or another, she and her party would get the answers and reclaim their stolen property.

CHAPTER TWO

Ever since Danny Ryan had been anointed executive director of the Cook County Democratic Party, he and Nancy Rae Mitchell, his most trusted and cherished accomplice, had celebrated après election in exactly the same fashion. Once all the tallies were verified and the staff released, they'd open the first bottle of Chivas Regal and trade hyperbole of once and future victories, then open a second bottle, which would be handed back and forth until one of them passed out. The one who remained upright was responsible for making certain the "loser" was safely situated before securing a cab home.

The next day, no matter how late it was, or how fierce the hangover, they would complete their ritualistic celebration with a trek to Leo and Heather's Irish Deli for greasy whatever and talks of vacations contemplated but never taken.

In the early years, the party included Danny's wife, Shannon. But that was before Danny had succumbed to the celebratory Scotch before Nancy Rae, presenting a scenario even the most understanding wife might question. It was one thing for the Ryans to entertain the beautiful, sexy Nancy Rae Mitchell on their couch in an alcoholic stupor, but entirely another not to know exactly where her husband had slept—or, potentially, with whom. One thing had eventually led to another. Danny Ryan was now free to wake up wherever it suited him.

This year's designated bout of inebriation had more or less ended in a tie. With a groan, Nancy Rae awoke at headquarters with her head face down on a cold steel table, her nose bent in an interesting shape. If her head didn't hurt so much, she'd be elated. Somehow she'd avoided the bed of chip and pretzel residue that Danny had apparently been using for a mattress on the floor. They'd never even made it home last night...correct that, this morning. With the closest coffeehouse too far to navigate given the pounding in her head, she nudged Danny awake with her foot. To hell with tradition. This was an emergency. An emergency that called for warm Diet Coke and leftover pepperoni pizza. At least until they made it to the deli.

The charm of Leo and Heather's Irish Deli is that it has none. Dating back to the zenith of Chicago's meat packing district, it occupies the same South Side corner where the first draft was poured and the first plate of C&C—"Chicago's finest corned beef and cabbage"—was served. Fourth-generation owners and wait staff represent the only changes to an otherwise perfect blend of comfort food and locals. Other than the Irish whiskey—the seasoning of choice in most of the dishes— the fact that Leo and Heather's had become a favorite haunt of the Democratic Party chieftains, including visiting national luminaries, was its worst kept secret.

It was also where Danny Ryan had held patronage court for many years on alternating Tuesdays and Fridays, dispensing jobs and mediating disputes among rival Democratic committeemen. The infamous Shakman decrees, a series of legal rulings to limit city-wide political corruption, had allegedly ended patronage—at least the kind that was openly bartered at Leo and Heather's and other neighborhood joints across the city. With insiders now wearing more wires than watches, the shake-of-the-hand and the report-for-work-on-Monday verbal contract had morphed into clandestine exchanges much further down the political food chain.

Nancy Rae well remembered her first meeting with Danny Ryan at Leo and Heather's. She was the foster child of a precinct captain and had, in short order, demonstrated the cunning and tenacity the party coveted. Wielding her uncommon beauty like a sword, Nancy Rae had been projecting a come-hither sex appeal at an age when most young women were still stuffing their training bras. To his credit, Danny instantly grasped the untapped intellect and hustle that belied her relative youth. That had been almost twenty years and umpteen plates of C&C ago. Now they were each other's best friend and confidant, and they had a silent pact to serve and protect, no matter the cost.

The short cab ride from headquarters this morning was absent of small talk. Even hungover, Nancy Rae was formulating her agenda, saving it for their time in their customary corner booth.

Once the waitress had taken their orders and they had mugs of steaming jet fuel and a full pot in front of them, she began.

"Danny, you made a promise to me last year. At this very table, as I recall. I have been waiting patiently for this day. It's time for you to honor your commitment."

Danny moaned. "Are you kidding? Now? My head feels like it's being crushed by an anvil."

Nancy Rae felt a twinge of remorse. But only a twinge. "Too bad."

"So…what…? Are we getting married?" Danny's words mocked, but his eyes shone.

"No," she chuckled lightly, "and don't change the subject."

"Okay, okay, I give," said Danny, pouring his second cup of coffee.

Nancy Rae plowed on. "I'm determined to make you crunch some brain cells here. On the other hand, I hadn't figured on your sleeping on the floor."

Danny shook his head and closed his eyes in pain. "Last thing I remember is that great decision to finish the bottle in one ginormous swig before carting you off. Next time, remind me that 'waste not, want not' does not apply to a four-shot equivalent of 80 proof. Either that, or at least remind me to sweep the floor before we crack the seal on the first bottle."

Nancy Rae grinned.

"Listen, Danny," she said, and her tone was suddenly serious. "I really just want to say thank you."

Danny looked at her curiously.

"Okay," he said. "I'll bite. For what?"

"Just…thank you," she said. "For always looking out for me. You've never sold me short. Not ever."

"That there's a heavy line, Rae. Care to expand…expound…fill me in?"

Nancy Rae smiled sweetly. "Happy to. But not until we take off."

Danny put his mug down heavily. "Come on, Rae. I'm not prepared for riddles today."

"Take...off," Nancy Rae repeated slowly. "You know, as in the trip to Mexico we're taking a week from Saturday. I bought the tickets right after Tom Robinson announced for governor. Come on, tell me you don't need to get away."

Danny looked at her with big raccoon eyes.

"Yeah," said Nancy Rae. "Exactly. Plus, you promised me a post-election vacation. I expect you to honor that promise."

"Stephanie," Danny called to the waitress, "we're gonna need lots more coffee here."

* * * * * *

While Nancy Rae Mitchell had been busy delousing Danny Ryan of pretzel crumbs with Scotch tape, the dwindling E Party celebrants had concluded that champagne and caviar was not the breakfast of champions. On a whim, their political guru, Mark Stone, had whispered an inspired suggestion to Atlas. Then, all it took was a nod and a phone call.

Lou Mitchell's, on Chicago's Near West Side, is to breakfast what Leo & Heather's is to Irish fare. Since its opening in 1923, Lou's loyal customers could not remember ever seeing a "Closed For Private Event" sign posted on the door during the breakfast rush hour. Today, that changed.

For the past two-plus years, Lou Mitchell's had been home to regular clandestine information exchanges between Mark Stone and Nat Carson. From the day Mark had slipped Nat the dossier on the first group of E Party legislative candidates, the passing combination of Stone to Carson had scored many editorial touchdowns. Mark's well-timed news tips had also resulted in a welcomed bump in *The Back Bench's* subscriber base.

Today, nestled in adjoining back booths, Illinois Governor-elect Tom Robinson and the original E Party cadre were honoring a self-imposed cell phone abstinence in a sop to their brains. In a sop to their stomachs, they were ingesting the best omelets, toast, potatoes, and coffee ever.

The group was unusually subdued. Contemplating the journey completed? Resisting notions of the adventure ahead? It was their resident public relations genius, Lisa Boudreau, who fired the first shot heard round the table. "So...now what?"

They all laughed as the bubble of silence above their heads popped. Atlas, more prone to action than contemplation, pointed a finger at Lisa. "Exactly. Now what?"

"Don't ask me why," said the General, "but I was just running the second Gulf War through my head. The Bush team spent all that energy deliberating and then executing the war, but when the victory was upon them it was as if they hadn't prepared for the inevitable."

"Well, I certainly hope the Robinson administration isn't facing the task of nation building," K.C. said.

"Amen to that," said the General. "I know we've just won the political battle. But honestly, I'll be damned if I've thought much about the long-term mission ahead."

"I'm betting none of us have," Atlas said. "Let's face it. Until Speaker Kennedy called last Thursday and offered to put Tom over the top, well, we didn't have a snowball's chance in hell. I'm dying to know what he had to do to swing the election our way." He held up his hands. "Then again, maybe I don't want to know. How much time do we have?"

"Well, without the benefit of a copy of the State Constitution, I believe the governor of Illinois is inaugurated on the second Tuesday in January," Mark said. "Let's call it two months."

"Two months, eight weeks, fifty-six days...who knows?" said Atlas. "What I do know is that I'm fried. I'm guessing all of you feel the same way. Physically *and* mentally. So here's what I suggest. We all take the next two weeks off. K.C. and I are long overdue for our belated honeymoon. As in, don't call. Don't text. Don't tweet. Don't even think about us."

"Great plan," said Mark. "But that's not how it works. Not in reality. Whether we like it or not, we are now on the clock. Under the microscope. All those clichés times ten. Anyone willing to venture an over-under on the number of press inquiries on Lisa's iPhone in the ninety minutes we've been incognito?"

"So the E Party goes rogue?" Atlas inquired. "What's the downside if we drop off the face of the earth for a couple weeks?"

"Well, one thing's for sure," said Lisa, "it's never been done. Winning campaigns take about two minutes to reboot before they start spinning their victory. Political honeymoons last only so long. Of late, that time seems to have shrunk to the size of a sound bite."

Atlas elbowed Tom Robinson. "Governor? What's your pleasure?"

"I assume you mean other than sleeping for the next seventy-two hours," Tom said. "I haven't even thought about being governor, if that's what you're asking. Based on this conversation, I may ask for a recount if the Republicans don't."

"How about 'make no decision before its time,'" said K.C., "as long as we're running with the clichés. Especially while hungover, sleep deprived, and unprepared. The only real problem I'm hearing is that the press needs its usual quantity of red meat. Beyond that, I think John Q. Public doesn't care what we do until Tom is sworn in." She turned to Lisa. "What do you think, Lisa? How do we feed the beast? And do we have to?"

"Screw the press," said the General. "Sorry, Lisa. But in the military they pushed us to leak crap at every turn. We're at war and the media prima donnas act as if they're entitled to know the plans in advance. Twenty-first century war—the ultimate spectator sport. Bull...shit! One thing that's worked for the past two years is that we handled those assholes strictly on a need-to-know basis. Why should that have to change?"

"I know I brought it up," Lisa said, regretting it, "but this is not a conversation I'm ready to have today. I agree with the General that we've had a successful, albeit unusual, run with the press. I'd like to keep it that way until we can't anymore. General, you've given me a great idea for a diversionary tactic. Mark, do you think Nat Carson can be coaxed to join us for breakfast?"

"Coaxed?" Mark echoed. "He'll come in his boxers."

E-MAIL

To: Atlas, K.C., General, Mark
From: Lisa Boudreau
Sent: 11/6 3:00 p.m. (CST)
Subject: Carson Interview

Tom and I thought the interview went particularly well, especially the part about "don't call us, we'll call you!"

Wishing everyone well on their downtime and their travels. Looking forward to Thanksgiving with Team Atlas in Aspen.

* * * * * *

THE BACK BENCH
"If you let it slip, we catch it"
November 7

In modern political America, victorious candidates for higher office spend the morning-after hitting the train stations in a ceremonial thanking of the mushrooms. And, of course, under the lights of TV cameras all too willing to help spread the manure. This is generally followed with a sweep of the morning shows, providing an equally ceremonial victory lap of sound bites to an allegedly adoring public.

As it turns out, Governor-elect Tom Robinson took his victory lap at Lou Mitchell's over fresh-squeezed, eggs, and toast before heading off on a much needed and deserved respite with family and friends.

Before taking his leave, he and E Party public relations maestro Lisa Boudreau granted me a brief interview. The full exchange is posted on the blog. Below are excerpts of our discussion:

Back Bench: Tom, Mr. Governor-Elect. Let me offer my congratulations. Are you as stunned as I am by the election results?

Robinson: I don't know if stunned adequately describes the moment. With all that the E Party has been through, no one could have predicted this outcome.

Back Bench: The most obvious question is, what's next? Something tells me you are not heading to Disney World.

Robinson: (chuckling) You know, I always wanted to use that line. It would have meant my team had just won the World Series and I was voted MVP. Any major leaguer would kill to cash that daily double ticket. Actually, I'm heading to Texas for a week or two of R&R. No phones, no Blackberry. In fact, the entire E Party leadership team has declared a two-week sabbatical. Don't call us, we'll call you.

Back Bench: Can't say I blame you. The past months certainly had to have taken their toll.

Robinson: It was especially tough on my friend, Alex Stein, aka Atlas. He was warned up front that things would get ugly if he found success with his third party idea. But that was some kind of ugly. The man's entire body of work, not to mention his integrity and reputation, was this close (gesturing) to, how would you say it…well…extinction. This is his victory, not mine. The entire E Party operation is due to his vision and a small, but very mighty, army. And, let's not forget, he afforded me the chance that allowed me to climb down off the ledge following a deliberate campaign of vicious rumor-mongering.

Back Bench: Come January, you'll have a new address at the governor's mansion in Springfield. What happens to Atlas—and General Smith?

Robinson: Probably the same thing they've been doing their entire lives. They'll find a mission and bring it home. For my sake, I hope that mission continues to be the E Party. There are great things to be done.

Back Bench: To that end, what do you see as your priorities?

Robinson: That was actually one of the topics at breakfast today. I think it was Lisa Boudreau who put it out there. *Now what?* And the thing is, I don't know for sure. Obviously there are a variety of tough issues to confront and we're already on the clock. You know how strongly I believe in the team concept, Nat, so assembling a team that can find a winning formula is critical. But you also have to appreciate that during its short existence the E Party has attempted to redefine victory within the confines of American politics. After what this state has been through, ethics and civility will dominate the culture of my administration. During the campaign, I was reminded about a saying that President Reagan had on his desk to the effect that you can do great things if it doesn't matter who gets the credit. That's what the E Party is about and that's what the Robinson administration will be about. Sure, I'd love to see the Getting to 21 program become a reality as soon as possible. But unless we rebuild the government's team and get that "we" mentality working, I can't see where any other priorities make sense.

Back Bench: Pardon me for stepping on your toes, Governor, but that sounds pretty Pollyannaish. There's an entrenched bureaucracy that chews up and spits out the best-intended politicians.

Robinson: There's a scary thought. And for that reason alone, I don't see rushing the process. The collegiality I'm talking about is not a creature of the inauguration. I've got a four-year contract. That, to me, is a workable time frame.

Back Bench: Fair enough. But you still have to turn on the lights day one.

Robinson: I'm pretty sure that will happen. We'll regroup in a few weeks. One thing I can guarantee. Politics as usual stops at the door to the capitol. Too many of our elected officials forget where the campaign ends and where governing begins. We will not hire to the polls nor govern to the polls. I think it was the first Mayor Daley who said 'Good government is good politics.' Somewhere along the line, we've turned that one on its head.

Back Bench: Thanks for your time, Governor. I'm sure the entire state of Illinois joins me in wishing you great success.

In other news...

CHAPTER THREE

The tradition dates back to Roosevelt's defeat of Hoover in 1932. At a particularly tumultuous moment in American history, the chairman of the Democratic National Committee invited the chairman of the Republican National Committee to a post-election détente. A modicum of one-upmanship was expressed, yet the occasion was not to gloat, but rather discuss the need to place national priorities above political bickering.

Over the years, a biannual post-election "discussion" between the two parties' leaders has become a ritual. The event usually takes place in either New York City or D.C., with an occasional detour to L.A. The losing chairman is afforded the choice of location, and the winner, by custom, pays the tab. No matter how vicious the rhetoric during the campaign, the respective party leaders well understand it is never too early to plot the course for the next election cycle. They, more than anyone else, understand the necessity of perpetuating the two-party system.

It was a mid-term election with a Democrat occupying the White House; it would have been aberrational for the Republican not to host. Mid-terms are generally brutal to the party of 1600 Pennsylvania Avenue. Therefore, it was RNC Chairman Scott Grusin who greeted his guest, DNC Chairman Eddie Cobb, in a private room at one of New York City's most exclusive clubs.

Chairman Scott Grusin is as cool and smooth as the underside of a pillow. Fourth-generation from one of Philadelphia's mainline families. Graduated at the top of his class with an MBA from the Wharton School of the University of Pennsylvania. Chairman of the family's manufacturing conglomerate at the age of thirty-seven following his father's untimely death. Distinguished by his inventive management style and impeccable insight, particularly during board meetings.

The Grusin family had a reputation for unbridled, competitive aggression in the business arena, and young Scott had not disappointed in that regard. During his stay at the helm revenues grew tenfold; profits, a staggering twentyfold. By the time he handed his proxy over to his children, Grusin Industries had become a member of the Fortune 100 privately held companies.

Scott Grusin's segue from the family dynasty coincided with his ascendency within the Republican Party. Shortly after assuming the reigns of the party, however, he realized that the demands of a dual chairmanship were insurmountable. He had worked a lifetime of magic at Grusin Industries. Under the circumstances, his goal was to direct any magic left in the wand toward political pursuits.

DNC Chairman Eddie Cobb was another matter altogether. Where Grusin exuded class, Cobb exuded crass. Grusin's competitive drive had always remained within the boundaries of conservative business ethics, even as he was exploding the family business. Cobb's creation of a West Texas oil drilling equipment monopoly was the product of every unseemly maneuver this side of not quite indictable. On those occasions where the line was crossed and charges threatened, Cobb's undeniable political acumen always managed to carry the day.

Strange bedfellows? Perhaps. But Grusin and Cobb got along famously. Party chairmen, not unlike presidents, understand and appreciate all too well the pressures their successors and competitors constantly face. It's easy to cast aside methods when there is a shared madness.

The first round of drinks was devoted to friendly banter about the outcome of the congressional races. Grusin gloated over taking the House. Cobb congratulated his adversary, not so subtly reminding him that in the face of an extended recessionary cycle, wars from which the public had long ago grown tired, and the endless venomization from *Fox News*, the Republican gains were underwhelming. His Democrats still held the Senate and the number of governor slots changing colors had also been minimized. Grusin countered. Cobb's president scored the lowest mid-term polling grades of any commander-in-chief in decades.

The second round of drinks was devoted to bashing the media and cursing how much money campaign ads cost.

"Those duplicitous assholes," Cobb spat, his southern accent dripping. "Bastards decry the state of campaign advertising, then charge premium rates and laugh all the way to the bank. By the next election, they'll be Facebooked and Twittered to oblivion. I tell y'all what, too. I'll be first to shovel dirt on their graves."

The third round of drinks accompanied T-bones the size of Texas, thus allowing a sidestep of Cobb's usual commentary about the "pathetic things that Yankees serve for steaks." Grusin ordered steamed vegetables as his side. Cobb ordered his usual complement of artery-cloggers. Grusin held back a comment, well aware that Cobb didn't take well to criticism.

Cobb couldn't wait to start chewing on the E Party. "So, what do you make of them sons-a-bitches E Party?"

"What I make of them depends upon what game your Speaker Kennedy is playing in Illinois," Grusin chewed back. "Liz DiMaggio tells me we can easily pick up that governor's seat. That is, if your guy doesn't intervene on Robinson's behalf." He tossed a card on the table. "Here's a palm card to prove it. Never thought I'd see the Democrats in Illinois, of all places, passing palm cards with a third party candidate as their headliner. So, you tell me, Eddie. What should I make of it?"

"Whoa, brother." Cobb held up his arms. "Don't shoot when there's no white left in my eyes. You and I are both the cowboys here. It's Kennedy who's turned renegade. I've been all over the E Party. If you haven't noticed, their counsel's stiletto heels are tattooed all over my ass since their funds were impounded." He leaned across the table, lowered his voice, and extended his finest Cheshire cat shit-eating grin. "As if I had anything to do with the tax fraud case filed by the Department of Justice against Stein and General Smith."

"You're telling me that the Democratic Speaker of the House in Illinois is off the reservation? And you know nothing about the crap they pulled to get Robinson elected?"

"On my mother's grave." Cobb raised his right hand as if in court. "Nothing."

"I'll need a little more than your mother's grave on this one, Eddie."

Cobb nodded. "And I can get you there right quick," he said. "I assume y'all plan to file an election challenge."

Grusin shook his head. "Not likely. In Illinois, any margin over two hundred votes is virtually impossible to overcome. Least that's what Liz DiMaggio tells me. And Robinson leads by over three thousand.

"Three thousand five hundred and eighty-two, to be precise," said Cobb. "Like I said. I'm all over this."

"Well, you may be all over it," Grusin said, "but this is not the land of hanging chads. If David Kennedy made this happen, we can't forget that the Illinois Supreme Court is his wholly owned subsidiary. Given that, I'm not inclined to waste the five-plus million dollars DiMaggio tells me the recount could cost."

"Now listen here, Grusin," said Cobb, pointing his finger with the enormous golden longhorn ring. "I'm telling you that will be the best five mil you ever spent. First of all, if you don't challenge, the redistricting map that gets drawn could be devastating for both of us. Second, my gut tells me you'll win." Cobb gave his gut a hearty pat. "And this baby ain't never wrong!"

"Eddie," Grusin said, suddenly sober. "I'm telling you this. If we contest the election—and by the way, I concede that having a Republican governor in control of the redistricting map would be worth risking five million—then you had better be light years away. Or Atlas Stein and his chain-dog counsel Elaine Richards will hunt you down and have you drawn and quartered. And I cannot—repeat cannot— afford to be associated with your business-as-usual nonsense."

Eddie put on his best Texas Hold'em poker face. "Light years it is," he agreed. "But this is a significant and timely opportunity, Grusin. And I suggest there are plenty of other ways to slow down this E Party juggernaut. Things we'd better get to asap or live to regret. Starting with redistricting."

* * * * * *

As soon as he was convinced that Cobb was out of earshot, Scott Grusin relished a spontaneous outburst of uncontrolled belly laughter emblematic of both his great performance and the undisputed domination of his foe that evening. The Republican accomplishments during the election were undeniably compelling. The people had spoken, their mandate was clear, and Grusin had used the occasion to lodge a proverbial stick in Chairman Eddie Cobb's eye. Their biennial gathering had produced agreement on a number of key political issues, including a plan to decimate the E Party.

It would be an all-out, take-no-prisoners assault, the likes of which had never been contemplated, even in the scummiest annals of American politics. Best of all, Cobb had made it abundantly clear that he was working to hand the governorship of Illinois over to the Republicans. Frankly, Scott didn't care how or why, as long as it was Cobb's fat, greasy fingerprints, not his, that would mark the crime.

* * * * * * *

As soon as he stepped out of Scott Grusin's lair, Eddie Cobb lit a fresh cigar, savoring both it and his flawless performance at dinner. He had dominated his foe one hundred percent. Talk about shoving the proverbial stick up his opponent's you-know-what! The icing on the cake was their collaboration on some of the more sticky political issues, including a plan to flatten that damn E Party and to control the decennial redistricting process.

Eddie rubbed his hands together at the thought of such an all-out, take-no-prisoners assault. One that would give free rein to his truly dazzling abilities as a political assassin. It's what made American politics so great. Best of all, he was about to unleash his inner James Bond to perpetrate the subterfuge that would change the world as they knew it. Regrettably, the brilliance of his sophistry would, by necessity, never come to light.

* * * * * * *

After her most recent mission impossible, a herculean three-day effort to transpose Democratic votes for governor to the E Party candidate, Tom Robinson, Nancy Rae Mitchell found herself reflecting on the past twenty-plus years, more than twelve of them as girl Friday (aka the Black Pearl) to Danny Ryan, as though she were contemplating retirement. In fact, she was. At least from politics.

Operation E Party—that was how she still thought of it—was the stuff of political legends. But now it was over. Still, the facts were indisputable. In the twenty-three precincts for which she and her team had responsibility on Chicago's South Side, Robinson had, on average, tallied an astounding 75 percent of the votes cast. These were Democratic Party strongholds where anything less than an 85 percent plurality for the Democratic candidate is justification to neuter the committeeman.

With the benefit of the Ryan imprimatur, Nancy Rae had parlayed her political relationships into an annual, seven-figure lobbying gig. In its simplest form, lobbying is about generating votes favoring the client's desired outcome. And if there was one thing the Black Pearl understood, it was how to apply her cunning and seductive ways to achieve success. Assign Nancy Rae Mitchell a legislator on a particular piece of legislation and, no matter how complex or controversial the issue, you could be sure her record of scoring the vote would remain intact.

Nancy Rae looked at her phone, surprised to see how much time had passed. She ordered another glass of sauvignon blanc from the cute, attentive bartender in the airport lounge and took a long appreciative swig. She didn't often get time to herself, but found she required more and more of it to balance the rest of her crazy life. She thought back to when the E Party was in its formative stages and seemingly so vulnerable. How Danny Ryan had asked her to obtain its source code from the handsome, winningly honest Tom Robinson. Speaker David Kennedy himself had tasked Danny with identifying the E Party's brain trust and, even more important, their financial backers. Danny, in turn, had naturally tasked Nancy Rae.

Though Nancy Rae well understood strategies necessary for conquering your run-of-the-mill male legislator, she'd been completely flustered about how to approach a nationally beloved sports icon. Her decision to transform herself into Nicolette Lawson, reporter for the *National Politics Quarterly*, had been an inspired choice. Too bad the whole thing had been an utter failure. A fiasco, in fact.

Not only had she failed to secure the information the Speaker so desperately coveted, the outcome had landed her in a year-long funk bordering on depression. Tom Robinson was unlike any person she had ever known, and the world in which he traveled was unlike anything she had ever experienced. He was unwaveringly compassionate toward the common man and had a zest for life that her kind abhorred and worked to destroy. His caring and devotion to the betterment of young Black ghetto kids had been nothing short of inspirational. Knowing Tom had made Nancy Rae more aware of her own duplicitous nature... and more aware that, like a coat she'd outgrown, that nature might not fit so well anymore.

When, she had asked herself on a daily basis since then, had "Illinois politics" and "inspirational" had seats at the same table—or on the same planet? Lincoln's era? Certainly not during the reigns of the recent string of governors currently wearing orange prison jumpsuits.

Her keen intellect only exacerbated things. As Nicolette Lawson, Nancy Rae had easily been drawn into fascinating and scintillating conversations with Tom Robinson on topics with context and meaning. After three months as a satellite circling the man's intellectual universe, how was she supposed to return to the day-in, day-out land of "Hey, doll, watta you say?" "Just fuck doze guys!" and "I don't give a shit how you do it. Just get 'er done!"

Nancy Rae remained adamant, however. There would be no keeping her down on the Cook County political farm. And she was determined to repay Danny Ryan's loyalty and kindness by taking him along.

Speaking of... where was Danny anyway? The flat screen at O'Hare gate C-14 flashed: FLT. 936 BOARDING IN 14 MINUTES.

I never should have agreed to let him meet me at the gate.

Nancy Rae checked her cell phone and the boarding sign for any new input. Her emotions alternated between nervous-angry and anxious-excited. Either way, whatever happened, she was leaving. They both knew it. She planned to start over. She'd made that very clear. She wanted her partner-in-crime to share the journey with her. She couldn't have been clearer on that either.

Suddenly, there was a voice over her left shoulder.

"Hey, good-looking. Imagine meeting you here."

Danny Ryan's hackneyed wit was a bald attempt to avoid a scolding at his down-to-the-wire arrival.

It worked.

* * * * * * *

Atlas Stein's instructions to Liz had been honored to every exacting detail. She'd been his assistant for over forty years, but only very recently, following his unexpected elopement and marriage to K.C., had she seen his romantic side. Workaholic bachelor into his early seventies finally marries his college sweetheart after the death of her husband. Who could blame him for jumping in feet first? Atlas, more than anyone she knew or could imagine, deserved such a Hollywood ending.

He'd laid it out to her in his usual concise fashion. "Watch the Hitchcock classic *To Catch a Thief*. Think about the honeymoon Grace Kelly would choose to have with Cary Grant. Create an unforgettable, luxurious, and romantic escape. Spare no detail and certainly no cost."

With the exception of a picnic overlooking the Mediterranean outside Cannes, trying to channel Grace Kelly was no easy task. But, with the benefit of a week of advance work in the French Riviera under her belt, Liz had dug into the research like the librarian she had planned to be before Atlas had met her all those years ago and invited her to become part of his team. She knew that in this case she would exceed his and his bride's expectations.

The yacht she booked was appointed with every comfort known to royalty. It had sailed on schedule with a staff of thirty, trained and dedicated to indulging their guests' every whim and fantasy, 24/7. The chef was five-star caliber, as was the sommelier and wait staff. There was an on-ship concierge. The yacht docked in the Maldives and used the Hotel Du Cap as their land base.

She imagined Atlas and K.C. filling their days with sightseeing, deep sea fishing and diving, and unmitigated relaxation. She pictured their evenings, the on-board helicopter whisking them off to enjoy unique, romantic repasts of the local's finest offerings and venues. Despite his staggering wealth, she knew that Atlas had never ever indulged in this level of luxury before. What better time than now when he was celebrating his marriage to the love of his life and the political coup of the millennium?

CHAPTER FOUR

Spencer Hawkins had been tracking the E Party experience for the better part of a year. As a senior editor at *Time* magazine, he was charged with knowing when a trend or story rose to the level of national prominence, especially where the treasured cover was concerned.

The E Party had been on the cusp a few times. Brief sightings on both *Nightline* and *NBC Nightly News*, along with their two-year record of innovation and button-pushing, were remarkable. But with a down economy and a dumb-downed readership, decisions regarding content were increasingly more difficult and critical. For the YouTube generation, producing an informative, widely-read weekly was rapidly becoming an oxymoron.

R.I.P., *Newsweek*.

The post-election edition had been mapped out for months. The Republicans would dominate the mid-terms, pick up enough seats to take the House, and fall excruciatingly short in the Senate. They'd also win the bulk of the open governor slots. And voilà, the interminable race for the presidency would commence. Not much to captivate the hearts and minds of the average newsweekly reader.

Suddenly, *There, in the sky! Is it a bird? Is it a plane? No, it's Tom Robinson, Governor-elect of Illinois.* But how best to posture Robinson and his Superman aura on the cover of *Time* and support a story with potentially long legs?

Like many professions, if you stick around long enough, attend enough national-level trade association events, and learn the favorite late-crowd watering holes, you eventually know the people who matter, or know the people who know those people. Six degrees of separation not required.

Spencer Hawkins and Nat Carson had stuck, attended, and drunk enough, for long enough, to be in each other's Rolodexes before LinkedIn was a binary code in the womb. They were sufficiently close enough for Hawkins to admire the tenacity and skills required for Nat to build the subscriber base for *The Back Bench* and for Nat to feel the pain of his once-mighty journalist compatriot fighting to retain the level of respect and integrity that had been kidnapped by the seldom fact-checked Internet whirlwind.

It hadn't happened with guys at Spencer Hawkins' level—not yet. But on average, Nat was fielding at least one call per week from some once-revered, currently unemployed journalist desperately wanting to know how he'd put his run together. *There but for the grace of God,* he'd mutter to himself after each call.

When Nat heard Hawkins's voicemail begin, his heart sank in anticipation of yet another "Hey, old buddy, mind if I pick your brains?" entreaty.

Then the intent of the call became clear.

Nat, never one to physically move all that quickly, pounced on the replay button and put his brain on speed dial.

* * * * * *

E-MAIL

To: General
From: Atlas
Cc: Mark
Sent: 11/15 3:12 p.m. (CET)
Subject: Read any good books lately?

The Riviera is spectacular. A touch cool, but November isn't exactly high season. We haven't seen a cloud since arriving and the sunsets are breathtaking. K.C. has already made me take an oath that there will be at least one secluded multi-week vacation each year. Fact is—she beat me to it!

I'm risking her wrath by sneaking this e-mail, but I think I've found our roadmap for the Robinson administration. Check out *If We Can Put a Man On the Moon...* by William D. Eggers and John O'Leary. If nothing else, it's a guide for what not to do when running a government.

Cruising the Italian side today. Ciao!

* * * * * * *

When Nancy Rae surfed the Internet for vacation spots, she'd used keywords like "Cabo," "secluded," "relaxing," and "five-star." Las Ventanas appeared at the top of every search. What she overlooked was the fact that many guests found the resort by searching "romantic," "couples," and "honeymoon."

Accordingly, the front desk staff had shot them confused glances when Danny Ryan and Nancy Rae Mitchell checked into the two-bedroom cabana usually occupied by multiple couples. When the housekeeping staff gossiped about the handsome, bi-racial couple's separate sleeping arrangements, the speculation only grew. "Definitely not siblings," came the assessment.

Nancy Rae had never cared what anyone thought about her and wasn't about to start now. She was on a mission to chart her future, and this was the first phase of Operation Nancy Rae's do-over.

Danny Ryan had decided he was merely fulfilling a promise to a great and trusted friend. Because he had not been on a vacation longer than a weekend since honeymooning with his ex-wife almost ten years ago, it was already proving to be a shock to his system. There was that horrifying moment when he discovered that the sign posted above the registration desk requiring all electronic communication devices to be checked and stored was not a joke. Nancy Rae claimed to have been unaware of this "irritating little nuance" when booking the trip, but Danny saw the look in her eye and suspected foul play.

Their luxurious cabana was a sophisticated white-on-white with a wall of glass doors leading to the beach. Their private pool and spa offered respite from the afternoon sun and heat. The six bars, including the obligatory thatched-hut version specializing in sunset views and margaritas where they would start each evening before dining, were strategically placed for easy access.

For Danny, the first few days felt like the equivalent of jonesing from drug withdrawal. But on Dr. Mitchell's orders, the beach, margaritas, and daily massages were slowly doing their job to exorcise the demons of his frenetic lifestyle—so much so that on the second night, he'd slept for an unprecedented twelve uninterrupted hours, and the next morning had taken a long walk on the beach for the sole purpose of contemplating the soothing rhythm of the waves. He could now call Dr. Mitchell's emergency brain-dump procedure an official success.

The adorable sight of Mr. Take No Political Prisoners Ryan darting in and out of the Pacific Ocean and rediscovering his boyhood was the signal Nancy Rae was waiting for. They were sipping on after-dinner drinks on the third night of their stay.

"Isn't this heaven, Danny? I never thought I could endure more than two consecutive days of sun and surf, but I'm getting used to it. I'm thinking of taking up meditation."

Danny smiled. "All these years I thought that chips and beer and a Sox game was the height of relaxation. But I could get used to this."

It was the opening she needed.

"I'm just happy you're here with me, Danny. And now that we're both feeling so *relaxed*…"

Danny put down his drink. Something was coming and he wasn't sure he was going to like it.

"…I think it's time to discuss our future."

Yup. There it was, as predicted. Danny sat back, aggrieved. "There you go again, Rae. Ruining the moment. Isn't it enough that we're here at this beautiful resort enjoying each other's company and—and—"

"No, Danny," said Nancy Rae. "It's not enough. You were there when we agreed we would talk about it and that's what we're going to do.

"I want to get out, Danny. Politics was fine for a while. For a long while. But it's not fine anymore. If anything, our stay here has only reinforced my desire to take my life in another direction."

"Yeah? And where you gonna go, Rae? You've got a very lucrative lobbying gig. You've just proved once again that you're the best field operative there is. From where I sit, the Speaker has us perfectly positioned for the future, as you call it. Let's face it, we both know our candidate for governor was headed for defeat. It's thanks to you that Robinson and the E Party know we put them over the top. Plus, the Speaker still controls the Illinois House of Representatives. Am I missing something?"

Nancy Rae sighed a dramatic sigh and reached for her perfectly concocted pear martini. According to dining etiquette, it was really time for a fine port or something, but she was never one for sticking to the rules. "Actually, you are. You're missing the forest *and* the trees," she said. "Don't you get it? When you asked me to dig deep and run the traps on Robinson and the fledgling E Party, I took a walk outside our narrow political world. I always thought the sun and the moon revolved around the world of Illinois politics."

"Well, doesn't it?"

"Come on, Danny, listen to me. You dropped me into the deep end. All of a sudden, I'm hanging out with baseball icon Tom Robinson, someone who is completely outside the live, eat, and breathe politics that we take for granted. And I find out this guy's not only apolitical, but genuine."

Danny looked at her, surprised. "What exactly are you telling me, Rae?"

"Just this, Danny. At first, I didn't believe it. I couldn't relate to any of it. Robinson shows up out of nowhere and stays out front as a spokesperson for the E Party. He messages the benefits of a third party to every church in Chicago. Pretty soon he's all over the media. Yet when we sit down to talk about Tom Robinson so I can write the story of his life—okay, okay, *allegedly* write the story of his life—there seems to be nothing of the slightest interest to him in the realm of politics. I mean, the guy really isn't interested. He doesn't have a political gene in his body. It's non-stop baseball, kids, church, family. The next time it's the same stuff in a different order. And the next time."

"So?" said Danny. "I'm lost. Who cares what his life story might have been about? Had you been a real journalist and written it, that is. What's this got to do with your stellar career as a ball buster?"

Nancy Rae grimaced. "Danny," she said carefully, "I'm trying to tell you something. Bottom line is the man has values. And not just values, but character, too. He must be one of the last men standing who has faith in his country and his fellow man. It made me—I felt so—I just can't do it anymore. I hated myself for lying to him. For sticking a pin in that deep river of faith." Nancy Rae took another sip. "You know, just like that old cowboy in *City Slickers*, I have to go find that one thing."

If Danny caught the film allusion, he ignored it. "Rae, you're scaring me here. I'm hearing what you're saying, but…"

"Danny," Nancy Rae said. "I know this is hard. I know you don't understand. But think about it. Think about what I've said, okay? We can leave it here for now."

Danny nodded, but his face was etched with thoughts left unspoken—and they didn't look like pretty ones.

Nancy Rae placed her warm hand on his.

* * * * * * *

"Nat? It's Spencer Hawkins. How's my favorite political ragmeister?"

"Well, if it isn't Father Time," Nat said. "At least you're still breathing."

"Barely. We're not killing as many trees as we used to. Fact is, some of our editions don't have enough news content to justify turning on the presses."

"Yeah," Nat acknowledged. "Fuckin' Internet. Any monkey can put out a story and no one cares about the facts. The damn thing gets tweeted, takes on a life of its own. How do you compete with that?"

Spencer kept it going. "How do we produce a weekly in the world of instant news gratification? We haven't found a coagulant to stop the hemorrhaging. Not even close. But me? I'm on the down slope to retirement. Think about the lost souls who majored in journalism this past decade."

"Yeah," said Nat. "Never thought our so-called golden years would be such a coaster ride."

They paused.

"Well, *Time*'s not throwing in the towel just yet," said Spencer. "Which brings me to the reason for this call. I have an idea."

"That spells trouble," said Nat.

"Hear me out...I know you're the news maven of the E Party."

Nat scoffed. "I've got my sources, if that's what you mean."

"Modesty becomes you," Spencer said. "I've taken the liberty of reviewing your entire repertoire since their inception."

"So you're the one."

"Nothing like doubling your readership," Spencer parried. "I've got to hand it to you. Must have been some run."

"Time of my life," Nat said, meaning it.

"How'd you like to take that to the national level?"

"I'm listening," said Nat. "For a byline in *Time* and the right ka-ching? I'm all over it."

"Good. As I see it, one of the ways to keep weeklies relevant is to run serials. Give the reader a reason to stop by in consecutive weeks or months. If this E Party is the real deal, why not have a continuing update—the E Party saga. Penned by the one journalist capable of providing the insight and timeliness necessary to pull it off."

"Ahem," coughed Nat.

"Yeah, yeah," Hawkins said. "I have no doubt we can accommodate sufficient ka-ching to hold your interest."

"Not bad," Nat said. "Not bad at all. But, frankly, I have no interest in abandoning *The Back Bench*. I've got me a nice little niche. Sounds like the horse you're riding has gone from prohibitive favorite to long shot."

There was a short silence.

"How much time do I have to decide?"

"Well, if we can take Tom Robinson at his word from your last interview, the E Party is taking a two-week sabbatical. In a perfect world, I'd like to kick this off right after Thanksgiving."

"Well, this world's a far cry from perfect," said Nat, "so I'll need some slack. I won't hold it over your head, but you're right. There's no one else who could pull this off."

* * * * * * *

E-MAIL

To: General
From: Atlas
CC: Mark
Sent: 11/18 2:12 a.m. (CET)
Subject: Wake-up call

We've been cruising the Amalfi coast for the past few days. Now working our way back to France. None of this can be reduced to words, let alone an e-mail, but it'll have to do for now.

You can't imagine how the gentle swaying of a boat, the heavenly scent of seawater, and a staff ready to bludgeon you with warm milk and every freshly baked cookie known to mankind—not to mention the love of your life beside you—helps you sleep like a normal person.

But I'm still human. Yup, violated our self-imposed E Party code of silence after less than 48 hours. Thank God K.C. cracked first. And don't go getting all excited. We're limiting the chatter to meal times. Course, yesterday we took a four-hour lunch, so....

I'm betting the two of you are chomping at the bit, too. Let's face it. Two straight weeks of time off for good behavior? Until this trip, I think my personal record was less than 72 hours. We've sketched out some random thoughts and plans, and Liz will be forwarding a package to each of you later today. (Laugh all you want, but you'd be doing the same thing, I guarantee it.) There's a lot there, so just take your time.

Think I'll go see about those cookies.

* * * * * *

"Spencer? It's Nat. You got me. I'm definitely intrigued."

"That's what I hoped you'd say."

"Before I make your day, though, I have questions. Lots of them. All swimming around my Second City brain. How 'bout I catch a flight to New York this weekend. You can wine and dine me like the hotshot celebrity I've never been. We just might be able to make this happen."

"I can do you one better. E-mail your flight info. My assistant will book the whole trip. I do hope the Carlyle will be adequate for your newfound status."

Nat laughed. "If not, I can always upgrade."

* * * * * *

After the initial ninety-six hours of decompression on their luxurious tropical getaway, Danny Ryan's mind and body had lost the will to argue. It was as if he'd entered a transcendent state where politics and party spin didn't exist. Where the sea air and sun and the scent of the exquisitely alluring woman at his side was all that mattered. After ten years and ninety-six hours, Danny Ryan's libido had re-engaged.

Nancy Rae had again downshifted the conversation to her exit strategy over dinner the next evening. This time, she'd focused more on her need to put the last vestiges of life to date behind her. She'd never before shared all the details of her foster upbringing, for one. Or the sexual abuse she'd suffered. Appalled, he had listened, realizing for the first time the extent of her extraordinary strength. How it had transformed her crumbled existence into a highly successful political career...a highly successful life. He saw clearly for the first time that he'd never bothered to examine too deeply, or really at all, why Nancy Rae had so easily employed her physical assets to achieve her goals when circumstances called for it. For the first time, Danny felt he was beginning to understand the real Nancy Rae Mitchell.

He'd let her talk. When she described her undercover role as Nicolette Larson and her growing feelings for Tom Robinson, the feeling in his gut was akin to eating bad clams. For all these years, he'd left Nancy Rae to her own devices. All the better to plead plausible deniability. But even he was shocked by the lengths to which she'd gone to unearth Tom Robinson's E Party secrets, the complexity of her charade, and the countless hours she'd spent in his company.

It was then that his bad-clam gut had begun to churn with a lot more than compassion.

Now the big green monster of jealousy stung as it had when his fourth-grade crush Mary Sue Decreamer had spurned him with the abandon of a praying mantis. How had Nancy Rae fallen in (and out?) of love with Tom Robinson without Danny's noticing even the slightest difference in her demeanor? What did that say about him?

Danny's stomach continued to roil. How could he possibly provide the advice she was seeking with his emotions at such a dangerous intersection?

In an impulsive and daring gesture, he'd snaked his arm around the wine glasses to take her hand.

Nancy Rae had stiffened noticeably, but had not withdrawn it. After a moment, she'd relaxed and smiled a tentative smile. It was at that point they'd risen together and left the restaurant.

For the remainder of their stay, the hotel staff was pleased to note the continuous presence of the "Do Not Disturb" placard.

CHAPTER FIVE

Alexander "Atlas" Stein came from stout German stock. The story went that the family originally arrived in Chicago from somewhere around Leipzig, Germany, in early November, just in time for the onset of winter and the inevitable continuous parade of dreary stratocumulus. Chicago met the family's needs for its business connections, but the closest relatives were nearly 800 miles away in Philadelphia. Without the familial bonds with other hometown transplants, life could have been very difficult. Instead, the Steins were welcomed into the arms of the neighboring Schoenbergs and their first American Thanksgiving.

Decades later, Thanksgiving was still considered a special mitzvah in the Stein household. Atlas's mother had happily accepted the baton of hospitality when the Schoenberg matriarch passed away, expanding Mrs. S's blessing to include not only new neighbors, but those in need in the community. Her last such event had fed over 300 people at the local YMCA, in addition to the usual forty or so regulars who annually descended on the family residence.

In honor of his mother's memory, Atlas continued to be generous. Very generous. In this case, creating a seemingly obscure foundation that provided over two million Thanksgiving dinners to people each year through charities across the country.

Atlas was both proud and humbled by these efforts. Yet more and more he found himself home alone for the holiday. Especially since moving to Aspen. This would be his first Thanksgiving in a long time in the company of someone else—a lot of someone elses, as it turned out. When he'd known K.C. in college, he had no idea how big her family was.

* * * * * * *

E-MAIL

To: Atlas and K.C.

From: Liz

Sent: 11/21 8:16 a.m. (CST)

Subject: Thanksgiving

Welcome home! I loved all the e-mails and pictures. So happy the honeymoon lived up to expectations. Unpack fast, though, you two. Only 72 hours to review and finalize preparations.

Here's what to expect: The General and Mark have insisted on "surprising" you on your return to Red Mountain. Governor Robinson arrives the day after tomorrow. And Lauren is bringing her husband and the kids, but has elected to stay at The Little Nell where Lisa and her husband will also be. It seems they had some strange idea that if they stayed at the house they'd be doing a lot more work than the holiday warrants. They'll relocate to the house on Sunday when their families depart.

Now, for K.C.'s family. There are 18 Kerstens and 23 Covingtons arriving from Tuesday through Saturday morning. K.C.'s grandkids, Aunts Jane and Betsy, and Uncle Bernie will all be at the house. The balance will be at the Hotel Jerome.

At current count, there are 277 confirmations from the extended E Party clan. Not all of the accommodations have been finalized, but the Aspen Skiing Company assures me it'll all be taken care of by close of business tomorrow.

The "feast" will be held at the Jerome. I am still working on meals, skiing arrangements, etc., through the weekend. Planning activities for kids of all ages is a new one for me. Thankfully, I'm working with a generous cast of hotel concierges in that department.

It's all itemized in Attachment A. Let me know when your jet lag will accommodate a call to lock down the final details.

Oh, one more thing. Those E Party officials who can't make it out for the Thanksgiving festivities will arrive over the weekend. We'll kick off the business meetings with dinner on Sunday night. The initial all-hands meeting is set for Monday. Breakout sessions are scheduled for Tuesday and Wednesday. Housing, meetings, and food are at the Aspen Institute. Details are itemized in Attachment B.

Once again, welcome back!

* * * * * *

Filling time on the flight back from Mexico went much the same as the flight down. Nancy Rae and Danny each took turns catnapping, reading, and channel surfing on the airplane's armrest media center, without much in the way of conversation. Their body language, however, spoke volumes. On the flight down, they were valued friends. On the flight back, they wore an intimacy on their sleeves and in every fiber of their bodies. Nancy Rae still lacked answers, but had at least tossed out the questions. Danny had no answers either, but was done questioning things that would never have been framed but for their recent interlude.

They gave each other a quick, inquisitive glance when the cab driver asked, "Where to?" Following airport protocol, the driver headed for the Kennedy Expressway before fielding their response. Even a rookie would know that this couple was not headed to the burbs. The outcome of the ensuing whispering campaign between passengers was determined and announced just short of the junction. For the time being, it would be her place.

* * * * * *

It wasn't a fear of flying, more a loathing, that had led to his reliance on meds.

Nat Carson's pre-flight routine was sacrosanct: get to Midway Airport ninety minutes in advance to avoid any undue TSA delays; grab his favorite Potbelly sandwich, the latest edition of the *Economist*, and a bottle of water; find a seat at the gate with a view of CNN on the tube; eat, read, and pop a pill; sleep through the flight. Thank you, Ambien.

It wasn't a fear of flying, more the nightmare from having flown countless missions in Nam as the navigator on a Bell "Huey" helicopter and always wondering which flight might be his last. Now, other than those few unavoidable times he forced himself to step on a plane, his pre-flight routine helped him relegate the horrors of that detestable term of duty to the remotest recesses of his subconscious—to a degree. Unfortunately, even all these years later, being airborne occasionally awaked the demons he worked so hard to suppress.

Today was a break from his usual pattern. Today there would be no pharmaceuticals. Nat Carson had boarded his two-hour flight back to Chicago, and the excitement radiating through his body and brain required immediate attention and reflection.

He adjusted his seatbelt one more time. Damned if Spencer Hawkins hadn't been true to his word. Over the course of four days in the Big Apple, Ned had been wined, dined, strategic-planned and game-planned to the max. Hawkins had also been true to his word in structuring an outrageous financial package. Ten thousand per monthly column with a guaranteed run of twenty-two columns leading to the next general election. Nat would have a comfy travel budget, be backed by the full research capacity of the magazine and, if he wanted, have a dedicated staffer to produce a blog. Why sleep when millions of sugarplum fairies are dancing in your head and videos of a future Pulitzer Prize are playing?

Best of all, there would be no impairment to his publishing *The Back Bench*. In fact, they wanted Nat to use it as a forum to link to his pieces in *Time*. Subscriptions would skyrocket. *The Back Bench* would be elevated to the national stage, and the entire residual was his.

Ka-ching, ka-ching.

And Pulitzer.

* * * * * *

E-MAIL
To: Elizabeth DiMaggio
From: Scott Grusin
Sent: 11/23 4:02 p.m. (EST)
Subject: Allen Election Challenge

Upon further consideration, let's be prepared to file the election challenge. At a minimum, find and hire the top election law attorney. Have him/her prepare a thorough briefing memo, ready for discussion by next Tuesday. Plan on a Wednesday morning conference call and, if all systems are go, we'll do an all-hands the following Monday. I assume this initial phase can be handled for under $100,000. The Republican Governor's Association will wire $50,000 upon confirmation that counsel has been engaged, with the balance as required.

E-MAIL
To: Scott Grusin
From: Elizabeth DiMaggio
Sent: 11/23 3:46 p.m. (CST)
Subject: Allen Election Challenge

Consider it done. Thank you.

* * * * * * *

As they stepped off the elevator on the fifty-first floor of her apartment building, Nancy Rae was reminded that not once in all the years they'd known each other had Danny Ryan ever seen her digs. Her plush one-bedroom-plus-den condo in Chicago's Gold Coast district had panoramic views of the lake to the east and the Loop to the south. She braced for his reaction.

Danny didn't disappoint. He'd always been a bit curious about where Nancy Rae lived, but this was crazy. "Holy shit," he said. "Holy fucking shit." He slowly worked his way along the continuous panel of ten-foot-high thermopanes. "I knew you were doing pretty well all these years. But...*this?*"

"Yup. And it's all mine," Nancy Rae said, setting aside false modesty. "I've made some good investments, too," she added. "But we both know I couldn't have done any of it without you. If you hadn't kicked me out of the political nest and set me up with those first clients..."

"Maybe it's time to kick myself out of the nest," said Danny quietly.

They looked at each other, not sure who was more surprised by his response.

*   *   *   *   *   *   *

As if Mexico had been only a click on life's snooze button, Danny Ryan awoke at 5:30 a.m., just as he had done every other Chicago morning for his entire adult life. He cast a perplexed yet adoring glance at the luscious woman beside him. He was still attempting to synthesize and assimilate this new Nancy Rae Mitchell, especially the part that was the sexual beast. He liked it. All of it. But learning what he needed to know might take a lifetime of work.

He rose without waking her to find the instant coffee. Thank goodness for these newer versions that tasted almost like the real thing. He put his mug in the microwave and turned to the window. The sun was just rising over Lake Michigan. Being back at his Chicago-style bungalow with its view of Mrs. Flynn's rock garden would be like watching Alvin and the Chipmunks perform the Nutcracker after seeing the Moscow Ballet.

Sighing, he slipped into a comfortable armchair strategically positioned for just such morning sightseeing. The one constant in his life had always been punching the clock at seven thirty. He'd set his life by that one act and he wouldn't stop now. At least not yet. It was time to face the realities of the current political situation.

For the first time in over a decade, despite Danny Ryan's best efforts, the Democrats would not control the Illinois executive branch. Patronage, he thought to himself, shaking his head. How was he going to replace the jobs, the lifeblood of his political army, those who served as government workers by day and Democrat field operatives by night and weekend? Danny himself had started that way. It's how the system perpetuated itself. Sure, there was still the city and the county, but the job demands of their troops were insatiable. Truth was, the state had become a deep, reliable reservoir that might soon become a dry well.

Maybe, he thought, recalling the Speaker's last-minute deal with the E Party that snuck Robinson over the goal line, just maybe, the Speaker, as always, was one step ahead. Maybe he'd negotiated a continuing flow of union jobs. Certainly wouldn't be the first time Speaker David Kennedy had peered into his crystal ball and come up with things that no one else could or would have dreamed.

Danny was about to make his second cup of coffee when he heard a rustling from the bedroom. He thought of Nancy Rae naked in bed. The visual reached him in places he'd thought no longer existed. He put down his mug, coffee forgotten. An hour later he was rushing to get dressed for work. Nancy Rae's come-hither call had led to another bout of real-time sexual fantasy that almost scared him in its intensity. He looked in the mirror. Would everyone know when they looked at him? *No. Don't be ridiculous. Go back and do your job. No one will be the wiser. No one will have the faintest idea that you've spent nearly a week having crazy sex in the arms of Nancy Rae Mitchell, femme fatale.*

As he tied his tie, Danny wondered if this was the home of her *nom de plume* Nicolette Larson. And what any of it might have to do with the next general election. Because the new governor wasn't a Democrat, he'd have to replace all those juicy contracts—the lawyers, the consultants…so many mouths to feed.

It was the governor who controlled pinstriped patronage as well. Secure a law firm a bond deal or two and they'd be there in spades for that occasional election challenge or voting rights case litigation. If it hadn't been for James Wallace, they never would have defeated the constitutional challenge to tort reform. How many bond deals did that victory win for Tristan, Dahlstrom & Peirce?

Danny's brain moved into political hyperdrive as his feet found their way into shoes. He grimaced at how tight they felt after days in flip-flops. *The map! Redistricting!* What would happen with the map—the holy grail? Admittedly, they had nothing. In almost every decennial census, Danny's party had controlled both the legislative and executive branches. Slam dunk. Draw districts to insure the Democratic majority in the legislature and put political life on automatic pilot. And now, suddenly, zippo.

Danny froze as the realization and accompanying fear of losing the map took hold.

But wait. It had to be. *Fucking Kennedy. That fucking genius.* Kennedy was the one who'd made the deal to put Robinson over the top. In exchange for the map. There was no other explanation for that frenetic last weekend when the entire organization was told to abandon their candidate and "make it happen" for Robinson. *Fucking Kennedy!* He'd known their candidate Stewart was dead in the water. He knew there would be no dealing with the Republicans on the map. No fucking way.

Thank God for David Kennedy!

CHAPTER SIX

Within heartbeats of fielding Scott Grusin's e-mail signaling that the Republican Governors Association would help fund the recount, Elizabeth DiMaggio was on the phone with Joseph Cole, the Michael Jordan of Illinois election law attorneys.

Election law, like many legal disciplines based in statute and otherwise heavily regulated, is dominated by attorneys that begin their careers in government and eventually roll the dice on private practice. In that regard, Joseph Cole was like all the rest. After graduating from the University of Illinois College of Law he went straight to his first job as staff attorney for the Illinois State Board of Elections. Before rolling a seven, he rose to general counsel and served a brief final stint as interim executive director. Snake eyes isn't probable when the great majority of the judges are law school cronies and the staff overseeing your caseload is comprised of disciples whose paychecks you once signed. And it hadn't hurt that his departure from the Board of Elections immediately preceded legislation limiting revolving-door scenarios.

Election law, unlike many legal disciplines where the number of ambulance chasers cause daily traffic jams, is an intimate cabal. The trick is how to survive in a field where the busy season occurs only biennially and you can count the number of potential clients on one hand. And where, in most cases, only the winner is in a position to pay.

When the big case pops, it's like rainy season flooding the Serengeti, providing an abundance of sustenance for those at the top of the food chain to stay satiated until the next monsoon. This time, the head of the Republican Party in Illinois had just engaged Joseph Cole to represent Robert Allen's challenge to Tom Robinson's alleged victory on Election Day. His retainer: $2.5 million against an hourly rate of $1,000 with quarterly retainer adjustments as required. *Allen v. Robinson*, the battle for governor of Illinois, would be the fee equivalent of a biblical flood.

* * * * * * *

"Mark? Nat Carson. Back to Earth from cloud nine yet?"

"I snuck off to Vegas for a few days," Mark Stone, the E Party's political director, admitted. "Week-long binge of poker and debauchery on the General's orders. Now there's a guy who knows his way around. But, as they say, we'll leave all that in Vegas for the time being. Remind me to share a few highlights next time I see you."

"I'll hold you to it," said Nat.

"Wouldn't expect less."

"So, what now?"

"By the time I got back, my brain was exploding with ideas for the Robinson administration. Atlas was sneaking e-mails from his honeymoon after a day or two."

"Why am I not surprised?" said Nat.

"Yeah, well, long story short, I've been cranking out memos and strategic planning crap for the past week. I can tell you this, if I'm only half wrong, Governor Robinson and our contingent in the legislature are going to kick butt."

Nat created a new Word document and put his hands on the keyboard. "Are you saying you're headed for the cabinet?"

"Haven't gotten that far," said Mark. "But I can see going in a number of directions. Don't forget, we took legislative seats in Pennsylvania, Indiana, and Iowa. Lots of opportunity."

"Funny how easy it was to forget about those other states," Nat said. "Hawkins and I completely missed them."

"Hawkins?" Mark asked, confused.

"Sorry, got ahead of myself," said Nat. "One of the reasons for this call was to share some news. Just after the election, Spencer Hawkins from *Time* reached out. He and I go way back."

Nat paused.

"And?" Mark prodded.

"Well, the upshot is that Hawkins called with the proverbial offer I couldn't refuse. Effective—let's see, nineteen hours ago, yours truly gets to pen a monthly column on the E Party."

"You're kidding me—"

"Wait," said Nat. "It gets better. You know those boxes on the cover that highlight key stories? Well, yours truly gets his own box. As in, I'm as big a gorilla as Joe Kline."

Mark expelled a breath. "This is wild. Am I hearing you right? You're telling me this column—your column—will be dedicated to the E Party?"

"Bingo! Hawkins and the other brass need readership. They think the serialization of the E Party story for the twenty-two months leading to the next general election will be a huge draw. If they want to throw beaucoup bucks at me to prove their point, who am I to disagree?"

"Outstanding," said Mark, "simply outstanding. And you started yesterday?"

"Signed the papers in the Big Apple at 3:27 p.m., to be exact. As they say, a moment that will live in *Back Bench* infamy."

Mark looked at his calendar. "I've got a few Vegas stories and you need to celebrate. What works for you?"

* * * * * * *

E-MAIL

To: Atlas, General, and Lisa
From: Mark
Sent: 11/26 10:10 a.m. (CST)
Subject: Nat Carson's news

Popped a few corks with Nat Carson last night. He's been hired by *Time* magazine to write a monthly column on the E Party. I shared some of my long-range thinking. The keypad was already clicking in that crazy brain of his. Any objection to including him at our post-Thanksgiving retreat?

E-MAIL
To: Mark
From: Atlas
CC: General, Lisa
Sent: 11/26 9:16 a.m. (MST)
Subject: Nat Carson's news

Congratulate Nat for me and definitely invite him. What'll it take to get Tom on the cover? How about Man of the Year?

* * * * * * *

Millions of stars were caressing Aspen, a miniscule dot on the Colorado Rockies. It was one of those evenings where earthly mortals contemplate the majesty of the universe. Like me, Atlas Stein thought. Aging had brought out his desire to pay increasing homage to this natural wonder. And who knew how much time he had left to make a difference?

He turned to the faces at the table, those of the de facto hierarchy of the E Party as well as Illinois Lt. Governor-elect Barbara Jenkins, Treasurer-elect Olivia Van Straten, and Comptroller-elect Paul Richmond. Kellie Morgan, defeated in her run for attorney general, Anthony Manzella, defeated in his run for secretary of state, and leader representatives from Pennsylvania, Indiana, and Iowa were also there, along with K.C.'s son, Patrick Covington Jr., who had expressed interest and was granted fly-on-the-wall status.

Atlas felt like the starter at the New York Marathon, ready to unleash a torrent of energy with a single gesture. There would be no holding back. The clock was ticking.

"Well," he began with Reaganesque hesitation, "I was thinking back to our impromptu post-election brunch in Chicago. I'm fairly certain it was Lisa who touched a nerve in all of us when she ventured to query those two little words—*now what?*"

"Way to go, Lisa," came the collective response. Everyone laughed.

"Since then we've had almost three weeks to contemplate the answer to those two prescient words. Now, ready or not, tomorrow we convene our first ever E Party plenary session. I am not sure any of us fully grasp the enormity of the challenges that lie ahead. Having spoken to most of you over the past few days, it isn't surprising that the list of 'now-what' questions is growing exponentially, while the list of answers is growing arithmetically, at best. Hopefully, a workable intersection where the Q's and A's meet will be found over the next few days and the weeks heading to the inauguration in January.

"What I hope to accomplish tonight is to review and finalize the program that Mark has prepared with assistance from Lisa and Anthony, and to agree who among us will take ownership of the various tasks before us. Before Mark grabs the reins, does anyone wish to propose any additions or amendments to the agenda?"

"No amendments," announced the General, coming out of his chair. "However, I would first like to offer a toast to our host and hostess." Extending his Scotch and soda to two o'clock, he raised his glass to Atlas and K.C. "Thank you for all you do to make the world a better place. And to the rest of the Atlas Superheroes, here's to great success on the mission ahead."

"Thanks, General," said Atlas. He wasn't someone known for his emotion or sentimentality, but his friend's comments made their mark.

When no one came forward to seek the floor to offer amendments, Atlas turned control of the session over to Mark Stone.

"I trust you have all taken time to review the materials," Mark began. "As Atlas indicated, I would also like to thank both Lisa and Anthony for their assistance. What we're proposing is to begin by dumping all the puzzle pieces on the table. Unlike your usual puzzle, though, since none of us has ever been here before, we don't have the box cover handy—in other words, we don't exactly know what the finished picture will look like.

"Short term, we know we have to form a government. That means creating and implementing a transition organization and preparing for the inauguration. It also means setting goals and priorities. Medium term, like it or not, we have to create a full-fledged political organization and prepare for the next election cycle. Short term, medium term, and long term, we have to put some meat on the bones. If nothing else, we need a manifesto. To a certain extent, it's a simultaneous equation, and I doubt we'll come close to starting, let alone finishing, during our meetings here.

"We also have to focus on process. This is no longer about seven people talking on the phone, exchanging e-mails, and shooting the breeze in Aspen every once in a while. If I may be so bold, what currently stands as four constitutional officers in Illinois and ninety-two legislators across four states could easily see those offices and legislative seats grow tenfold in the next election cycle. Given that this is a redistricting election cycle, it also presents a once-per-decade opportunity to consider an E Party assault on Congress. All of which makes fundraising the one hundred million dollar question.

"Monday's meeting schedule has four two-hour sessions on the key topic areas. One, transition to Robinson administration; two, inaugural and related festivities; three, developing the E Party organization and structure; and four, preparing for the next election cycle. On Tuesday and again on Wednesday morning, we'll run concurrent breakout sections on each topic with smaller work groups. On Wednesday afternoon, we'll regroup with reports from the work groups, including next steps.

"This came together faster than a two-step, so I'm really pleased with our facilitators. Having said that, I hope all of you are comfortable with your leadership assignments."

"Mark, if I could just interject something here?" said Atlas.

Mark nodded.

"While K.C. and I were traveling, she reminded me, rather emphatically, as I recall"—K.C., on Atlas's left, gave him a playful kick on the shin—"of the original E Party concept of developing a think tank primarily to serve as a training ground for future legislators and government officials. To that end, one of the projects that she and I will focus on over the next few months is the creation of that program. If all goes well, the plan will be fully operational by next summer here in Aspen, possibly in conjunction with the Aspen Institute's annual Ideas Festival. Probably not worthy of time on this week's docket, but I wanted to at least alert everyone to one more puzzle piece."

As was her custom, Barbara Jenkins had thoroughly studied and digested the materials prepared for the meetings. It wasn't until Mark had made his presentation and Atlas had spoken that she was finally able to wrap her brain around the concern that had been percolating for days.

Without question, Barbara Jenkins was the academic giant of the E Party's elected officials. In a pool of highly educated people, her summa cum laude degrees from MIT and Columbia created the greatest wow factor. Through her role as the titular head of the E Party legislators in Illinois during their first General Assembly together, she had also gained stature for her leadership and communication skills. She would be missed in the legislature, but the assembled E Party hierarchy was counting heavily on the new lieutenant governor to do some very heavy lifting as the right-hand person to Governor Robinson.

When the General had first approached her about running for state representative, Barbara's initial reaction reflected her lifelong aversion to politics. She was content teaching math in her East St. Louis hometown and saving the world, one exceptional student at a time, through her Reach for the Moon Foundation.

The General, however, had struck a nerve—one that had previously been tweaked by friends and family who had prodded her to elevate her game to what they deemed a more "appropriate level." She resented the suggestion that someone with her "talents" should "escape" a city trapped in time and forever be relegated to impoverished ghetto status. What she found most distasteful, though, was the elitist tone of her predominantly East Coast classmates who had uniformly chased fame and fortune, and who had, for the most part, achieved both. The e-mails and calls had dried up slowly as her lack of interest became too clear to ignore.

The political system had also long ago abandoned her hometown, completely stripping the dignity and pride that come with meaningful jobs, competent education, and expansive culture. Sure, there was great rhetoric and the occasional blue ribbon report, but in her thirty-something years, the trajectory of vital services had proven to be a continuous downward spiral.

It had taken almost two months for her to call his cell number, the one on the card he'd left behind: GENERAL SAMUEL HUNTINGTON SMITH, E PARTY OF ILLINOIS. Two months of stepping back and contemplating the challenge he'd presented. Sixty days … every one of them wondering if he was the Pied Piper or the genuine article. Every one of them digging deeper into the cause and effect that had led her to travel paths less taken.

Early research verified that the General and his E Party were the real deal. "Make a difference, Barbara," he had said over and over, strumming the same nerve. "Take your great work and leverage its potential. People like you have to fill the void when no one else can or will. Help *us* fill the void. We need people like you."

Never one to leap without having made a complete analysis of all of the angles, Barbara had contacted Billy Shakespeare, her most accomplished protégé, whose considerable artistic talents had allowed him to escape a world into which no child should be born. Barbara had watched, along with the rest of the world, as Billy's musical abilities propelled him from the streets of East St. Louis to achieve super stardom—the kind of stardom that had made his life a living fishbowl.

Billy was not someone who allowed others to dictate the way he lived his life. Accordingly, as Barbara's friend, and now advisor, he assured her that the chance of enacting meaningful public policy reform, particularly in education, was worth the risk of living a life in which her every movement and comment would be open to public scrutiny. The clincher was his commitment to continue serving as her sounding board through thick and thin. It was a promise he had already fulfilled myriad times throughout two grueling election campaigns. His words of support continued to circle her brain.

"I'm sorry to interrupt," Barbara finally said, "but I have a concern that I wish to share. Now seems as good a time as any."

Mark nodded.

"Thanks. First off, I agree that Mark, Lisa, and Anthony have done a phenomenal job of organizing on short notice." She looked around the table. "Here's what I'm thinking. One of the things that has always galled me about American politics is that, following each election, the so-called victors claim they have a mandate. In most cases, their mandate is based on a very weak mathematical case. I'm troubled by the fact that we're meeting and planning with respect to so many issues of critical importance to Illinois...that we seem to think that elected E Party officials and a few targeted outsiders are the repository of all wisdom. I don't see it that way. And I certainly don't view a point zero two percent plurality in the governor's race as a mandate to operate as though we're the chosen ones."

There was a pause as the group considered Barbara's strong words.

"Well said," said Atlas finally. "So what would you do differently, in light of the fact that our cast has already been assembled?"

Barbara shrugged. "I was afraid you'd ask that. Under the circumstances, I'd say we proceed as planned, but agree to quickly establish some protocols—for lack of a better term—to both open the process and solicit contrary viewpoints. In math, it's called proving to test a theorem."

"Makes perfect sense," said K.C. "All sorts of political theorems need proving. And thank you for using the M word. The day the E Party cops a mandate attitude is the first slippery step toward losing the edge that got us here. Barbara, I can guarantee you that our think tank will be anything but one-dimensional."

"I'm on board, too," said PR guru Lisa Boudreau. "But we have to deliver on that promise. Part of the rhetoric of every new administration is the 'we're going to reach across the aisle' spiel. We all know it never works out that way. Personally? I'm pretty sure that our opposition has little to no interest in helping us succeed. So, I guess what I'm saying is that we should do some looking before we leap."

"I understand your concern about perception," said Atlas, "but as I see it, we have no choice but to take that leap. Mark? How would you evaluate this risk?"

Mark took his time answering. "Well, I agree with Lisa that neither the Republicans nor the Democrats have any interest in seeing our experiment succeed. I do feel, however, that the public needs to see that its government is open to new ideas and able to perform basic tasks at a high level of efficiency more than it needs to believe we are adding members of both parties to the team. The problem for Democrats and Republicans isn't that they load their administrations with party loyalists, it's that they load them with party slugs and retreads who are more dedicated to the whims of party constituencies than to the public-at-large. It's a farce. Show me the last administration—state or federal—that built its cabinet around talent to the exclusion of party loyalty and big donor preferences."

He paused to take a drink of his all too rapidly cooling coffee. "I'd go the other direction. In the interests of reinventing government, we should steer clear of anyone with ties to either party. If I remember correctly, that was one of our guiding principles in fielding candidates. Why not build the bureaucracy the same way?"

"Interesting legal question," said Anthony Manzella. "Can we deny employment on the basis of political affiliation?"

"I'm pretty sure we can for exempt employees, not so sure for others," said Mark.

"Exempt employees?" asked the governor-elect.

"I'll take that one," said Anthony. "In preparing for the transition, we sought counsel from labor attorneys familiar with Illinois law. Simply put, there is a discretionary level of hiring referred to as 'exempt' for which you, as governor, have total latitude. All the rest—and the percentage is a rather staggering ninety-plus percent in Illinois—are called 'non-exempt' and are subject to predetermined standards for hiring and firing. My guess is that our hands will be tied if we deny hiring based on political registration or any other political litmus test, but I'll check with counsel first thing in the morning."

"Over ninety-plus percent union employees?!" said the General. "No wonder government's a joke. Maybe someday someone can explain to me why any government worker needs to be unionized. The day the army's unionized is the day we get our asses kicked in the next war."

"Well, before we fire everyone in state government," Atlas said in the General's direction, "does anyone else have issues for the conference agenda?"

"Not about the agenda," said Mark, "but just as critical. There's the potential of an election challenge as well as our planning for redistricting."

Atlas nodded. "I don't think anyone here would be surprised if the Republicans challenge the election. If there's no objection, we'll use Elaine Richards to head up our legal team. Her work to date in *U.S. v. Stein* has been a difference maker—a great balance of juggling law, politics, and the media. Just what we'll need if a challenge comes to pass. As for redistricting, I recommend holding off for the time being. Our plate is beyond full and, as I understand it, the census data won't be released until sometime in late January at the earliest. Now, anyone for a cocktail?"

* * * * * * *

The General's late-night knock at the door was an old habit from past visits to the Stein compound. Many an evening had culminated with a few fingers of Scotch and conversations about everything and nothing. Atlas's marriage to K.C. had not interfered with tradition, simply obligated less testosterone. And more Scotch.

"You kinda left me hanging tonight," he said, sinking into the first of two worn leather chairs by the fireplace. "What's the deal with Elaine Richards, and what's happening with *U.S. v. Stein*? Remember, I've got skin in that one, too."

"My fault entirely," said Atlas, settling into the chair to the General's right and setting his glass on the side table next to K.C.'s. "Elaine contacted me while we were cruising. Evidently, you were having too much fun in Vegas to pick up your voice mail." Atlas winked at his friend who had a reputation for playing as hard as he worked. "Anyway, she wants you to get back to your buddy at the Justice Department, see if the case can go away quietly now that the election is over. Otherwise, we're in a holding pattern until a new judge is appointed. That's why the U.S. attorney in Chicago is not currently engaged."

"Hmm," said the General.

"Yeah," Atlas continued. " And if it's true, as she believes, that all this started high—very high—up in the food chain, that's where the deal will have to be cut as well. It makes sense to me. That's where Eddie Cobb's best contacts lie, and there's little doubt left that he orchestrated the bogus complaint."

"Funny you should mention that SOB," said the General. "I was thinking about his tactical blunder a few weeks back. I can understand his motivation to create legal fiction in an attempt to freeze your assets. Let's face it, in the short run, it had the desired effect. But he underestimated our response. If that case is never prosecuted, we don't run Tom as our candidate for governor and there's no Elaine Richards on the scene to drive public opinion so forcefully to our camp. One of the first rules of engagement—let sleeping dogs lie."

"And, let's not forget," said K.C. "If Mr. Cobb hadn't frozen our hero's assets, I might never have conned him into marrying me. How's that for a rule of engagement?"

"Well said," said the General. "Which sounds to me like a 'see you in the morning,' so I'll bid you newlyweds adieu."

* * * * * *

Eddie Cobb's ears had to be ringing down in Texas.

As the General and Atlas Stein were discussing the Democrat's role in the situation at hand, so were Mark Stone and Nat Carson similarly engaged in belated Monday morning quarterbacking of the same election sequence. Only instead of fine Scotch in the library, it was brewskis in a number of Aspen saloons.

"So, for the sake of argument," Nat said, emptying yet another mug. "I can buy the story about Cobb's involvement, but how does that lead to Democratic palm cards with Robinson's name on them being passed around on Election Day?"

"I'm not sure the two are that closely connected," Mark admitted. "But at some point just a few days prior to the election, the Speaker called the General to offer a deal."

Nat perked up. "What kind of deal?"

"Well, first of all," Mark hesitated, "let's be totally clear. This is completely off the record, as in this conversation never happened. I mean it, Nat. Every word."

"Done."

Mark nodded. "Okay, so the Speaker calls and offers to run a late blitz for Robinson. Our analysis is that he knew his candidate, Stewart, was burnt toast. The thought of a Republican governor capable of completely throwing a monkey wrench into the redistricting process was too much for him to risk."

"Yeah, but it's not like the E Party is gonna just roll over," Nat observed.

"True. And I will tell you that we internally discussed redistricting at great length before making the deal. But, as you'd suspect, what Kennedy primarily wanted in exchange was our guarantee to re-elect him Speaker of the House. Let's face it, for him, that's the end-all and be-all. The repository of all power from which his political empire has evolved.

"Under the circumstances, how could we guarantee votes for Speaker? If anything, with *U.S. v. Stein* hanging over his head, the focus was on proving a Chinese wall exists between Atlas and the E Party legislators. Regardless, there's a bond that has formed between General Smith and Speaker Kennedy. A throwback kind of trust level you don't see in politics anymore. Hard to explain."

Through slightly bleary eyes, Nat looked at Stone. "Mark, you don't have to convince me. I'm not the jury. But as the House currently stands, Kennedy needs only six E Party votes for Speaker out of the twenty-five seats you now hold. The General can arrange that in his sleep. As I see it, you cut a deal, Speaker Kennedy puts on a full-court press, and Robinson hits a long shot to win at the buzzer. Sweet."

"Let's hope so," said Mark. "But, to use your analogy, our decision was no slam dunk. If the E Party can't deliver on its promises with Robinson as governor, electing him will turn into a political death sentence. After almost two weeks of wrestling with transition issues, I can tell you it won't be easy. Illinois is a fiscal nightmare. In hindsight, we may rue the day we made the deal. But we also scored a few other trinkets in exchange that should come in handy."

"Such as?"

Mark grinned. "Let's save that for another time, shall we?"

"As for Cobb? The Speaker made it eminently clear to the General that neither he nor any member of his team have been involved with Cobb's bullshit. He has even offered to help us seek our revenge at the right time. You know the first rule of politics: Get even, but never leave fingerprints."

"Politics. Love it or hate it," said Nat.

CHAPTER SEVEN

As soon as he pushed the button, the answering machine at Cook County Democratic Headquarters told Danny he had forty-seven messages. Not too bad for ten working days away. Of course that didn't take into account the Blackberry confiscated at the hotel that had over one hundred voice messages and 400-plus e-mails in the queue.

Over a dozen calls were from the Speaker's executive assistant, Dawn Eckersley. She knew that Danny was on vacation, but nothing could stop the Speaker from insisting she try, just in case Danny was checking in.

He picked up the receiver and dialed, bracing himself for the onslaught. "Dawn, it's Danny. *Buenos dias, Señora Eckersley.* I understand the Speaker has been looking for me."

Dawn snorted. "That's an understatement and you know it, Danny. Welcome back and *buenos dias* to you, too." She lowered her voice. "You know how he is. And consider yourself lucky. For every message I left, I didn't leave another three. Off the record, I'm happy you took a real vacation. I trust you enjoyed yourself."

You can't imagine, thought Danny.

"Hang on," said Dawn. "I'll get him for you."

The Speaker's voice boomed through the phone. "I see you're finally back," he said. "I expected you two days ago. I *suppose* it's possible I misread the itinerary."

Danny held his peace. If the Speaker thought Danny was going to give in here, he had another thing coming. Two could play at this game.

"Hello, Mr. Speaker," he said, hoping to sound conciliatory but not contrite. "I did land on Friday, but ended up in bed the entire weekend." Well, at least it wasn't a lie.

"Um-hm," the Speaker acknowledged vaguely.

Lack of interest or disbelief? Danny didn't know and didn't have time to wonder.

The Speaker got right down to business. "Dawn will send over a packet this morning. It contains Al Taylor's analysis of the election. As I'm sure you're well aware, we're down to fifty-four Democratic votes in the House. We'll need to find six for the election of Speaker of the House. I want those six locked down as soon as possible."

"I trust our focus will be on the E Party?" Danny asked.

"Agreed. No doubt Elizabeth DiMaggio is on the same scavenger hunt so the Republicans can grab control."

* * * * * * *

Note to our readers: The article below is part of a series that *Time* will run at least monthly through the next general election. Nat Carson, editor-in-chief of *The Back Bench,* one of the nation's leading political dailies, will chronicle the activities of the E Party. In addition to these monthly columns, Mr. Carson will further document the E Party's journey in a new and exciting blog, posted at www.time/carsonblog-eparty.com.

WHENCE THE E PARTY?
By: Nat Carson

Over the past three years, a fledging third political party known as the E Party has been reinventing politics. Founded by Aspen billionaire Alex "Atlas" Stein just over two years ago during its maiden electoral voyage, the E Party initially won eight seats in the Illinois Senate and fourteen in the House of Representatives. Last month, they gained six more Senate and eleven more House seats in the general election to clearly establish the E-Party as a legitimate legislative force. In a stunning upset, they also elected former baseball star and Hall of Famer Tom Robinson Jr. governor of Illinois. Along with Robinson, a young political dynamo named Barbara Jenkins was elected lieutenant governor. They also claimed the state treasurer and comptroller offices. Beyond Illinois, they expanded their horizons by taking legislative seats in Pennsylvania, Indiana, and Iowa.

As you might suspect, overcoming the political prowess of legendary Illinois Speaker of the House David Kennedy and the all-powerful Cook County Democratic organization was not for the faint of heart. But this is no rag-tag outfit. They have assembled a talented, dynamic team (see accompanying article introducing the personalities comprising the E Party brain trust) that knows how to take the fight to the Democrats and Republicans. Billionaire Stein has already committed in excess of $40 million of his personal wealth and continues to hint that the spigot will remain wide open.

There are, however, at least two significant challenges to the E Party's financial wherewithal. Last August, both Stein and Gen. Samuel Huntington Smith, Stein's top political co-conspirator, were named co-defendants in a pending tax fraud case in the federal district court in Illinois. When the case originally broke, in what has since come to be publicly viewed as a politically motivated gesture, then sitting Judge Suffredin froze all assets of both named defendants and the E Party. In a scene reminiscent of a classic cavalry oldie, Stein's recently widowed college sweetheart, Julie "K.C." Covington, rode to the rescue with sufficient interim funds to save the day. Although the case is pending, Judge Suffredin recused himself once the political heat intensified. A replacement has yet to be named.

With the election having concluded and immediate financial pressures concomitantly abated, the greater challenge lies ahead.

Incredibly liberal campaign contribution laws in Illinois were an integral component of the party's foray into the prairie state. But—and it's a significant hurdle—the laws of most states mirror the feds in severely limiting individual and corporate contributions. The E Party now finds itself in the unchartered fundraising waters that have sunk many political newbies.

Professor Sonja Cassidy from the University of Arizona James E. Rudgels College of Law, a national expert in campaign finance, predicts that the E Party will respond with a vigorous Internet campaign. "The Internet is the game changer," says Professor Cassidy. "Eight percent of all political funds were raised over the Internet six years ago. That figure rose to nineteen percent in the last presidential election cycle. And I suspect we will see that rise significantly again during the presidential campaign cycle over the course of the next two years. The E Party is no stranger to the political power of the Internet and I predict that they will launch a nationwide viral fundraising campaign."

While the E Party's capacity to raise funds through the Internet remains untapped, their prior efforts at electronic messaging have been nothing short of spectacular. For that, Stein tapped Lauren Chevez de la Rosa, a former business associate and nationally recognized technology guru who now heads the Chevez de la Rosa Corporation. This entity, funded by Stein, has in just a few short years created a multitude of cutting-edge Internet applications specifically tailored for political campaigns.

Cynthia Faraci, an expert in web-based technology for Goldman Sachs, says of de la Rosa, "She is very highly respected, particularly for her creativity. She has already developed new political adaptations for social networking, and her company is rumored to have re-engineered Twitter sequencing. It would not surprise me if her company issues an IPO or is acquired by one of the major industry players, such as Microsoft or Google. At the same time, they could sign an exclusive licensing package that would give the E Party unbridled capacity."

Assuming the financial obstacles can be met, the E Party also finds itself at organizational crossroads. Not dissimilar to a business with a new patent in its pocket, it has to determine if it should continue to grow at a controlled pace, state legislature by state legislature, or launch an all-out national effort that includes Congress. Does it seek executive branch offices, as it recently did in Illinois, or does it keep its focus strictly on a legislative model?

These, and other organizational matters, were heavily debated last week when the E Party convened its first-ever national convention. Staged in tony Aspen, Colorado, where Stein makes his home, the party's leadership, elected officials, and national policy experts on a wide-range of disciplines met over the course of three days just after Thanksgiving to plot the party's future.

The outcome of those discussions remains under lock and key to this point. With General Smith at the helm, the E Party prides itself on military-like precision and secrecy. Its spokesperson, Lisa Boudreau, would comment only that "typical of the E Party, the debate regarding its future plans was spirited and innovative. The party plans to continue to grow and to provide the people of America with a distinct and responsible voice on issues of importance."

Had not Boudreau previously set the bar very high for succinct and frank discourse, her announcement would have been viewed as typical political non-speak. But, if nothing else, the E Party has proven itself capable of messaging in a way that cuts to the heart of the issue. Their focus to date has been on, as they call it, the "three E's": economy, ethics, and education.

Leslie Fischer from *Political Weekly* predicts that "As it evolves, the E Party will begin to equivocate on issues as it panders to a broader audience. What they have accomplished to date, although unique and remarkable, can be attributable in great measure to the country's thirst for a viable third party. What remains to be seen is whether this proves to be mirage or oasis."

Regardless, the legislative target for the Robinson administration will be education reform and the bull's eye will be a program the governor-elect calls "Getting to 21." Its essence is devoting resources and planning to avoid the severe impact to our society and economy created by the considerable population of high school dropouts. Robinson's vision is that this lost generation be trained for vocational work, contribute to society through many volunteer organizations such as the Peace Corps, or join the military through conscription. Regardless of the choices made, the goal is to turn dropouts into functioning members of society.

Accordingly, a major portion of the E Party meetings was dedicated to education and, in particular, Getting to 21. Lt. Governor-elect Barbara Jenkins has been chosen to shepherd the program through the legislature. Jenkins has a remarkable curriculum vitae of achievements in the field of education. But does her one term in the Illinois Legislature as an E Party state representative qualify her to take on the likes of Speaker Kennedy and the state's Republican Leader, Elizabeth DiMaggio?

The E Party has focused on education reform from day one, but has continuously been thwarted by the political maneuvers of Speaker Kennedy. However, speculation is rampant that Speaker Kennedy engineered an eleventh hour effort to swing the election to Robinson. Courtney Grant, a long-time observer of Illinois politics, and currently serving as political correspondent for the NBC affiliate in Rockford, Illinois, says, "It's no secret that Kennedy's political army worked relentlessly over the final seventy-two hours preceding the election in favor of Robinson. The Democratic candidate was slipping in the polls and Kennedy, as usual, made an astute political decision and drove home the winner."

If Kennedy was truly behind Robinson's win, it would not seem farfetched that he would help pass legislation to codify Robinson's pet program. Together, the Democrats and E Party have the votes to pass any legislation they agree upon.

Others are not as sanguine regarding Kennedy's motives. Erik Garvey, chair of political science at the University of Michigan, suggests a different scenario. "Kennedy's candidate for governor was headed to defeat. However, Kennedy is fiercely loyal and would not jeopardize his party's best interests. His latest maneuver sets up the E Party for failure, while keeping the Republicans out of the redistricting picture. What could be a better scenario for the long-term future of the Democratic Party in Illinois?"

Whether, as Professor Garvey suggests, the E Party has been set up to fail remains to be seen. However, what has become immediately apparent to them is the magnitude of the test before them. At their recent convention, a stream of eminent presenters discussed the challenges they face in forming their executive branch team and then running a $60 billion operation with approximately 65,000 employees.

In typical E Party "out of box" planning, they have engaged *If We Can Put a Man on the Moon…* authors William D. Eggers and John O'Leary. In their presentation during a plenary session of the convention, Eggers and O'Leary focused on the seven "traps" discussed in their book.

As an example, what they refer to as the "complacency trap" is caused by a whole host of barriers to change inherent in democratic systems that lock us into "what is" and prevent us from trying "things that could be…" The dangerous task of staying the same when the circumstances of the world around you change.

Although Messrs. Eggers and O'Leary did not pull any punches with their E Party audience, they ended on a high note by identifying a series of steps the Robinson administration needs to take to be successful, and then demonstrated how each of these steps had been successfully implemented in highly effective government programs such as President Kennedy's challenge to the country in 1961.

With respect to substance and policy, other speakers were not quite as confident. From the Illinois budget, to its education system, to its infrastructure and beyond, a series of distinguished presenters lamented the current state of affairs.

In her review of the state's fiscal crisis, Professor Cate Arnold from the University of Chicago called the situation "a cruel Ponzi scheme that makes Madoff's look like child's play." As she described it, "They could double the income tax, property tax, and sales tax and still not achieve a structural balance for almost five years."

Not to be out-hyperbolized, in his review of the state's education system, Wallace Kingsly from the Heritage Foundation suggested that "particularly in the city of Chicago, if its high-school graduates were measured like a product, they would be the functional equivalent of typewriters."

Yet, in the face of adversity, Tom Robinson and the E Party appear appropriately and cautiously optimistic about the future. In his closing remarks, General Smith reminded them of historical military battles where success had been achieved against great odds. Then, in a stirring close, he sent his troops off to battle.

* * * * * * *

"Scott, Eddie Cobb."

"Eddie. Happy holidays."

"I assume you saw the Carson article in *Time*. This monthly E Party series could be devastating."

"I saw it, Eddie. I'm not pleased about it either. But it's not as if we can demand equal time."

"Fuck equal time!" snapped Cobb. "If we don't stop this parasite in its tracks, there's no telling what legs this gets. This Carson guy is totally in the bag and has complete, unfettered access. For all I know, Lisa Boudreau writes the fuckin' articles for him. Are you getting this, Grusin?"

"Calm down, Eddie," said Grusin firmly. "Hysterics won't help and I don't appreciate your tone. My team is already developing a strategic response. Remember, this is a marathon, not a sprint."

"Then you better marathon your ass into Illinois state court and get that election overturned! This race is going to the swiftest, and your team isn't looking so swift."

"Eddie," said Grusin slowly, "I told you we'd look at it and we have. But I'm not about to share our plans or our pleadings with you. I thought we covered that at our last dinner. As for Carson, I know the people who will be cutting his checks. Don't take your eye off the ball. If redistricting comes off the way we discussed, this *Time* stuff too shall pass."

Shit, thought Eddie. First Kennedy and now Grusin. Was he the only one who got it? But it wouldn't do to alienate Grusin. They needed each other.

"All right, all right," Eddie placated, dialing down the rhetoric. "I'll grant you that we've still got a couple bullets in the chamber. We'd just better be taking very careful aim—starting with that election challenge."

There was a pause. "I have every confidence we'll be hitting the target on that one, Eddie," said Grusin. "And now, if that's all..."

I'll tell you when that's all, you sonnova—

Cobb heard the phone disconnect in his ear. The asshole had actually hung up on him. *Unbelievable!* Quickly, he stabbed a new number into the phone and waited impatiently while it rang.

"Listen, get in touch with Jack. Yeah. I have reason to suspect that package will be delivered soon. What? Yeah. *Now.* We've only got a week to ten days at best. We'd better be ready on our end. And don't screw this up."

"Got it," said the voice on the other end. "Consider it done."

* * * * * * *

E-MAIL
To: Elizabeth DiMaggio
From: Joseph Cole
Sent: 12/3 11:01 a.m. (CST)
Subject: Election challenge

Great news! Yesterday was the last day for county clerks to transmit certified copies of the tabulated statement of returns to the Illinois State Board of Elections. Based on information we have obtained from our sources, Allen has closed the gap from 3,582 down to a mere 189. If this bears out, it is a complete game changer.

As I predicted, whatever tricks Speaker Kennedy pulled that last weekend to shift votes from Stewart to Robinson were not reflected in the absentee vote, which has driven numbers to our side. Accordingly, we have Allen winning in excess of 63 percent of the previously uncounted absentee votes as compared to the 38 percent he tabulated on Election Day. That accounts for almost the entire difference.

The State Board of Elections has set December 6 as the date for proclamation of the final results. We will then have five days to file our Petitions for Discovery Recounts. Discovery will include examination of the ballots, ballot applications, records relating to the absentee ballots, comparison of the voter's signatures on their registration records and their applications for ballot, and an examination of the voting equipment used.

Although we can seek discovery in up to only 25 percent of the precincts in any election jurisdiction, we intend to maximize this effort on a statewide basis. No chad left hanging.

Remember, our discovery efforts will not result in any change in the official proclamation by the State Board, but rather establish the grounds for our election contest. The Petition of State Election Contest is due just ten days after we start discovery, which adds up to an intense amount of work conducted in a very short time.

* * * * * * *

THE BACK BENCH
"If you let it slip, we catch it"
December 6

EXTRA EXTRA EXTRA EXTRA EXTRA EXTRA

The State Board of Elections has released its final tabulation of the vote for governor, and it would seem as though things are about to get *very* interesting.

Election night reporting had Tom Robinson with a seemingly insurmountable 3,582 vote lead. That total has now shrunk to a steam room-sized 189.

Sources speculate that the bulk of Allen's vote pick-up comes from late arriving and previously uncounted absentee ballots. At the national level, absentees generally tend to swing Republican, given the tendency of overseas servicemen toward conservatives. However, the so-called experts were not expecting such a dramatic shift given that Illinois has a high percentage of minority servicemen more likely to support the Democrat, Stewart, or the Black candidate, Robinson.

The guess here? Timing. Robinson's victory is generally credited to a late surge, somewhat aided by a rumored Democratic push in his favor. Many of the absentee ballots would have been sent long before the signal to switch was given.

Who wouldn't want to be a fly on the wall in the Republican and E Party boiler rooms right now? What had to be a tense decision in the Allen camp in terms of whether to file an election challenge has just become a no-brainer. Fasten your seat belts!

In other news...

CHAPTER EIGHT

Joseph Cole was now officially on the clock. Under state law, he would have only ten days to conduct discovery. For a recount of this significance, it would be unthinkable to analyze data in fewer than the maximum number of precincts allowable. As he saw it, there were two major hurdles: staffing and choosing the key precincts.

Cole considered the numbers as his feet pounded the rubberized pavement of the treadmill. At 5 a.m. the sky was still dark, but getting up before the rooster crowed had proved beneficial in a profession where billable hours were given the status of a deity. Staffing was arithmetic, pure and simple. Multiply each warm-bodied attorney or paralegal times an average of three to four hours, per precinct, plus travel, times 11,271 precincts...equals approximately 40,000 man hours required. Then divide by eight hours a day available at each county clerk's office times ten days, not forgetting to apply an appropriate fudge factor for bureaucratic confusion and waste. Then there was the support staff necessary to handle copying, Fed-Exing, whatever. Call it roughly 200 attorneys and paralegals and twenty-five to thirty staff.

Been there, done that.

Choosing the key precincts would be trickier. More like calculus. Find the districts where Robinson had the most to lose and Allen had the most to gain by vote total. The third leg of the triangle would be a combination of experience and visceral intuition.

The real challenge? Extrapolating from forty-plus years of experience with two-party elections. Joseph Cole could handle R v. D in his sleep. Historical patterns had been gleaned from voting tabulations run through continuously upgraded algorithms. But did they have statistical validity in a three-party race? Doubtful!

Joseph wiped the sweat from his brow and neck and considered his more visceral reaction to the situation, based on his twenty-plus years of trying election cases. There was always a decisive factor, no matter the circumstances. Sometimes it stared him in the face. Sometimes it came to him slowly, like a cat—stealthy, but hell bent on pursuing its prey.

The beeper on Cole's device went off. The app on his phone showed he'd run five miles. Blood pressure steady.

Joseph stepped off the machine and began his stretching exercises, his mind and pulse still racing. Yeah. It was crazy. That note he'd found left under the wiper blade of his Benz. Normally he paid to park in one of the many underground garages to avoid any possible theft or damage. Figures. The one time he'd left it on the street because he was running late for a meeting that something like this would happen. The note was typed in all caps: FOCUS YOUR ATTENTION ON THE LAST PRECINCTS REPORTING FROM CHICAGO. YOU WON'T BE DISAPPOINTED.

It didn't get by Cole that someone knew who he was and knew his vehicle, too. The reactive shivers that had traveled up his spine at the note's discovery had been both from discomfort and, if he had to be honest, excitement.

"… THE LAST PRECINCTS REPORTING FROM CHICAGO… "

To address his curiosity, he had instructed his team to run a new series of statistical tests.

Preparing for the designation of discovery precincts traditionally meant looking for statistical outliers based on standard deviations from turnout, party voting tendencies, campaign funding, and, if known, each campaign's television and mail saturation. If a precinct usually saw X percent turnout and the voting percentage in a particular election showed 1.5X percent—bingo! You knew something was wrong. If a precinct usually saw X percent of votes for a certain party and voting in a particular election showed 1.5X percent...again, bingo! Time to pay attention. If candidate A had significantly more resources and either the turnout or the party vote percentages were off? Right. Bingo! Again.

In the shower, the words on the scrap of paper under the windshield wiper of his car clicked over and over in Cole's mind like a ticker tape... *THE LAST PRECINCTS REPORTING FROM CHICAGO...THE LAST PRECINCTS REPORTING FROM CHICAGO...*

Other than in obvious situations, they had never used timing of votes reported as a factor for initiating discovery. Sure, there always were a few precincts or counties that came in late, but the great majority of the time it was nothing more than a technological failure or antiquated tabulation methodologies or equipment. Sometimes, a judge made the decision to keep the polls open late or some county chairman liked the attention and drama of late-night reporting of results. There were famous exceptions, of course, such as old man Daley's reputed last-minute maneuvering that elected JFK. But, for the most part, no statistical connection between vote fraud and the time when results were submitted from the precinct to the clerk, or from the clerk to the state, had ever been established.

Would this be the first?

* * * * * * *

THE BACK BENCH
"If you let it slip, we catch it"
December 11

Well, that didn't take long. At exactly 10 a.m. on the first day available to file Petitions for Discovery Recounts, the Allen campaign filed the necessary paperwork. That officially starts the clock on a ten-day discovery process leading to a Petition of State Election Contest.

Also no surprise is the fact that Allen will be represented by Joseph Cole. Every election case of any prominence over the last decade has seen Cole carrying the Republican banner. And who can blame them? The guy doesn't lose.

In a press briefing yesterday afternoon, Cole stressed that his job was made much easier by virtue of the final canvass reducing the deficit to less than 200 votes. As reported by *The Back Bench* last week, rumors on the street are that absentee votes had significantly broken Allen's way. Cole confirmed that yesterday.

Cole acknowledged that he had been contacted by Republican State Chairwoman Elizabeth DiMaggio shortly after the election and had assembled a legal team well in excess of one hundred attorneys who would now begin the arduous task of reviewing ballots and procedural compliance in 110 jurisdictions and over 2,800 precincts.

While Cole stopped short of tipping his hand on strategy, a quick and dirty analysis of their petition indicates they will be placing great emphasis on voting in Black city wards where Robinson accomplished staggering vote totals—wards that usually run 80-plus percent Democrat and went big for Robinson.

Was it his Hall of Fame stature and name recognition in the Black community? Was it Speaker Kennedy's alleged last-minute dumping of Stewart? Was it legendary Chicago vote fraud at work? All of the above? We're about to find out.

In other news…

* * * * * * *

Cole pushed back in his king-sized desk chair. *The Back Bench* was right. In Cole's assessment, after their analysis had been calculated and recalculated for accuracy, the evidence was all there. One hundred precincts in the city had reported more than one hour later than their historical pattern. Fifty of those precincts had reported over two hours late; another handful over three hours behind their usual time. Of the one hundred precincts, Tom Robinson had averaged 55 percent of the vote against 48 percent citywide. In the fifty precincts where the votes were over two hours late, Robinson's numbers had shot to well over 70 percent. *Bingo!*

The Back Bench was right about one other thing, too. Joseph Cole didn't lose.

* * * * * *

"Good morning, Scott. It's Elizabeth DiMaggio. Do you have a moment?"

"Absolutely! I was meaning to call you. I saw that Joseph Cole filed the discovery petition. Pretty miraculous narrowing of the vote, wouldn't you say?"

"First positive news in quite a while," DiMaggio agreed dryly. "Could it be our luck's changing?"

"Let's hope so," Scott Grusin said. "So, how can I help you?"

"Well," said DiMaggio, "I just got off the phone with Cole. He feels this is the time to challenge the Act, now that the discovery petitions have been filed. If you remember, when we first contacted Cole, he advised that there had never been a legal challenge to the constitutionality of the Illinois law regarding statewide election recounts. This particular version was passed almost forty years ago, after problems arose during the last meaningful statewide challenge.

"The section he wants to attack calls for Robinson to be sworn in as governor if the challenge is not timely resolved. Now that the race has tightened, Cole thinks that places significantly more pressure on the court to overturn the law."

"What's the downside, then?" asked Grusin.

"Well, according to Cole, there are a few risks. First, and most obvious, is cost."

"Not to worry," Grusin said quickly.

DiMaggio silently acknowledged this declaration of monetary backing from the national party. "Next is the delay factor," she went on. "Cole thinks it could add two to three weeks minimum to the election challenge. Maybe a month or more." When Grusin did not respond,

DiMaggio continued. "And third—and here's where it gets dicey—it's not clear who the alternative caretaker would be. The E Party will argue that, as successor to a gubernatorial vacancy, their lieutenant governor candidate Barbara Jenkins fills the position."

"Hmm. That doesn't help, does it?" Grusin said rhetorically.

"Not in the least. But our argument is that since the two candidates run as a combined ticket, neither can serve. Next in line under the constitution is the Attorney General."

"So, if I hear you correctly," Grusin said, "under that scenario, a Democrat becomes interim governor. That complicates things, doesn't it? When do we have to decide?"

"We can take it right up to the inauguration. At the same time, the longer we wait, the greater the chance the court upholds the statute to avoid a vacancy."

DiMaggio waited as Grusin considered for a moment. "Cole also cautions that if we raise the issue, we run the risk of losing in the court of public opinion. The Supreme Court reads the papers, too. If we come across as too heavy-handed on the temporary position, there could be repercussions for the recount."

Grusin sighed. "Have you discussed this with Allen?"

"Of course. As you can imagine, he focused immediately on the last point. He has no interest in taking any chances with the outcome of the election."

Grusin and DiMaggio parted on this note, agreeing to talk after the weekend.

* * * * * * *

E-MAIL
To: Atlas
From: General
Sent: 12/14 8:06 p.m. (CST)
Subject: U.S. v. Stein update

I just had a lengthy conversation with my guy at Justice today. Typical good news/bad news scenarios. When's a good time to talk?

CHAPTER NINE

"Does the name Andrew Mellon mean anything to you?"

"Sure," said Atlas. "Financier extraordinaire. Secretary of the Treasury under Hoover, if I remember correctly. Maybe the wealthiest guy on the planet in his day. Is that sufficient or should I use a lifeline and phone a friend?"

"If the friend's name is Elaine Richards."

"Okay. Let's see. Andrew Mellon, as in one of the so-called robber barons that FDR skewered during the Great Depression? An act which put the entire Justice Department on Mellon's case over bogus tax fraud charges?"

"Warmer," said the General. "You're in pretty impressive company, my friend. If you recall, Mellon beat the criminal charges, but got hoisted on his petard with civil charges. His loss, Roosevelt's gain."

"So, what you're trying to say," said Atlas, "is that they'll drop their bullshit criminal case but attempt to destroy our reputations by overdramatizing a civil tax case—at least as far as inflicting pain on the E Party is concerned."

"I think it's fair to say yours will be the first civil tax case since Mellon's to have captured the attention of the president," the General said.

"Lucky us," said Atlas. "And the good news?"

"My buddy at Justice says that all of this goes away if, and I said *if*, you and I go away."

"I'd like to meet this 'buddy' someday. In the meantime, how exactly does he define our disappearance?"

"He refrained from specifics," said the General. "But that might be a good question for Elaine—and whoever else is assigned the case at the Internal Revenue Service. But it sure seems likely that it's one that our good friend Eddie Cobb and the U.S. attorney general already have mapped out."

* * * * * *

THE BACK BENCH
"If you let it slip, we catch it"
December 15

EXTRA EXTRA EXTRA EXTRA EXTRA EXTRA

In a move that could potentially turn Illinois politics on its head, former Democratic candidate-for-governor Jeff Stewart filed a discovery petition today in preparation for a challenge to the election of Tom Robinson.

Republican candidate Robert Allen filed his petition four days ago on the opening of the filing period. With the State Board of Elections final canvass showing Allen within 189 votes of Robinson, Allen's challenge was expected. However, virtually no one saw a challenge from Stewart in the offing.

While focused solely on Allen, the media, including this reporter, failed to note that Stewart had also crept within striking distance. Based on the canvass, Allen gained over 3,000 votes to pull within 189. At the same time, Stewart gained enough votes to come within 5 percent of Robinson. Five percent is the statutory minimum separation required for standing to file an election challenge.

Statewide election contests are very expensive and, in this case, guesstimated to be well north of $5 million. Someone is placing a huge wager on Stewart. But who?

Stewart is represented by attorney Jessica Myers. Myers is a seasoned election lawyer who historically focuses on federal races. While based in Illinois, she has litigated election challenges in many other jurisdictions across the country.

Neither Stewart nor Myers has been available for press inquiries, but they did release a rather vanilla joint statement. What's missing is an indication of the funding source for their effort. While it's not known who stands behind Allen, the Republican Party is the likely suspect.

However, given Speaker Kennedy's reputed last-minute push for Robinson, it would be inconsistent for him to bankroll Stewart, especially while he's in third place. Then again, that might be a small price in order to deflect growing criticism that Kennedy helped elect Robinson. As the criticism grows, Kennedy's re-election as Speaker could be at risk.

In other news…

* * * * * * *

"Joe? Jessica Myers here."

"Jess? This is a surprise. I didn't think I'd be hearing from you until the first court date."

"I have been directed to call to determine how best to coordinate with you regarding discovery and all aspects of the election challenge."

"Come again?" said Cole, too stunned to react to Myer's lack of phone etiquette.

"You heard me correctly," Jessica said. "My client has instructed me to offer my services in support of Allen."

"Um, then I must be missing something," Cole said, nonplussed, something that rarely happened. He rose from his desk to pace. "Why would he do that? Why file without an expectation of winning? I have a healthy respect for your fee schedule, and that's a big number to spend on a presupposed defeat."

"I can't give you an answer," Jessica said. "I took the case predicated on doing everything in my client's best interests. I've since checked the ethics canons, however, and believe I am on firm ethical footing in following his wishes. In the event you have not had time to review my pleading, and I would be surprised if you had, you'll see that I've filed for discovery in precincts that complement your petition. Without overlap."

"So, if I understand what you're saying," Cole said guardedly, "you have filed a case for which your client has no expectation of winning and, to that end, are attempting to deliberately facilitate my client's case."

"That is precisely what I am saying," said Myers.

"I'll need to run the ethical and legal traps on this before responding," said Cole, growing more cautious and suspicious by the second. "At a minimum, I do not want to engage in any *ex parte* conversations that risk my client's case. In the meantime, I suggest you vigorously pursue your client's petition and the discovery included therein. I don't have to do any research to know that I have no interest in being accused of tampering with your case."

* * * * * * *

E-MAIL

To: Atlas
From: General
cc: Mark
Sent: 12/15 11:16 a.m. (CST)
Subject: Meeting With Speaker

I received a call requesting a meeting with the Speaker. His assistant asked if you could join me.

E-MAIL

To:	General
From:	Atlas
cc:	Mark
Sent:	12/15 10:47 a.m. (MST)
Subject:	Meeting with Speaker

I'm in. When and where?

E-MAIL

To:	Atlas
From:	General
cc:	Mark, Barbara
Sent:	12/16 1:36 p.m. (CST)
Subject:	Meeting with Speaker

The meeting with the Speaker was extremely productive. He was sorry you could not join us on such short notice, but stressed his desire to meet with you in the near future. He has commitments over the holidays, but is interested in your offer to spend a long weekend in Aspen.

I thanked him for all his help in electing Tom. As you would suspect, he offered no specifics, but his body language was that of a proud peacock.

The agenda proved to be very narrow, along the lines of our pre-election negotiations:

(1) Election of Speaker and Senate president: He presented an analysis, prepared by Danny Ryan, demonstrating his judgment as to which E Party representatives are best positioned politically to vote for him to retain the speakership and for Fred Welk to continue on as Senate president. I informed him that, based on our November meetings, we believe we can produce at least the six votes he needs and the five votes Welk needs.

(2) He reconfirmed his commitment to move our education agenda in the spring session of the General Assembly. I indicated that Barbara Jenkins will be our negotiator for purposes of drafting the bill to be introduced on the first day of session. His negotiator will be Majority Leader Kapama. He is waiting for Welk's negotiator to be identified. He suggests we exclude the Republicans. I told him we would consider the suggestion and get back to him.

(3) He brought up redistricting before I did. We again reconfirmed our understanding. In light of the tightening of the election results, however, he cautioned that our negotiations should be put on hold for the time being. Obviously, neither of us wanted to broach the election challenges, but I couldn't help noticing that at this point his comportment and body language were anything but strong. I sensed an element of stress that I had not seen in him at previous meetings.

(4) He then threw me a curve ball, offering an unsolicited recommendation that we not cut a deal when our tax case is recast as a civil filing. The man obviously has impeccable sources. When I see you, I'll fill you in on his compelling observations.

(5) Finally, we talked staffing. He gave us his list of those holding state jobs he considers "must stays." As you might expect, nothing over the top. The man's a pro.

He asked how we were coming on putting Tom's cabinet together. Over a few Scotches, we had a very informative *tête-à-tête* about government, bureaucracy, and patronage. And I thought I had war stories!

Bottom line: He'll work with us on a shadow basis to make sure the lights get turned on and stay on.

E-MAIL

To: Atlas, General
From: Elaine Spencer
Sent: 12/17 9:11 a.m. (CST)
Subject: Need to talk

Please have Liz set a call as soon as possible. Our initial review of the petitions indicates that we could be knee-deep in foul play.

CHAPTER TEN

If Elaine Richards were a man, her nickname would be "the Duke" from the inevitable comparison to the prototypical John Wayne movie character. Strong, tough, born to lead, cool under pressure, no bullshit and, above all else, always the last "man" standing. As it was, Duke was only one of the pseudonyms she'd earned from enemies she had vanquished throughout her legal career. Of the public variety, she had one that she specifically preferred for her epitaph, a comment coined by a thoroughly defeated opposing counsel in Dallas after a particularly lengthy and difficult trial. "Richards," he'd said ruefully, "is one tough broad."

If Elaine Richards were a man, she also would not have been so frequently passed over early in her career for key political appointments, board of director slots, and partnership in her firm. As it was, she'd let nothing get in the way. She'd served a stint as U.S. attorney in Houston and was now a senior partner in the prestigious Frazier, Santona firm. For the most part, the sky had not been the limit, but the glass ceiling below it. And even that had cracked and crumbled under her continued pressure.

When Atlas and the General needed the second coming of John Wayne in the person of their legal counsel, Richards had been a surprisingly easy choice.

"Evening, gentlemen," Elaine Richards began in a manicured Texas dialect. "I am sorry to call for the cavalry on such short notice, but we've been ambushed."

"Evening, Elaine." Atlas, the General, Mark, K.C., and Tom Robinson were all in on the call.

"If you'll allow me, then, I'll cut to the chase."

This was Richard's trademark segue. They waited.

"As you know, both Allen and Stewart have filed discovery petitions as a precursor to officially challenging the election. Statistically, Allen is the only real threat. No way does Stewart leapfrog two places. He has to know that. Yet, someone is bankrolling a very pricey legal operation.

"Under Illinois law, in an election challenge, discovery is allowed in up to twenty-five percent of the precincts in each election jurisdiction, which essentially means each county. There are 11,271 precincts in Illinois, so the law contemplates discovery in up to 2,817 precincts—exactly the number included in the Allen petition and the Stewart petition.

"Our legal team has just analyzed the two petitions and discovered there is not one single precinct overlap. In other words, an effort has been very carefully orchestrated to result in discovery being conducted in fifty percent of all precincts and, therefore, roughly fifty percent of all votes cast. Equally curious, the Stewart petition is decidedly skewed to Republican-leaning precincts where Allen, not Stewart, is more likely to pick up votes.

"If nothing else, this is a logistical nightmare for which we are not prepared, and it significantly increases the chances of the election being overturned."

Though Elaine sensed hearts thumping, apparently the chorus knew better than to interrupt counsel. And she hadn't even moved to cautionary yellow yet.

"In the case of Allen, we are convinced his legal expenses are being covered by a combination of the Republican National Committee and the Republican Governors Association. The state Republican Party coffers were totally exhausted last October, and those two groups were already funding the campaign in the waning days. It's all in the D-2s, the political financial reports filed with the state.

"What's not so clear is the source or sources of Stewart's funds. Speaker Kennedy has adequate sources at his disposal to make the commitment, at least initially, as do various other local Democrat organizations, including the Cook County organization. It could also be national or DGA. For that matter, it could also be the Republicans. Regardless, it's not about Stewart.

"As your attorney, I wanted to get this information in front of you immediately. Bottom line, this case just became significantly more complicated, one that raises constitutional questions and, unfortunately, escalates costs considerably."

Not normally reticent, the chorus members individually collected their thoughts, each waiting for someone else to jump in. The General went first. "Who would serve as governor if, as you are suggesting, the case is not decided by early January?"

"Tom, pending the outcome of the hearings," Elaine said.

"I assume Tom would possess the entire panoply of constitutional powers, even if only temporarily serving as governor," said Mark.

"Absolutely."

Atlas sought and received an outrageous budget guesstimate for the cost of the proceedings.

As a follow-up to Mark's query, Tom expressed concerns about the executive branch team he could assemble under such tenuous circumstances.

It took approximately three hours of spirited debate before a revised game plan was unanimously approved.

* * * * * * *

E-MAIL

To: Lisa
From: Atlas
cc: Tom
Sent: 12/17 11:11 p.m. (MST)
Subject: Change of Plans

Elaine Richards has just briefed a few of us on recent developments—and a host of new complications—in the election challenge. She'll brief the entire leadership team on a call later this week once she can ferret out a few additional details.

In the interim, we've decided to re-double our PR efforts leading to the inauguration. Among other things, we're playing to a new principal audience—the Supreme Court of Illinois.

Please revise the plan according to the attached notes. Call me with any questions.

* * * * * *

"Cobb, what the hell are you doing?" This time it was Scott Grusin doing the shouting through his headset. "You agreed to stay out of the recount. From where I sit, your thumbprint is embedded in Mr. Stewart's forehead, if not stuck up his ass. If that isn't enough, our lead counsel just tendered his resignation. He says this case has indictment written all over it."

"Whoa there, cowboy!" Eddie said. "Not so fast. What I *told* you was that my gut tells me you'll prevail if you spend the five mil. So far I haven't changed my mind about that. As for Stewart, I'm not sure I like your insinuatin' such a thing. Sure, I may have convinced a few patriots to pony up some cash, but unless his counsel violates attorney-client privileges, those providing the funding shall remain forever nameless. And don't go pretendin' you don't know how it works, Grusin," he added meaningfully.

"Besides, anything I might have set in motion was entirely consistent with a thorough and competent legal analysis. Once your lead counsel calms down, his own research will confirm that the Stewart petition is squarely within Illinois statute and case law. In fact, if he finds otherwise—and I'm talking anything less than four square, rock solid— you give me the word and Stewart's petition rides off into the sunset. Otherwise? I'll wait for your thank-you note."

Scott sputtered, but said nothing.

"Furthermore, there's nothing tying yours truly to this matter. And, in case Mr. Cole hasn't yet enlightened you or Ms. DiMaggio, he's just been handed a gift of almost 3,000 precincts' worth of free discovery with which to win his case."

Scott fumed silently.

"Now," said Eddie, feeling positively gleeful at the turn of the table, "anything else we need to discuss?"

Grumbling, Scott tore at the Bluetooth at his ear and disconnected. It was hard medicine to swallow that Eddie Cobb had actually done him two favors. Three thousand additional precincts, especially in Allen territory, were the godsend he'd described. The unpleasant reminder that his cohort was the ultimate loose cannon had also clarified that the better course was to avoid Cole's constitutional challenge inquiry to the election law, particularly if it induced Kennedy to insert himself.

* * * * * *

E-MAIL

To: Elizabeth DiMaggio
From: Scott Grusin
Sent: 12/18 5:06 p.m. EST
Subject: Joseph Cole

Please tell Mr. Cole that my sources report that there is nothing to suggest his case has been or will be tampered with.

Please implore him to reserve his decision to resign pending the completion of his ethics research. As for Cole's question regarding a constitutional challenge, I suggest we defer to our candidate's wishes and take a pass.

* * * * * *

THE BACK BENCH
"If you let it slip, we catch it"
December 19

In an election case that has already broken the mold with two statutorily enabled challengers in the mix, things have gotten even more interesting. On the day before discovery was to commence, E Party counsel Elaine Richards filed the first ever motion to dismiss based on a count of conspiracy.

Count One of her petition, filed on behalf of E Party candidate Tom Robinson, alleges that Illinois Election Law caps the number of precincts in which discovery can be conducted at 25 percent of the precincts in each election jurisdiction. Because challenges have been separately filed on behalf of Allen and Stewart, the effect is to cause discovery in 50 percent of the precincts.

Count Two alleges that the challenges reflect a conspiracy in that there is no overlap between the precincts for which discovery has been requested. Further, with Stewart still over 5,000 votes in arrears, Count Two alleges that the precincts for which discovery has been requested on his behalf statistically favor the Republican, Allen. Accordingly, the motion asks that the Stewart petition be struck as an unconstitutional attempt to bolster Allen's petition.

Finally, in a separate motion, in the event the court rules against Richards/Robinson, they ask for an additional thirty days to prepare for the unprecedented scope of discovery.

Regardless of the outcome, Richards's motions already have the desired effect of delay as the Illinois Supreme Court has set a hearing date for December 28, just over one week from now. The Christmas holiday gives the E Party a needed, if brief, respite in this electoral battle. At the same time, the Court has effectively granted the E Party a stay of discovery.

This delay will also provide much needed time for Richards to organize her legal team for discovery, including the possibility of having to contend with discovery in 50 percent of all precincts.

The motions also have the effect of virtually guaranteeing that the recounts will not begin until after the constitutionally mandated swearing-in of the new governor. Should that occur, various election scholars from whom *The Back Bench* has sought an opinion unanimously agree that Tom Robinson will be sworn in as the governor of Illinois!

In other news…

CHAPTER ELEVEN

While the universe of political speculators was obsessed with the twists and turns of the early round machinations of *Allen v. Robinson* and *Stewart v. Robinson*, Speaker David Kennedy was obsessed with the fact that, for the first time in over twenty years, his stronghold on the Democratic Party of Illinois was in jeopardy.

To anyone less than the grand master of Illinois political chess, the election case would hold center stage. But grand masters see ten moves ahead or risk checkmate. Kennedy's review of the pieces on the political chessboard had revealed that someone or multiple someones were financing a $5 million-plus legal challenge on Stewart's behalf that had no prayer of succeeding and that Stewart's discovery request had been deliberately skewed to Allen's benefit.

Kennedy himself had personally spoken with Stewart prior to launching the last-minute push to elect Robinson. Stewart had appeared to understand unequivocally that, in defeat, the Speaker would arrange a patronage position with an inflated salary designed to greatly enhance Stewart's state and municipal pensions. In addition, Stewart's wife would be chosen by the outgoing Democratic governor to serve on one of the state's plum-flavored citizens boards, complete with a near six-figure compensation and an embarrassment of perks. Was it possible that Stewart would have put all that at risk without the promise of significantly greater financial rewards, rewards far in excess of the Speaker's package?

There was only one possibility. Stewart would never risk his deal with Kennedy if not for a very sure thing. And there were very few very sure things this side of the president. Given a choice between currying favor with the President of the United States or the Illinois Speaker of the House, the outcome was predetermined. It was a matter of when, not if.

Then there was the fact that anyone seeking to increase Allen's chances for success would all too well grasp the power of the Kennedy/E Party alliance. If nothing else, such a move was designed to disrupt Kennedy's plans for redistricting. More than likely, this was a precursor to an all-out attack on his political dynasty.

And finally, there was only one person capable of connecting all these dots: Fast Eddie Cobb. Cobb, while formidable and ruthless, was all too emotional. And that made him prone to mistakes.

The Speaker of the House prepared himself to engage in another round of wizard's chess.

* * * * * *

Nancy Rae Mitchell idly checked the items on her list of Christmas gifts against those she'd already purchased. There weren't many, but this was the first year she could remember that she had both the money to buy presents and the time to shop. Next, she found herself going through her life checklist. Vacation in Cabo with Danny. Check. Decompress from the 24/7 stress-packed election. Check. Plot her exit strategy. Check. Well, maybe half a check.

She scrolled through the Bergdorf Goodman website for gift packs of lotions and bath salts for one of the women she knew through work. Nancy Rae couldn't call Carole a friend—Nancy Rae had no time for close friends. But Carole Zupancis was an acquaintance, and Nancy Rae had an abundance of acquaintanceships. She chose an expensive set of Tom Ford body and face lotions and added it to her shopping cart. She'd have to pay a lot more for shipping to get the gifts before Christmas Eve, but that didn't faze her. It was only money.

Only money! What are you saying, Nancy Rae Mitchell?

Shocked at her own thoughts, Nancy Rae sat back. Money— money through her looks and political savvy—had been the *raison d'être* for her entire life. As soon as she was old enough to understand the concept that money bought things you needed and that some people had it and some people didn't, she'd made the decision to be one of the ones who did. So, how was it that now she sensed there was something more she should be doing...thinking...being...

Clicking on the "submit order now" button, Nancy Rae filled in her address. She didn't need to add her credit card information. Bergdorf Goodman already had that. Which reminded her that she had recently purchased a sexy new Agent Provocateur black negligee, now hanging in her closet, to try out on Danny. Smiling, she made a note to titillate his senses that very night. She sure was enjoying their exploits. Danny was a willing partner, and adventuresome. Nancy Rae liked feeling that she didn't always have to be the one controlling the situation...the outcome. That, too, was new for her, this deferment to someone else's needs and wants.

But now that she had determined a change was in order, the emotional holes refused to fill themselves. She'd never been one to look within—in fact, had derided the entire field of psychotherapy along with the myriad counselors who were always trying to worm their way into her foster child's brain. Who would have thought she'd be thinking about what it would be like to explore her screwed-up psyche now?

One of the most unexpected results of the recent election was that the pendulum of change and doubt had swung Danny Ryan's way. Danny's job had always consumed him, even in the happiest, most fulfilling times of his marriage. A type A before they'd been invented, his compulsiveness and drive had left no room for passion or spousal companionship. Nor had he apparently ever perceived a need for either one. His job, his commitment to excel, were wife, mistress, and whore for all the years Nancy Rae had known him.

Nancy Rae wandered into the kitchen to see if the 2010 Bonneau du Martray chardonnay she'd set in the refrigerator had sufficiently chilled. Danny liked merlot, so she took out a bottle of his favorite and set it on the counter for later. The chardonnay bottle was cold to the touch, so she uncorked it, poured herself a healthy glass, and took a deep appreciative sip. Good wine was just one more thing financial abundance had afforded her.

What was really interesting was that the more Nancy Rae felt herself relax into "political retirement," as she was thinking of it in her own head, the more Danny seemed willing to go along with her. The first week they were back, his usual eighty hours slipped to sixty-something. Then fifty-something. The alarm clock's insistent badgering went from five thirty to six thirty to seven thirty.

She could remember how he used to fall asleep on the couch in the office with his clothes on, tie askew, so tired from the day that he could barely speak. Now their evenings consisted of vintage wine, delivery, and their clothes abandoned on the floor in the heat of the moment.

Nancy Rae took out a wheel of brie and set it into the oven to melt a bit. Cheese and crackers were one of her standbys. Funny about that pendulum shift in Danny's direction. It was December, following a November election, the slowest month in the world of politics. But January was around the corner. This would not be just any January, either, given the possible contested election for Speaker and decennial redistricting posted at the starting gate.

Normally, redistricting was Danny Ryan's finest hour. It set the table for a decade of Democratic dominance. It created fealty from the candidates who understood that their careers were made by Danny Ryan's careful drawing of districts and it assured political contributions from those who understood the power and predictability of a well-conceived and implemented map.

Nancy Rae hoped that the pendulum would hold. That Danny Ryan's holiday season and the new year would guide him one step farther toward a new life.

* * * * * * *

Note to our readers: The article below is part of a series that *Time* will run at least monthly through the next general election. Nat Carson, editor-in-chief of *The Back Bench*, one of the nation's leading political dailies, will chronicle the activities of the E Party. In addition to these monthly columns, Mr. Carson will further document the E Party's journey in a new and exciting blog, posted at www.time/carsonblog-eparty.com.

OPERATION GRASSROOTS DEMOCRACY
By: Nat Carson

Over the past two years, the E Party has assaulted the political establishment. The results speak for themselves. They now hold 18 percent of the legislative seats in Illinois, 12 percent in Pennsylvania, 12 percent in Indiana, and 11 percent in Iowa. In addition to capturing legislative seats, in the November general election they elected the governor, lieutenant governor, comptroller, and treasurer in Illinois.

As with any growth company, it can be expected that they will look to new markets and new opportunities for expansion in the next election cycle. President? Doubtful. But don't be surprised to see them field candidates in all fifty states and possibly take a run at Congress. In a redistricting year, just about everything is up for grabs.

Somewhat overlooked in their political ascension is the way they've gone about it. They find fresh, vibrant candidates, shun negative campaigning, make their Internet messaging state-of-the-art, and their television and radio spots engaging and informative. In short, they have begun to reinvent politics and political campaigns.

Guy Kroft, political commentator and former executive director of the DNC, offers this cautionary advice to his former flock: "The American public has been awakened to the possibility that the political world is undergoing a revolution. If the Democratic Party does not forsake its traditional campaign philosophy and approach, the E Party will not only continue to prosper, it will also spawn additional players and forever change the landscape." He further cautions, "There are only so many dollars available for political contributions, and contributors want to be with the winners. Once either or both of the two major parties lose that edge, it will be nearly impossible to recapture."

As if the entrenched duopoly didn't have enough on its political plate, the E Party has just announced an assault on patronage and the bureaucracy! But if taking on the Republicans and Democrats is a six-inch tap-in for par at the country club scramble, taking on the bureaucracy is a forty-foot downhill twister for birdy on the 18th hole at the Masters to avoid a playoff. Were Vegas oddsmakers to handicap the effort, the odds against taking on the bureaucracy and succeeding would fall just between lasting peace in the Middle East and growing corn on the moon.

Leading the party's mission impossible is Anthony Manzella, a disciple of General Samuel Huntington Smith and a decorated veteran of both Operation Desert Storm and Operation Iraqi Freedom.

Henry Bellock, Senior *Fox News* war correspondent, has seen Manzella perform logistical miracles. "He possesses a unique blend of micromanaging and big picture talents. His brain is ambidextrous. During Desert Storm, he literally oversaw the building of a metropolis in the heart of an unforgiving desert, complete with an airport, transportation system, and accommodations for over 50,000 troops. Not only was it completed in record time and below budget, it was so well conceived and developed that it still functions today with almost no modifications or adaptations in over two decades of heavy, stressful use. But his true genius is manifest in the way his vision facilitated the human element, as if one were living in one of the world's great cities. If anyone can envision and implement the redesign of the bureaucracy, it's Tony Manzella."

If nothing else, its name—Operation Grassroots Democracy—reflects the military vision and precision that Smith and Manzella bring to the E Party. To many, it's the ultimate oxymoron, given that their pedigrees are a byproduct of the world's largest bureaucracy—the U.S. military establishment.

However, to view the military as an entrenched bureaucracy is to misunderstand the avenues of its success.

"Of course, the military is the classic bureaucracy," observes retired Admiral Holland, CEO and president of the George Street Institute, one of the nation's leading think tanks for modern warfare tactics, "but primarily in the sense that the success of any military operation requires unwavering loyalty and precision. At the same time, the true genius of the U.S. military is the constant change that derives from the intramural competitiveness of the four primary branches as well as the constant upgrading and reinventing of hardware and technology allowing us to stay well ahead of any competitive forces. Those who choose to observe structure to the exclusion of functionality do so to their detriment."

To that end, anyone looking at the E Party and seeing a traditional political party structure will do so to their detriment, given its record of innovation on the political battlefield. Operation Grassroots Democracy is modeled after the party's successful launch of a grassroots effort to overhaul and revitalize the Illinois budget process.

Taking a page from the popular television show, *Who Wants To Be A Millionaire*, last spring the E Party launched an Internet platform from which the newly empowered man on the street could have a voice in budget matters. The best idea submitted qualified for a seven-figure award, while other qualifying proposals carried sufficient remuneration that, within two short months, submissions resulted in over 700 amendments to the state's budget for total savings in excess of $2 billion. In the copycat world of American politics, the simulation was adapted by sixteen other states then still in the budget process and will almost certainly be applied in every state next year.

Lisa Boudreau, E Party spokeswoman, says Operation Grassroots Democracy will build on lessons learned from their budget experiment. "Our new effort will incorporate much of the technology and educational adaptations developed by Lauren de la Rosa's group during the budget exercises. However, there is heightened complexity and organizational challenges with Operations Grassroots Democracy. It will be a multifaceted effort combining our search for top talent with organizational and functional considerations, and all this across dozens of executive level agencies, many of which have thousands of employees and multiple layers of bureaucracy to contend with. De la Rosa's team has done an incredible job of developing Internet applications to address this challenge."

Comparing the relative size of the two programs, Boudreau points out that "the budget process was predicated on participation by registered voters in Illinois, whereas the recruitment phase of this operation has a national focus designed to draw the best and brightest from across the country."

As can be expected, the rhetoric has already escalated from the unions. Honey Golden, spokesperson for the American Federation of State, County, and Municipal Employees (AFSCME), cautions that "the Robinson administration has announced its intention to totally overhaul government operations. We wish them well, but also wish to point out that the state currently delivers a wide range of critical services from education to healthcare to public safety, and it is important to guard against rushed decisions and disruption to the education of our children and services to the infirm and elderly."

With the E Party having also won seats in other states, tremors have spread far and wide. Witnessing how quickly others rushed to incorporate the E Party budget model, union representatives at the national level have been meeting in an attempt to launch a preemptive strike where possible. Abigail Stephens of the P.T.I. Institute notes that "the E Party threatens to upend the longstanding paradigm of unions thriving under Democrat administrations and peacefully coexisting under Republican administrations."

In particular, governors facing re-election in the next cycle will want to be out in front of the E Party in reforming government or face the likelihood of a third party challenge. It did not go unnoticed that Governor-elect Robinson was the media darling at the recent biennial National Governors Association Orientation Program for those newly elected. And that the attention was not solely focused on the celebrity of his historic election. He and his E Party entourage came prepared to engage on issues of substance, particularly Robinson's pet project, Getting to 21.

Tom Robinson has yet to be sworn in as governor of Illinois and, with aggressive court challenges to the election results, may never do so. Regardless, Operation Grassroots Democracy looks to be a game changer and the process will be fascinating to watch.

Historically, executive branch transitions are ostensibly a feeding frenzy for party hacks seeking either positions within the new administration or the outward appearance of access and clout from which to leverage consulting and lobbying gigs. A newly-elected president, governor, or mayor stokes these desires with the creation of innumerable committees and task forces purporting to study and report on the failings of the outgoing administration while recommending policy and organizational chart changes necessary to restore efficiency and accountability to government—at the same time extracting additional campaign contributions in the finest tradition of P.T. Barnum.

"Hogwash!" says Garrett Fogarty, former governor of Wisconsin and author of *Re-inventing, Re-inventing Government*. "I've yet to see a transition that did more than kill trees and find ways for the party regulars to rearrange the deck chairs. At the end of the day, not much changes as far as the bureaucracy is concerned. The level of talent needed to truly affect change is held hostage to the demands of the major contributors and political heavyweights, most of whom, no matter how well intended, have out-of-work sons, daughters, nephews, nieces, and other sundry relatives with well-appointed resumes. I have few regrets from my time as governor, but starting off with a superior talent pool to support the administration would have been well advised."

* * * * * * *

E-MAIL

To: Scott Grusin
From: Elizabeth DiMaggio
Sent: 12/19 11:04 a.m. (CST)
Subject: Operation Grassroots Democracy

We're in a perceived bind and I'd like your thoughts before moving ahead. I do not want our decision to cause problems with national.

You probably know that Tom Robinson has announced Operation Grassroots Democracy to serve as his transition mechanism. The scope is far in excess of traditional transitions both in terms of the range of issues and the government operations coming under the microscope.

Anthony Manzella heads the operation. He has personally asked me to provide names of elected Republican officials and any other "scholarly types," as he put it, who can help.

He has also invited Robert Allen to work directly with Tom Robinson so that Allen can help shape and take advantage of the work product in the event he ultimately wins the election.

As you might imagine, it's a PR disaster waiting to happen. They're playing it up beautifully in the media with the usual big tent crap oozing from every announcement. Speaker Kennedy's public statements in support of Robinson's plan are also influencing our position.

Allen wants to graciously decline, as do I, but I fear a backlash if we sit this out. After much consternation and discussion, we have decided that Allen will issue a statement in support of Robinson's efforts to clean up the damage caused by Democrats' having controlled the state, just as Allen will do if his election challenge succeeds, blah, blah, blah. In the end, Allen will decline and defer his attention to the election litigation.

At the same time, I'll play ball just enough to avoid our being labeled as obstructionists...walk that tightrope of public opinion between good and evil, while in no way unduly assisting Robinson or risking any PR damage to Allen's case.

Needless to say, this is one catch-22 I do not relish. Regardless, we will give you advance copies of any press releases for review and comment.

Again, I look forward to your input.

CHAPTER TWELVE

Not unlike the wilds of Africa, the political jungle is dominated by alpha males and females. Not unlike the wilds of Africa, for every alpha leader there are dozens of cubs born each year that are destined to fulfill the circle of life by challenging the throne. And, not unlike the wilds of Africa, most political alpha leaders face disputed, and often abrupt, endings.

That Speaker David Kennedy had vanquished alpha challengers for well over twenty years was the stuff of political legendry. His success and prowess was ubiquitous throughout national political and governmental circles. Such was the reach of his renown that, on his occasional tours outside the country, the release of his itinerary attracted unsolicited inquiries and invitations from the highest ranking dignitaries and monarchs.

It was Kennedy's good fortune that the world of politics and government, unlike the jungle, offered untold opportunities to deflect alpha pretenders. There had been countless challengers he had easily diverted during his reign. Hundreds he had swatted to higher office, alternative political tracks, cabinet positions and, occasionally, private sector paths to fame and fortune. Most of them came to understand that the consequences of merely wounding the king were of themselves fatal and, for that reason, shrank from the enormity of the task.

But not Javier Sanchez. The current prince-in-waiting.

It was Nancy Rae Mitchell who'd unearthed and tapped Javier's potential. Constantly on the lookout for talent, she'd been quick to notice that he possessed the intellect, tenacity, and guile that, properly channeled, would eventually catapult to leadership. Accordingly, she'd tested him from precinct to precinct, from campaign to campaign.

She saw in him many of the attributes that had facilitated and advanced her own career. With one major exception. Whereas Nancy Rae was destined to flourish behind the scenes, he had the itch, the style, and the cojones to put his name on the ballot.

Following the last remap, and contrary to her wishes and Danny Ryan's orders, Javier had challenged a longstanding state representative from the West Side of Chicago. Although Ryan selectively and covertly used his powers of persuasion to avoid or minimize primary battles, it was the party's longstanding tradition not to actively involve itself at that level. The winners of the Democratic primaries, however, whether or not they had been preferred, would always enjoy the party's unrequited love and support in general elections.

The incumbent, Martin Winger, enjoyed the advantage of funding and organization. But it was a remap year, and he'd found himself defending a large swath of new territory, including areas of burgeoning Hispanic population. The incumbent enjoyed a career replete with ribbon-cuttings and parades. But it was a remap year and a legacy of tough votes, when strung together in the legislature, became easy targets for the arrows in his challenger's quiver. The incumbent enjoyed press connections and a voluminous, good ole boy Rolodex, but aging hips and knees kept him from knocking on as many doors as he once would have.

Javier Sanchez won that first campaign by less than one hundred votes and never looked back. At the state level, he rapidly climbed through the legislative ranks to become chairman of the powerful House Transportation Committee. Within the party, he was now a state central committeeman, and was in line to become chairman of the National Hispanic Caucus of State Legislators.

It made Javier's blood pulse a little faster just to think about the trajectory of his career and about the fact that it was aimed dead set at a bull's eye with David Kennedy's face on it. It was nothing personal, of course. Javier wasn't hostile or antagonistic. Simply self-confident the way a seasoned pro who understands that time is on his side can afford to be.

Still, he reminded himself constantly to be cautious, to survey the political landscape for opportunities to cement his status as next-in-line, no matter how distant from the top. Admittedly, had Kennedy not been so skilled, he would already have succumbed to the political reality of a Democratic Party reflective of its ever-increasing majority base. Javier Sanchez knew that when the chips fell, he would not only be the next Speaker, but the first minority—Black or Hispanic—to rise to a level of true leadership in the Illinois Democratic Party, at which point, he would reshape the party's image to the realities of census and demographics.

When his cell phone called out the first few notes of "La Bamba," Javier was jolted back into the moment. A quick glance at the screen told him it was Eddie Cobb on the other end. Another alpha male who enjoyed—no, reveled—in the status commensurate with his role as national chairman. Sadly for Cobb, the shelf life of his position was dependent on whether or not his party held the presidency, and therefore notoriously brief. Not that it kept him from thoroughly enjoying the infighting below. With no reason to heed the advice of Satchel Paige, Cobb had clearly looked back a long time ago to see who might be gaining on him. It hadn't taken binoculars to see Javier Sanchez on the path. And wasn't it convenient that the object of Cobb's immediate obsession was the same face that Javier had affixed to his own target.

"Mr. Sanchez," boomed the phlegmy cigar smoke-filled voice. "I hope I'm not catching you at a bad time. Chairman Cobb, here."

Javier feigned ignorance. Thank God for caller ID. "Not at all, sir. What can I do for you?"

"Well, son," Eddie Cobb began.

The endearment made Javier's hands close in a fist.

"It seems I'll be in your neck of the woods in a week or so. You think you could manage to squeeze me into your busy schedule? I have an opportunity that you just might find intriguing."

Squeeze you in? Please. They both knew that Javier had no choice in the matter. Not that he wanted to have a choice. His brain had gone numb after the word "opportunity" had left Eddie Cobb's lips.

* * * * * * *

MEMORANDUM
To: Transition Team Leadership
From: Anthony Manzella
Subject: Transition Issues Update
Date: December 20

Set forth below is a status report on the key transition issues identified at our Aspen retreat. Overall, our efforts to date are consistent with the timetable. PLEASE NOTE: various decision points are set forth in anticipation of our call next Wednesday. Please feel free to contact me in the interim with any questions.

Robinson Campaign Transition Update
1. Governor Robinson has spent the majority of his time meeting with leaders and key constituent groups regarding the list of major action items and legislative initiatives identified. Attached is a chart showing his meeting schedule to date, as well as meetings currently set through year-end. In each session, the attendees have been asked to identify (a) their top issues for consideration by the new administration, (b) a reasonable timeline for implementation, (c) cost to the state for issues needing funding, and (d) other parties having a stake, pro and con. A complete matrix is available in the secure area of the transition website, and a final report will be released to the public and the legislature via the website commensurate with the inauguration.
2. Governor Robinson has also been conducting a wide range of public relations-type interviews across a varied spectrum of media and geography, the bulk of which is Illinois-centric. Lisa has done an excellent job of tailoring the scope to background and big picture, specifically including Operation Grassroots Democracy. Mark and Lisa

have commissioned weekly polling on the governor's favorability ratings, which remain consistently high and are trending up. Attached is a list of completed interviews as well as those scheduled and Liz will have all the interviews available for you to download.

As you are aware, although we had planned to begin publishing issue papers at this point, the recount has necessitated a change in plans. No reason to test the waters on anything that could become controversial when we need the court of public opinion behind us.

Although not yet confirmed, Lisa remains hopeful that Kathryn Collins will host Tom on her talk show during the holidays. Her ratings are higher than normal during that period and it could match nicely with the anticipated court schedule.

3. Operation Grassroots Democracy is now in full swing. I will circulate a progress report under separate cover. The most pressing issue is whether to defer cabinet appointments until the recount has been resolved. Obviously, that would greatly delay implementation of our agenda.

4. It is imperative that we finalize Tom's key governor's office staffing during our call. Attached are recommendations and complete briefing papers for chief-of-staff, press secretary, budget director, and general counsel. All candidates have been vetted by Elaine Richards's legal team. Once finalized, Mark proposes to provide background information to Nat Carson for staged release through *The Back Bench*, similar to our roll-out of candidate resumes during the campaign.

5. Barbara Jenkins has begun negotiations with the Speaker's staff and Senate president's staff on the education bill, which will be filed as House Bill No. 1 and/or Senate Bill No. 1 once the legislature convenes.

6. Inaugural festivities are still on hold. Attached are various scenarios for a scaled-back production in respect for circumstances and wanting to show deference to the court. Given the late date, many decisions require immediate attention.

* * * * * * *

E-MAIL
To: E Party Leadership Distribution
From: Barbara Jenkins
Sent: 12/21 8:16 p.m. (CST)
Subject: Negotiations update

It was a shock-and-awe honor to have the Speaker sit in on the first working group session for the education package. I was told afterward by a member of his staff that he never attends drafting sessions.

Not surprisingly, the Speaker has little apparent interest in the nitty-gritty. He was all about politics, process, and big picture. Among other things, he recommends moving the bill quickly, before the election challenge is resolved. He said Tom's ability to show strength on this legislation will give the court pause if it comes down to a close call. He also wants to avoid the end of session "food fight," as he called it, over the legislative remap.

He cautioned that, for the entire month of May, if not sooner, each legislator's entire focus will be on drawing and finalizing their new districts. Evidentially, self-preservation totally eclipses the people's business in a remap year. The Speaker's candor was unexpected, but greatly appreciated. It almost seemed as though he was reaching out to me personally.

As to the big picture, the bulk of the discussion was devoted to whether Getting to 21 should be included in the package. The Speaker presented an insightful list of pros and cons and went into great detail regarding the politics of each.

Bottom line: He agrees to add Getting to 21 to the package. But he strongly cautioned that it is too new and controversial to pass without a full-fledged PR campaign and that we should be prepared to use it as a bargaining chip.

After the meeting, he took me aside to embellish on the PR campaign and offered to lend one of his top lieutenants to the effort. More about that on our next conference call.

* * * * * * *

As national chairman of the Democratic Party, a common figure on Sunday talk shows, and a key participant in celebrity-hosted golf-outing fundraisers and other events generally featured in gossip columns, Eddie Cobb was not likely to arrive unnoticed in Chicago. Equally unlikely was the possibility that he could set a meeting with Javier Sanchez that would remain undetected by Speaker David Kennedy's radar. Accordingly, Eddie decided the best tactic was to hide in plain sight.

First, he accepted an invitation to U.S. Senator Appleby's annual holiday party at the Drake Hotel. That would place him at the scene without turning any heads. Then he tasked Representative Javier Sanchez with finding a quiet, out-of-the-way location where, as he'd carefully phrased it, "they could have a private, confidential exchange."

Sure, Eddie could have flown Sanchez to Texas, and done it discreetly. But why shouldn't he test his understudy to determine if he was sufficiently savvy and trustworthy? Should Sanchez fail this simple trial to successfully orchestrate a clandestine meeting in the Speaker's backyard, he would be the wrong man to play one of the starring roles in director Eddie Cobb's rendition of *Mission Impossible*. Should word of their meeting leak, Cobb would eventually find out. That would be unfortunate for Javier.

* * * * * * *

"Oh, excuse me," Mark began. "I'm looking for the nationally renowned *Time* magazine columnist, Nat Carson. Is he available, please?"

"Cut the crap, Stone, " Nat snorted. "Last thing I want is a groupie. Especially one like you."

Mark laughed. "I'm offended. I'm your biggest fan, you know."

"Sure. And six is eight," said Nat. "To what do I owe this outbreak of groveling?"

"Nothing, really. Just thought you might have some time to catch up on your new celebrity and some E Party scuttlebutt."

"Well, then, why not?" said Nat. "Even us national celebrities can find time for an old friend. I'm feeling that festive holiday mood, too.

How 'bout we grab a big thick steak, some double-baked, and a bottle of something expensive at Gibsons? We'll let my buddies at *Time* pick up the tab."

"I say groupie status feels pretty good right about now. Can you do tomorrow night? I have a time-sensitive agenda that needs your attention."

* * * * * * *

E-MAIL
To: E Party Leadership
From: Lisa
Sent: 12/24 12:51 p.m. CST
Subject: Tom on Kathryn Collins

The taping went well. The downside is that Collins thinks it may have greater impact if the show runs closer to the inauguration. Although we had hoped for a holiday screening, January is a dead period for television ratings and their producer knows that Tom's appearance is likely to give the show a boost.

* * * * * * *

THE BACK BENCH
"If you let it slip, we catch it"
December 28

EXTRA EXTRA EXTRA EXTRA EXTRA EXTRA

With unexpected swiftness, if not a totally unexpected result, immediately following oral arguments this afternoon, the Illinois Supreme Court ruled that the discovery requests from both the Allen and Stewart campaigns are to be honored. The result of the ruling is that there will be an unprecedented discovery recount in 50 percent of all precincts. This is a huge boost to Allen and an equally huge setback for Robinson. Allen need only find 190 votes, and with almost two million subject to review in discovery, his chances are excellent. The court also denied attorney Elaine Richard's motion for additional time to prepare for the twofold discovery burden. All this clearly portends another Bush v. Gore, Coleman v. Franken knockdown, drag out.

In other news ...

THE BACK BENCH
"If you let it slip, we catch it"
December 28

EXTRA EXTRA EXTRA EXTRA EXTRA EXTRA

Just one hour following the Supreme Court's ruling on the motion regarding discovery, the E Party filed a new procedural motion requesting bifurcated discovery. Consistent with the order in which the petitions were filed, it asks that the Allen discovery proceed first, followed by Stewart.

It is somewhat curious that counsel Richards will be asking her legal team to sit through duplicate sessions. However, sources point out that conducting joint discovery would require double the staffing and double the coordination given that there is no overlap in the precincts identified by the Allen and Stewart petitions.

If the motion is granted, the total time allotted for discovery will double as well.

In other news ...

THE BACK BENCH
"If you let it slip, we catch it"
December 29

Yesterday, the Illinois Supreme Court dispensed with briefings and ruled in favor of Elaine Richards's motion to bifurcate discovery. The court also set a hearing schedule for preliminary motions that runs through late January.

In other news...

CHAPTER THIRTEEN

Democratic Chairman Eddie Cobb's DNC Ranch in McAllen, Texas, just outside San Antonio, contains the obligatory stables, fields, livestock, and ranch hands. It had also recently been reconfigured and rehabbed to serve as command central for his nationwide political activities, complete with state-of-the-art information and telecommunication technology. That it has parking for up to one hundred cars and a constant stream of white-collar workers and visitors does not prevent Chairman Cobb from enjoying a diverse basket of local, state, and federal tax benefits associated with raising cattle.

Upon arrival, Representative Javier Sanchez and his wife, Camilla, were escorted to a lavish suite and advised of the available relaxation and spa facilities for their comfort. Not exactly Tia Natalye's home in Jersey where they usually visited family for New Year's.

Although a large entourage would eventually descend to ring in the holiday, Javier was astonished to learn that he and Camilla were Cobb's only guests for both the twenty-ninth and thirtieth. Time well spent. Within forty-eight hours, he, Cobb, and Oliver Kiley, Cobb's chief-of-staff, designed the outline for a platform from which Javier could dominate the remap process in Illinois, raise untold millions in campaign contributions, and launch an attack on Speaker Kennedy. All in preparation—anticipation—of Javier Sanchez's rise to Speaker of the House after the next general election. And all predicated on a Robert Allen governorship.

The mere thought of it gave Cobb a chilling sense of certainty.

* * * * * * *

Against his better instincts and against the protestations of the E Party leadership, Atlas Stein had invoked his self-proclaimed veto powers to enjoin all E Party transition activity from Christmas Eve Day until noon on January 2. Time was their principal enemy in every facet of their race to build an effective executive branch operation to support Tom Robinson and Barbara Jenkins, Comptroller-elect Olivia Van Straten, and Treasurer-elect Paul Richmond. Upon their return, there would be less than two weeks on the clock.

Also of growing concern was the building tension and battle fatigue Atlas could sense among the troops created by the unanticipated stress and overhang from the recount. From his years of dealing with large-scale trauma victims throughout his professional career, who better knew the signs? He also knew that once the line was crossed, the journey back to normalcy was far more difficult than, in this case, the potential planning setbacks from an imposed hiatus.

To a lesser, but very personal degree, there was also his selfish desire to enjoy the festivities with his new bride.

He received no argument from K.C., who immediately set about planning an impromptu celebration. With Aspen in its seasonal glory, days of skiing, sledding, skating, snowmobiling, and snowshoeing along with nights of fabulous food, festivities, and family were precisely what Atlas would order if he'd had the time to think of it himself. As it was, K.C. delighted in handling all the arrangements.

It wasn't until the ceremonial clinking of flutes, filled to the brim with Dom Perignon on New Year's Eve, that the Atlas musketeers dared violate the gag order.

"To an amazing year," Atlas saluted. "To be surrounded by my three dearest friends and my new family gives me great hope for the year ahead. To borrow from the late, great Mr. Gehrig, I consider myself the luckiest man on the face of the Earth. Regardless of where the journey takes us, it's been one helluva run."

"Here, here," echoed K.C., the General, and Tom Robinson.

"Then I guess that makes me the luckiest woman alive," said K.C., smiling broadly. "Rest assured, I pinch myself each morning to be certain that the adventure lives. Even then, sometimes it still seems like some kind of delirium…a wonderful, extended dream."

"A little too much bubbly for my friends perhaps?" the General joked.

K.C. raised her glass in her own salute and Atlas filled it once again. They all laughed.

"But honestly," said the General. "What we've created isn't a function of luck or fantasy. It's a creature of the damnedest brilliance, dedication to cause, and steadfastness ever seen. Mark my words: what we've accomplished and what we will accomplish under Tom's leadership will be studied, copied, and written about for many years to come. Malcolm Gladwell will have to write a sequel to *Outliers* to try and explain how we got here. My only regret is that this old war horse will be out to pasture while Tom, Barb, and all those babies we elected turn the world on its ears."

"General," said Tom, raising his own glass, "if you even think of greener pastures, I will personally dispatch the state police to place you under house arrest. In fact, my first executive order will be to place all three of you under constant surveillance—G.P.S.-laden ankle bracelets included—so I can find you any time the need arises."

He pointed playfully to each of them. "You got me into this and you aren't going anywhere. *Capiche?*"

"*Capiche!*" they said and raised their glasses once again.

"As for greener pastures," Atlas said, "this young lady and I plan to make good on our threat to christen our institute this summer—that is, if Elaine Richards ever gets around to having my impounded fortune released."

"I'll drink to that," said the General.

"We aren't getting any younger, you know. And the institute has always been the second half of the vision. Our country needs ideas and leaders just as much as it needs the E Party. We're chomping at the bit to get started. We're also excited that Patrick Jr. is joining the parade. We're naming him executive director."

"From his brief exposure to the cause during Thanksgiving," the General said, "I had a sense you guys were working him over. You know how I feel about lawyers, but I guess he has enough K.C. in him to overcome his handicap."

"He does at that," Atlas said. "In fact, between the two of them, I expect to have a hard time keeping up."

"Well, if they kick you out for slacking," said Tom, "I can always find you a cushy job in the Robinson administration."

Atlas, to everyone's delight, blanched at the mere suggestion and the laughter rang out once again.

"I've been bursting at the seams with ideas ever since we got back," said K.C. "In some ways, I'm glad we delayed our plans for the institute because our brief exposure to politics and government overseas has given me an entirely different perspective on what needs to get done. For example, the European newspapers and television appear to have a, shall we say, unique slant on our nation's politics. As if they're using a different lens. And it wasn't very flattering."

"It was always that way in baseball, too," Tom said. "The local papers seemed to have rose-colored glasses. I don't know if giving us the benefit of the doubt is the right way to put it, but... I mean, sure, they took their shots when shots were due, particularly during slumps, but, for the most part, the glass was at least half full until we were out of contention.

"But on the road? Different story. Papers in other towns talked up their teams and literally had us walking around in our underwear. Our paper reported a bonehead play as a 'great try.' The homey's paper called it for the bonehead play it was. You can see how things might play out the same way in politics and government."

"Homies," said K.C., "I like that. Across Europe and the Middle East we're clearly the visiting team. The institute is going to have to undergo some rethinking."

The group waited, not sure if K.C. was finished or if she was doing what she often did—regrouping for her next onslaught of thought. Sure enough, in a moment she dug in again.

"Now that you mention it," said K.C. as if she hadn't jumped countries in the same sentence, "while Mr. Stein was working over Bill Eggers's book with his highlighter, I was totally absorbed with

Fareed Zakaria's work, *The Post-American World*. I don't know if you've read it, so I'll make it a belated Christmas present.

"Zakaria takes much of what we have been discussing for the past few years and applies it to the world stage. That seems to be exactly what the institute needs to do: build leaders who are ready for where the world is headed—economically, socially, and, of course, politically. As the Internet continues to make the world a smaller place, all our political systems will have to adapt accordingly."

Suddenly K.C.'s eyes came back into focus. "Oh, listen to me. I totally forgot where I was in all that. Forgive me. You must think I'm nuts. Why didn't someone kick me?"

"My dear," Atlas said. "Don't think for a moment that we'd do any such thing. Your passion is contagious."

K.C. grinned and planted a kiss on her husband's forehead.

"On the other hand," he said, picking up his glass with a few drops of champagne still remaining, "maybe we should pick this up at breakfast. My brain cells are spent.

"To a great new year with dear friends."

* * * * * *

As the E-Party enclave was counting down the new year in Aspen, Danny Ryan and Nancy Rae Mitchell were celebrating in their own unique fashion in Chicago until the wee hours of the morning, barely shutting their eyes before their prearranged breakfast arrived on New Year's Day at 11 a.m. At Nancy Rae's elbowing, Danny somehow managed to stumble his way to the door, where he suggested through the inch-and-a-half chain-guard opening to the room service waiter that two or even three in the afternoon would work much better.

It had been Nancy Rae's idea. Danny's only disappointment was that he hadn't thought of it himself. They had been officially in lust for some time, and they were undeniably falling in love. But each knew that an orgy in the bridal suite at one of Chicago's finest hotels, christened with as many reenactments of simulated nuptials as they could handle before the alcohol got the best of them, was as good as it was going to get—for now.

In the short run, Danny would soon be lost to the remap as well as to the scores of would-be emergencies declared by newly elected legislators with the driving need to shine, along with their faux ideas for legislation to save the world. At the same time, Nancy Rae would grudgingly find herself groveling to the same legislators in Springfield, Illinois, of all places, and managing her own share of the same ego-driven, would-be emergencies in her capacity as lobbyist.

It was their reality. Neither of them dared contemplate a viable alternative until session adjourned in late May.

In the meantime, an extended New Year's frolic was something they could cling to.

* * * * * *

While nostalgia reigned in Aspen, and animal pleasures governed at the Peninsula, contemplation commanded the mind of Eddie Cobb on the eve of the new year. Not one to ponder the wonders of the universe or the benefits of a loving relationship, it was unusual for Eddie to find himself in this slightly off-putting mood. Once his guests had departed, instead of his usual final call ritual in his library, he moved to the deck outside his bedroom, drink and cigar in hand, to ruminate. The night was clear and chilly, especially for Texas, but it was clearing his head, helping him visualize the play he had commissioned. After a while, Eddie nodded. He had set things in motion, and it was good.

He shivered, got up, walked into his bedroom, and shut the door.

* * * * * *

After honoring his usual uneventful family dinner ritual, Speaker David Kennedy spent time alone in his study moving chess pieces in his head and envisioning endgames for future sessions and elections and the like. For David Kennedy there was no more exciting way to ring in the new year.

* * * * * *

Legal combatants Joseph Cole, Jessica Myers, and Elaine Richards had made their required appearances to various events and parties. Now, all tucked in at home, they could finally give in to the thoughts that had been ruling all levels of their consciousness for months: the recount.

All in all, New Year's Eve was celebrated by most with gusto—with a large dash of anxiety thrown in for good measure.

CHAPTER FOURTEEN

THE BACK BENCH
"If you let it slip, we catch it"
January 2

Given the recent Supreme Court scheduling in *Allen v. Robinson* (note: both cases have now been consolidated under that title), *The Back Bench* has learned that over the next few days the Robinson campaign will begin releasing its plans for key governor's office staffing and the inauguration.

The Back Bench has also learned that implementation of Operation Grass Roots Democracy will be indefinitely delayed, including the extension of cabinet-level executive hiring deadlines through at least mid-February. The effect of this extension will allow for increased participation and comment for their nationwide Internet search that has already given the E Party tons of exposure. In a released statement, E Party spokesperson Lisa Boudreau says, "The additional time will guarantee that the highest quality cabinet members will be selected to serve Governor Robinson and the people of Illinois." Nice spinning, Lisa.

The delay also adds to speculation that Governor Robinson has decided to defer the majority of his cabinet appointments until after the election challenge is decided. It all makes sense. The E Party and Governor

Robinson gain a month or more in which to find top talent to serve in the new administration, but also avoid having their candidates for directorships make risky career decisions.

In other news…

THE BACK BENCH
"If you let it slip, we catch it"
January 3

Discovery begins today in the matter of *Allen v. Robinson*. As many of our readers are aware, *The Back Bench* editor-in-chief, Nat Carson, has recently affiliated with *Time*. The publishers of *Time* have graciously offered to assist *The Back Bench* in staffing coverage of the discovery process. That will allow us to provide daily updates on both *The Back Bench* blog and the *Time* blog. Real time Twitter feeds will also be available from both @backbench (BB Twitter) and @timemag (Time Twitter).

Discovery in the precincts identified in the Allen petition runs for ten consecutive business days. At that point, there will be a three-day break, followed by ten days of discovery predicated on Stewart's petition.

In other news…

* * * * * * *

Tweets from Team Carson quickly captured the nation's attention. At the conclusion of discovery, in excess of 500,000 daily tweets had been originated by *The Back Bench/Time* magazine group of observers and then retweeted and shared on Facebook, Instagram, and numerous individual blogs, as well as analyzed to oblivion on every network and cable show with any semblance of a political theme.

But for the limited twenty-day scope of events, the editors of *Time* would have launched a marketing campaign based on the volume and content of the Tweets. As it was, the operatives in the field held back sufficient tidbits of data to keep fresh the edition of *Time* containing Carson's January article, which was among the top twenty-five of all-time sales.

After engaging the most highly regarded election law experts, political consultants, and at least one well-known psychic, the conclusion reached in Carson's epic story: Too close to call!

* * * * * * *

THE BACK BENCH
"If you let it slip, we catch it"
January 8

Governor-elect Robinson has announced his first appointments to the governor's office staff. At first blush, it appears to be a highly talented and loyal crew that should well serve the new governor.

In an unorthodox selection, he has named Lt. Governor-elect Barbara Jenkins as chief-of-staff. Unorthodox in that the lieutenant governor is usually relegated to third-tier status in the very out-of-way office at the south end of the Capitol. Regardless, the initial reaction has been extremely positive.

In her one term as state representative, Jenkins earned a reputation for both brilliance and perseverance. She was elected caucus chair of the E Party and demonstrated leadership skills that caught the attention of General Smith, leading to her spot on their statewide ticket. She also possesses an amazing academic pedigree. If there's weakness on her resume as far as the chief-of-staff position is concerned, it's her lack of political seasoning. But, with the collective acumen of the E Party leadership team—Mark Stone, in particular—that would not appear to be a significant shortcoming.

With another unorthodox configuration of the ORG chart, the governor has created the position of chief operating officer and has designated Anthony Manzella to fill that role. COO is usually a corporate position without comparable government functionality. However, the assumption is that Manzella will focus on day-to-day operations of state government while Jenkins focuses on coordinating with the General Assembly, setting the agenda, prioritizing issues, and scheduling. Manzella has already been earning his E Party stripes, while serving as the head of Operation Grassroots Democracy.

Another familiar E Party face, Kellie Morgan, will hold down the general counsel post. The general counsel is usually tasked with watching the governor's back to minimize controversy. Although she, too, may not be accustomed to the political side of the job, her performance as their candidate in the recent race for attorney general proved that she is a quick study. A better choice was arguably Elaine Richards, but she is slightly preoccupied with the election challenge and otherwise might not have embraced the pay cut.

The final key governor's office position is that of press secretary. E Party spokesperson Lisa Boudreau will serve in that capacity on a temporary basis. Speculation is that Lisa will serve until the recount is resolved. Many talented names have surfaced, but they all hold current jobs and/or are not willing to accept a position that could terminate before their office furniture arrives.

None of these positions require Senate confirmation.

In other news...

CHAPTER FIFTEEN

E-MAIL

To: E Party Leadership Distribution
From: Lisa Boudreau
Sent: 1/9 7:14 p.m. (CST)
Subject: Airing of Kathryn Collins Show

The interview with Kathryn Collins will air the day before the inauguration. I think the timing could not have worked better. Because we taped a few weeks ago, they were kind enough to provide a transcript so I could anticipate damage control related to shifting events. Below are key excerpts. Let me know if you see any trouble spots.

> **Collins**: Today we are fortunate to have with us the Governor-elect from Illinois, Thomas "Jackie Jr." Robinson. If you recall, Tom graced our show last year, at which time he officially declared his candidacy. He promised to return, but I doubt many in our audience that day anticipated his stunning victory. I'm sure many of you are as fixated as I am with the three-way election challenge Tom is facing, all of which should make today's show rather engaging. So, please join me in welcoming Illinois Governor-elect Tom Robinson. [Applause]
>
> Tom, thank you ever so much for taking time out of your busy schedule to honor us today.

Robinson: Thank you, Kathryn. For the record, you have to include me among those who did not envision the stunning victory you just described.

Collins: Well, let's start there. When did you first sense that you could win the election?

Robinson: To be brutally honest, I never saw it coming. The pollsters had me in third place heading into the final weekend. The gap was narrowing, but it was still all uphill. As you may recall, at that particular moment in the campaign, I was taking considerable heat for a comment I made during the debates by suggesting I was not qualified for the job.

Collins: But, at the same time, I believe it was the *Chicago Tribune* that turned that line around in a salute to your honesty and integrity.

Robinson: Who am I to quarrel with the *Trib*?

Collins: Many political analysts think Speaker David Kennedy orchestrated a last minute deal to elect you in order to avoid a victory by the Republican candidate, Robert Allen.

Robinson: I'm afraid that's one I can't touch.

Collins: Fair enough, but your victory margin has shrunk considerably and that has to be a source of great stress.

Robinson: Any stress I bear is not a function of the election challenge. At the end of the day, the decision lies with the Illinois Supreme Court. They're the umpires and we all know the ump's word is final.

There is, however, great stress associated with planning for a transition, an inauguration, and a functioning Robinson administration. Sorry for again falling back on my baseball career, but it's kinda like an extended rain delay. Not much you can do but sit and wait.

Collins: But you will be sworn in as governor. And, I dare say, you will be immediately under the microscope.

Robinson: Unfortunately, it's also like being an instant lame duck. Take my administrative appointments for example, primarily for department heads. We are in the process of identifying the most talented people from around the country to help us reinvent government. Because of their talents, however, most hold current jobs and are in no position to risk their careers and uproot their families in the face of uncertainty.

Collins: It must be very frustrating to all concerned in the E Party. But you're still moving ahead with Operation Grassroots Democracy. How's that coming along?

Robinson: The best part, at least for me, is that the Internet has facilitated learning about and participation in the political process for the average citizen. These days, those who feel disenfranchised have only themselves to blame.

As you know, the principal function of the exercise is to help identify candidates from across the country to serve in the cabinet. After that, we hope to draw on them to rethink and reinvent how government delivers services.

I believe it was our political guru, Mark Stone, who noted at an early transition planning session that, for the most part, state and federal agencies are headed by the party faithful.

We actually crunched some numbers and, over the past twenty years, the significant majority of people holding cabinet-level positions in Illinois government were Illinois born, raised, and educated, and had strong party ties, whether they'd served in office, been a major contributor or relative of someone who had, or were lifetime bureaucrats who, at best, understood their role was to maintain the status quo.

With the possible exception of a closely held business, no other entity could contemplate or withstand such patronage and nepotism. Imagine if the Cubs or White Sox limited themselves to draft or recruit only home-grown players.

The Robinson administration is dedicated to the best and the brightest from throughout the country. If we accomplish nothing else, it will be to revitalize and re-energize government through efficiency and innovation.

If you'll indulge the pitch, anyone in the audience wanting to learn more about Operations Grassroots Democracy can check us out on Google or Facebook. We welcome all ideas for how to make government function better.

Collins: Very admirable, but that sounds more like a typical politician's cliché than what we've come to expect from the E Party.

Robinson: Changing government *is* a cliché, Kathryn. Both Democratic and Republican. What else do they have to sell? If, at the end of my term, we haven't moved the ball down the field, then it will be an E Party cliché as well, and I will have failed.

My life in sports taught me that success breeds from leadership and teamwork. Operation Grassroots Democracy will hopefully identify and produce leaders we can build around. The next step, forming the team and developing a winning attitude, is where the rubber meets the road.

We're working with some of the nation's top minds in systems and logistics. Anthony Manzella, who will become my COO, is a recognized expert in coordination and procedure from his days in the military. Above all else, we will establish realistic, sustainable goals.

To that end, we've adopted a fascinating book called *If We Can Put A Man On The Moon*, as our strategic bible. In short, the book chronicles historic successes and failures in government and identifies themes and patterns that can drive bureaucratic success. As the title suggests, if we can put a man on the moon, we should be able to fix our education system and solve other pressing problems.

Collins: Again, I appreciate your enthusiasm and commend your plans, but you can't do this single-handedly. As we see at the national level, partisan bickering and in-fighting have created a dysfunctional mess. Even if you survive the election challenge, the Democrats or Republicans will not want you to succeed. How do you overcome that mess?

Robinson [nodding]: And I'm told that the forthcoming redistricting process will further complicate matters. I think the answer lies in a quote from President Reagan that I have become fond of using. Basically, you can have success if you don't care who gets the credit.

Part of the problem with government today is that excessive energy is wasted trying to both assess blame and jockey for credit. I am convinced we can reverse the paradigm and I personally plan to set the example.

Collins: Atlas Stein and General Smith played prominent roles in the creation and implementation of your party. They also became very controversial with respect to a federal criminal trial challenging the party's principle funding source. If you don't mind my asking, what role do you see them playing in your administration and the party moving forward?

Robinson: I don't mind at all. Their story is fairly ubiquitous at this point so, needless to say, in great measure, the success of the party and my personal victory is because of them. However, as you point out, the case of *U.S. v. Stein* is currently before the courts and its determination could have a momentous effect on their future roles.

The way the case has played out, many speculate that it was politically motivated. Even today, no replacement has been named for the judge who recused himself, and vast sums of my good friends' personal fortunes remain frozen. In my opinion, the longer this persists, the more people will come to consider politics to be at the root of the case.

As for my administration, I doubt either will be involved in the day-to-day. I have, however, asked the General to chair a task force that will conduct a forensic audit of government agencies in conjunction with the state's auditor general. But I don't see that exercise lasting more than a month or so. As for Atlas, you must also know he recently married and I expect their extended honeymoon to outlast mine.

Collins: Last time you were here you briefly expounded on a program you called Getting to 21. Where does that fit into your plans?

Robinson: Still at the top of the list. But it will need legislative approval first. Lieutenant Governor Jenkins is currently working on an education package that will hopefully become the cornerstone of my first year in office. During the election, candidates Allen and Stewart both signed oaths to support the E Party education package. Even if I am not the governor, I will stay involved to make certain that whoever wins honors his pledge.

Collins: Governor, our time has flown. Thank you ever so much for being here today. Best of luck to you.

Robinson: Thank you, Kathryn. It's been a pleasure.

* * * * * * *

E-MAIL

To: E Party Leadership Distribution
From: Atlas, K.C.
Sent: 1/9 11:46 p.m. (MST)
Subject: Collins interview

Reads well. We're both pleased with the messaging and assume Tom accomplished it with his usual eloquent, charismatic delivery. Appears to be totally non-threatening to the Illinois Supreme Court. At the same time, very adept at setting the stage for hopefully settling *U.S. v. Stein* in the very near future.

E-MAIL

To: E Party Leadership Distribution
From: General
Sent: 1/10 8:01 a.m. (CST)
Subject: Collins interview

Ditto. What's this about me overseeing some damned audit?

CHAPTER SIXTEEN

Scowling her displeasure at the task ahead, with only days to the inauguration, Senator Elizabeth DiMaggio understood that she had no choice in the matter. As head of the Republican Party in Illinois and as the Republican leader in the Senate, etiquette dictated that she call to congratulate the new governor, and it was now two months since election night. Originally, it was the enormity of Robert Allen's defeat that had kept her from honoring the obligation. Then, it was the intensity of the election challenge that had diverted her attention. Now, the impediment was nothing more than utter and complete embarrassment.

Lt. Gov. Barbara Jenkins had called her to discuss the education package and to invite her to a pre-inauguration meeting of the legislative leadership. There was absolutely no way Elizabeth could possibly show up without having bit the bullet first.

She pushed aside a stack of files on her crowded desk and reconsidered her options. Prior to the last General Assembly, she and General Smith had met to negotiate who the E Party would support for Speaker of the House and president of the Senate. She'd been patiently waiting to hear from the man. Surely, he was still engaged in the process; still the go-to, behind-the-scenes deal maker. So what did it mean that she'd received no call, no email, no contact?

Could Speaker Kennedy have trumped her again? Everyone knew he'd packaged the election for Robinson. It didn't take a rocket scientist to figure out his price. He'd deliver for Robinson; the E Party would give him the votes he needed to stay in power.

Sinking farther back into her chair, Elizabeth heaved a great sigh. Two dreaded calls to make and, with the inauguration looming, very little time left on the clock.

She'd gone all in for Allen. Now, unless Cole found a net gain of 190 votes, she was about to be evicted, her career derailed like the train in that old movie—what was it?—oh yeah, *Silver Streak*.

Funny what you remember when your life is about to end.

* * * * * * *

E-MAIL

To: E Party Leadership Distribution
From: Lisa
Sent: 1/10 9:56 a.m. (CST)
Subject: Inaugural address

Attached are the two draft speeches for the inauguration. One is the "short and sweet, don't rock the Supreme Court boat" version. The other one is the "lay out the full agenda" version. Please let me know your preference and comments by the end of the business day tomorrow.

* * * * * * *

THE BACK BENCH
"If you let it slip, we catch it"
January 11

With the inauguration just days away, Governor-elect Robinson met today with legislative leaders. For the first time in Illinois political history, the leader group included six members, two from each party. The E Party has earned its seat above the salt.

For as long as anyone can remember, the Democratic leaders are Kennedy and Welk and the Republican caucus leaders have been Williams and DiMaggio. The E Party designees are Senator Benjamin and Representative Abernathy, each of whom was the E Party leader on education in their respective chambers during the last General Assembly.

In another display of mold breaking, Lt. Gov. Jenkins also attended. Whether in her role as lieutenant governor or chief-of-staff, there is a new paradigm shaping governance at the 10,000-foot level of decision and deal making.

In press briefings, the participants uniformly stuck to script in reciting that the meeting's agenda was brief and primarily to meet and greet. They all uniformly refused to address the status of the recount or its potential impact on the session before them.

Lt. Gov. Jenkins said she hopes to introduce an education package on the first day of session, but steadfastly avoided any specifics.

For their part, the Democrats and Republicans gave their usual muted response to questions about their own legislative agendas.

In other news…

* * * * * * *

"General Smith, Elizabeth DiMaggio calling. I hope I'm not catching you at a bad time."

"No, not at all," said the General, nearly choking from surprise. "It's been a while, Senator. How can I help you?"

"Actually, I was hoping I could help you," she said.

"With the session starting in a few days, I'm hoping we can chat about the pending elections for Speaker and Senate president. In the last go round, you went with Speaker Kennedy. I think the Republicans are better served to move your party's platform. Perhaps we can meet to discuss this mutually beneficial opportunity."

"You know," the General equivocated, not yet sure of the best maneuver to employ. "Under the circumstances, I may not be the best person for that conversation."

"Oh," said Elizabeth, taken slightly aback. "I see. Then who might that be?"

"I'll toss it around and see what I can come up with. Can I get back to you this evening?"

What else could she say, but "Sure, no problem." And quickly added, "Though if you've already cut your deal with the Speaker, we can simply move on."

"Let's talk tonight," the General insisted, again putting her off and upholding his reputation of gruff and to the point. "What's the best number to reach you?"

* * * * * * *

E-MAIL

To: E Party Leadership Distribution
From: Barbara Jenkins
Sent: 1/11 1:16 p.m. (CST)
Subject: Negotiations Update

Today was our fifth and likely final drafting session. We are taking the advice offered by the Speaker at our first session not to let perfection become the enemy of a well-drafted bill. He also emphasized that no bill of this complexity and importance ever escaped the sharp knives of the lobbyists or the amendment process.

Once the Legislative Reference Bureau finishes drafting the bill, it will undergo one last review by staff. Consulting with the House and Senate Education Committee staffs on this issue has been another valued lesson as to the inner workings of government. They are experts on substance, in most cases having served their respective committees for many years (while legislators come and go) and are valuable repositories of historical knowledge from legislative battles won and lost. If nothing else, their knowledge base has allowed us to avoid quite a few traps.

The last piece of the puzzle is the name. A few suggestions are attached. Kind of a shame that "No Child Left Behind" was already taken.

As an aside, when we staff up the governor's office, we will need to assess the importance of adding a few graybeards who can lend historical perspective in setting policies and practices.

* * * * * * *

E-MAIL
To: Atlas, Tom, Barbara, Mark, Lisa
From: General
Sent: 1/11 2:27 p.m. (CST)
Subject: Call from Senator DiMaggio

I got a call from Senator DiMaggio late this morning inquiring about the vote for Speaker. I punted and told her I'd get back to her tonight. Who gets the short straw on this one?

* * * * * * *

"Senator? Barbara Jenkins here. General Smith asked me to get back to you in response to your call from earlier today."

Senator DiMaggio had to think a minute. The General hadn't called back himself, simply foisted her off to a rookie. "Thanks for getting back so quickly, Barbara," she said politely. "I didn't get much of a chance to chat with you at our leader's meeting. Congratulations," she added. It might have been half-hearted and unenthusiastic, but it was also acceptable.

"Thanks," Barbara said, appreciating how hard it must be for this maven of political clout to offer an olive branch, however small. She quickly got down to business. "You were asking about the vote for Speaker and Senate president?"

"Why, yes. I trust you are authorized to speak for the party."

Barbara chuckled. "Let's just say that, as the new chief-of-staff, the bucks seem to be stopping at my desk."

"Well, at least they were wise enough to select a woman for the job. Another first for Illinois, and a welcome one," DiMaggio said, this time meaning it.

Barbara acknowledged the nod. The solidarity of women counted for something, despite party lines. "Another first would be installing a woman president of the Illinois Senate—if I were to be elected. Any ideas on how we can work on this together?"

"Interesting perspective on it, I'll grant you," said Barbara. "But, under the circumstances, Governor Robinson and the E Party representatives and senators are focusing solely on our education agenda. At least, that's where the conversation has to start. And that conversation has to include Mr. Allen."

"Allen?" Elizabeth did not like where this was headed.

"Yes," Barbara said, surprised by DiMaggio's sudden tone shift. "Under your scenario, should Allen ultimately win the election, both the legislature and governor's office would be under Republican control. We would have to know with certainty that our education bill would become law."

"Well, it's unlikely anyone could provide that kind of certainty," Senator DiMaggio said, acknowledging Jenkins the check-mate. "Even if Kennedy and Welk promise to deliver, you still have an Allen problem. It seems I'm being held to a higher standard."

"Fair point," Barbara parried, "but Speaker Kennedy has already delivered. From where I sit, I need a demonstration of your ability to deliver as well."

Grateful for the fact that Barbara Jenkins couldn't see Elizabeth's face as her eyes widened in shock, DiMaggio thought fast. Had she really just heard Barbara Jenkins confirm there had been a deal to elect Robinson and that the Speaker was personally involved? That it was the E Party agenda or nothing?

What was the alternative, though? To walk away now with the expectation that Cole would prevail on behalf of Allen...and empower her position as Republican leader in the Senate?

"Barbara," she said, hoping Jenkins couldn't sense her heart racing. "I truly appreciate your candor. Now that I understand the price, I'll need to talk this over with my leadership team and get back to you."

"Absolutely," said Barbara. "I'll look forward to it."

* * * * * *

"Elizabeth DiMaggio calling for Mr. Cole. Is he in?"

"Yes, Senator. Please hold. He's just finishing a call."

Elizabeth impatiently drummed her fingers on the edge of her laptop until Cole picked up the phone. "Elizabeth, how are you today?"

"Well, it sounds like someone's having a good day," she observed. The smirk in Joseph Cole's voice was irritating as hell, as always, but the man was too good at his job to let it get in the way. "I only hope it's due to the Allen case."

"You might say that," said Cole, "and I believe Mr. Allen is, too. With the recent court decision, things are headed in the right direction. A lot will depend on Stewart's discovery."

"Glad to hear it, Joe," said Elizabeth. "But I'm up against a deadline. I need to make a difficult decision predicated on the chances of an Allen victory."

"If you're asking me if I think we'll win," said Cole, "then the answer is yes. I believe so. But am I suggesting that I am sufficiently certain to drive your decision? No, I'm afraid I can't. Not at this time. I don't suppose you can give me a few weeks?"

Elizabeth silently hit her fist on her desk in frustration. "Unfortunately, not," she said solicitously. "How about some odds?"

"Hmm," said Cole, taking his time and only increasing Elizabeth's impatience. "As things stand today, I'd have to say it's probably forty-sixty Robinson. But that's a long way from where we stood on election night. If the discovery is as good as I suspect, the odds will rapidly shift in our direction."

Well, it was something. Elizabeth sighed—with her head averted from the receiver. "Okay. Thanks, Joe. Anything you need from me?"

"I'd still like to know what's behind Stewart's gambit," said Cole. "Has anything turned up?"

"I'm afraid not," said Elizabeth, "so I'll let you go. But, Joe? See if you can get me to eighty-twenty in Allen's favor, okay? Thanks."

She hung up before he could answer.

The space between the rock and a hard place was squeezing uncomfortably. Agreeing to pay Barbara Jenkins's price to be elected Senate president meant victory for the E Party and its education package. The boost that would give them would forever stabilize their party's political standing in Illinois—and to the severe detriment of the Republicans. But allowing Kennedy and Welk to hold the seats of power while they continued playing footsie with the E Party was just another route to the same address.

* * * * * * *

"Mr. Speaker, I have the General on line two."

"General, good to hear from you." They had not known each other for long, nor spent much time together, but had developed a reciprocal respect and admiration that had surprised the Speaker, who reserved his taciturn approval for very few.

"Mr. Speaker," said the General, as always short with his words. "I know it's late notice, but I'm wondering if you can spare me half an hour. I'll come to you."

The Speaker's curiosity was piqued. "I'll have Dawn get back to you as soon as possible."

* * * * * * *

E-MAIL

To: E Party Leadership Distribution
From: General
Sent: 1/12 3:02 p.m. (CST)
Subject: Vote for Speaker

I just finished meeting with Speaker Kennedy. There is no doubt in my mind he expected the question…and that he has nothing to do with Stewart's petition. Further, although he has his suspicions, as party chairman he "is not in a position to make inquiries."

As for the education package, he spoke highly of Barbara's efforts and negotiating skills and confirmed that it will be filed as House Bill No. 1.

In response, I took the liberty of assuring him that there would be sufficient E Party votes to re-elect him Speaker of the House and to re-elect Fred Welk Senate president. Unless there are any objections, I will call Elizabeth DiMaggio myself.

Finally, I asked his opinion of the sitting agency directors in the event we defer our nominations until Tom's election is finalized. He said that, for the most part, they are decent party loyalists and that he could play a role in assuring no undue mischief would occur. As he put it, "Most hold their jobs because of me, either directly or indirectly, and most will be coming back to me for help finding their next opportunity."

As soon as we give him the signal, he will circle the wagons to make certain all retained directors will run their departments using the Manzella playbook. He also offered to lend us one of his top patronage lackeys to crack the whip when necessary. I declined, but the offer stays on the table.

CHAPTER SEVENTEEN

THE BACK BENCH
"If you let it slip, we catch it"
January 13

Never before have so many press and permission-to-film credentials been issued to an event at the Illinois State Capitol. With a decided boost from the soap opera that has become the recount, the swearing in of Thomas "Jackie Jr." Robinson as governor of Illinois, not to mention the phenomenon that is the E Party, has captured nationwide media attention. It was the lead on every major channel's national evening news broadcast last night.

Governor Robinson chose to ignore protocol by not releasing the text of his speech in advance. That he then proceeded to give the shortest address in modern times was also a bit of a shocker.

However, Robinson's presentation was not lacking in emotion, style, or sound bites. He reflected on the journey, with appropriate attribution to how his battle with AIDS had impacted the decision to run. In perhaps the most compelling quote, he closed by saying:

"When I was first called up to the majors, I was a scared young kid, not knowing if I would be there a day or a decade. With the help of the Lord, I was blessed with a Hall of Fame career. I stand before you today with the same trepidation and the same hope. With that said, I pledge to the people of Illinois that I will bring that same level of commitment and team spirit every day I am blessed to serve them."

Anyone who remembers Robinson's great career could sense that, no matter how short or how long his tenure, Illinois is about to be graced by a very special person.

The speech was bereft of issues and needless platitudes. Alluding to the tenuous nature of the situation, he emphasized that the initial focus of his administration would be what he called "revisiting the spirit of excellence and pride in public service."

Just as he had done during the debates, Robinson spoke from the heart about education and his vision for Getting to 21. In doing so, he finessed both Allen and Stewart by invoking their pre-election pledges to support the E Party education agenda, referring to himself as a "torch bearer in a crucial marathon" and taking the high road by suggesting he "will be content to pass that torch to either man if and when required to do so."

In other news ...

* * * * * *

E-MAIL

To: Atlas, General
From: Elaine Richards
Sent: 01/13 3:57 p.m. (CST)
Subject: U.S. v. Stein

I understand from Lisa and Lauren that there has been significant Internet chatter since Tom's interview with Kathryn Collins—almost all of which appears to be running in your favor regarding *U.S. v. Stein*. Lisa also tells me you were named "patriots" by Bill O'Reilly.

So, I guess I should not have been surprised by a call from the U.S. attorney this afternoon, asking when we can get together. Nice bit of strategy to have Tom put the story back in the public eye. I'll keep you posted.

* * * * * *

THE BACK BENCH
"If you let it slip, we catch it"
January 14

As expected, David Kennedy was elected Speaker of the House and Fred Welk president of the Senate. This marks the fourth consecutive General Assembly to be overseen by that pairing.

Both offered rather bland remarks. The Speaker, however, went directly to the issue of the election challenge and confirmed that it will be extremely difficult to craft or pass complex legislation with respect to many of the day's pressing issues until there is certainty in the election for governor. Notwithstanding, he firmly committed to pass what he deemed long-overdue education reform legislation and, in somewhat of a surprise, announced that he would be cosponsoring the bill in the House with Representative Abernathy of the E Party.

In perhaps the most poignant statement of the day, the Republicans in the chamber did not display any approbation for the education agenda. Their apathy did not escape the media, particularly the national level holdovers. As a result, Robert Allen felt obligated to call an impromptu press conference to reaffirm his commitment to the E Party education agenda.

In other news...

* * * * * * *

"Mr. Cobb, Javier Sanchez. Sorry for the late hour, but I got a voice message to call you tonight no matter how late. I just got in from our inauguration day festivities."

"No problem, Javier. But how many times do I have to tell you to call me Eddie?"

"Uh, sorry...Eddie."

"That's better. I learned this evening that your Speaker's cosponsoring the E Party's centerpiece education legislation. I'm sure hoping you can enlighten me here, Javier, because I don't see how putting Robinson on a pedestal is in the interests of the Democratic Party."

"Well, Mr....uh, Eddie, I don't know that I have the answer to that one, but..."

"Of course you don't know the answer, son," Eddie snapped, his charm come and gone like a flash flood. "But I'm still turning to you. Now, tell me what you do know."

Javier regrouped. He didn't like being told what to do, not by Eddie Cobb or anyone else. For now, though, he'd let it go. "Well, for starters, there was no pushback in the Democratic caucus meeting today. There's no reason for anyone to be taking on the Speaker, of course. The man's impregnable."

"No one's asking anyone to take on the Speaker," Eddie cautioned, "particularly not now. What I'm thinking is that we need some good ol'-fashioned hardball lobbying. There must be someone out there, someone who—with the right backing, of course—would risk a battle over this education package."

Javier had no response to this. He always felt slightly out of his depth with Cobb and didn't appreciate the gamesmanship. If the man had something to say, he should just say it.

Finally Cobb went on. "See, here, Sanchez. I'm just asking you to take a step back, give it some thought. Bottom line, we don't necessarily have to defeat the bill. Just slow things down a bit until we put our plan in motion."

Javier opened his mouth to speak, but Cobb cut him off again. What else was new?

"But we won't solve this tonight. Give me a holler next week, ya hear?"

The phone went dead.

* * * * * *

"K.C., my love," said a perplexed Atlas, "seems there's trouble in River City."

"You would have made a great con man," said K.C. referencing the same *Music Man* song lyrics. "But what's so bad that it's causing all that trouble right here in Aspen?"

"I take it you saw the e-mail from Elaine Richards."

"Ah, yes. The one about the court's ruling in favor of Cole's motion to further expedite the evidentiary hearings?"

Atlas grimaced.

"Let's discuss it," said K.C. "But first, how about I buy you a drink?"

Once they were situated on their terrace, under the stars, warmed nicely by the fire pit, a couple of fur throws, and a bottle of Italian vino from their honeymoon travels, K.C. took her husband's hand. "What exactly has got you so tied up in knots?"

Atlas looked up at the infinite sky, wishing the answers he sought would fall into his lap, and sighed. "I've been stewing all day over Elaine's follow-up with the U.S. attorney," he said. "At first, it was as if the timing dovetailed with that cute bit of cheerleading from Tom on the Kathryn Collins show and the public volume it generated. Now, I'm wondering if it's tied more to the election challenge. According to Elaine, the dismissal of the criminal case and release of my assets—as well as the General's—is being tied to my agreeing to follow certain protocols regarding future campaign contributions, especially soft money."

Atlas looked at his wife. She nodded, but didn't speak, intent on his every word.

"On the surface," he said, "the request is reasonable and acceptable. But the language in the draft settlement agreement is sufficiently broad to restrict my further funding of the legal fees in the election challenge. Elaine wanted to know how to proceed.

"If she asks the direct question and is told the release is, in fact, designed to prohibit my paying legal fees, obviously the settlement falls apart. The cost of defending Tom's election has already blown past the budget. With the hearings expanded, we could be looking at an additional five to ten million dollars. I'm not sure where those funds come from. I've talked to the banks and our other sources of liquidity. Understandably, they're growing increasingly skittish. The banks, in particular, are concerned about audit findings since all of the collateral is technically frozen by the court.

"If Elaine doesn't seek clarification and we finalize a settlement, the fear is that the U.S. attorney moves to block continued funding of the recount. In that case, we get creamed in the media for violating the agreement and the well dries up very quickly."

There was a long pause, then K.C. said. "Oh. So that's all it is, then?"

That won a smile from Atlas. "Yeah, I guess that's about it," he said.

"I understand the dilemma as you present it," said K.C., serious now. "But I think you might be missing the point."

Startled, Atlas leaned in to hear her.

"It seems to me that it might be time to abandon the notion that Atlas Stein is the sole benefactor to the E Party. I know, I know, it's not ego. And maybe pride doesn't describe it either. But at some point— and from prior discussions you know I think that point has long passed—all this will have to fly on its own. Or not. You may be the founding father of the E Party, but sooner or later all children need to go off the payroll."

Atlas started to respond.

"Wait, honey. Just listen," said K.C.

"You know very well that Lauren is ready to throw the switch on Internet-based contributions. The same goes for a legal defense fund. It's inevitable. Particularly if and when we launch either federal campaigns and/or campaigns in states with tighter campaign funding restrictions. She throws that switch tomorrow and I guarantee money comes pouring in, especially to support Tom's legal costs and especially now."

K.C. put a finger to Atlas' lips. "The word that comes to mind is stubborn, my dear. You can ask the General, Mark, or any of the others. They'll all say it's time to let go. Just promise me you'll sleep on it, okay?"

After a moment, K.C. got up, placed a gentle peck on Atlas's forehead and went to bed, leaving her beloved, furrowed brow firmly fixed, to ruminate on what she'd said.

* * * * * * *

THE BACK BENCH
"If you let it slip, we catch it"
January 18

Governor Robinson and his top guns spent a very busy and productive first week in office. There was a continuous stream of visitors to his office, reminiscent of the annual wedding gown sale at Filene's Basement. Sources confirm that meetings fell into three categories.

The governor met primarily with senators and representatives, in groups of five or six. As the ultimate political outsider, he had never met most of them. The meetings were brief and introductory in nature. On the lighter side, many legislators took advantage of the opportunity to obtain the Hall of Famer's picture and autograph, no doubt suggesting it was for a friend or relative.

Lt. Gov. Jenkins met with major constituent groups to discuss the education package. The bill contains the concepts advanced by the E Party in the previous General Assembly. Whether or not controversial, they were familiar. However, sources confirm that the scope has been broadened to add the governor's pet concept, Getting to 21. At this stage, the lieutenant governor appears engaged in a dog-and-pony show designed to enlighten rather than to press for support. No sense breaking a sweat this early, especially with the Speaker on board.

Perhaps the more substantive meetings were conducted by Anthony Manzella, the governor's designated chief operating officer. Word has it he is interviewing all department heads one-on-one. Since Governor Robinson has deferred making new director-level appointments until the election challenge is finalized, Manzella needs to reach a meeting of the minds quickly with the holdover directors to confirm their willingness to honor and obey the Robinson playbook.

Allegedly, all sitting directors are being asked to sign undated letters of resignation. Anyone not acquiescing will be terminated *sua sponte*. It's a classic win-win. The directors extend their tenures and, in doing so, have additional time to seek new employment while building pension credits. From Manzella's perspective, anyone who gets the slightest bit off message is goneski.

Finally, the troika of Robinson, Jenkins, and Manzella held a late tête-à-tête with the leaders. Speculation is that the governor intends to institute new executive orders and wanted to brief the leaders in advance. Imagine that, open communication in government. How *avant garde*.

In other news...

* * * * * * *

E-MAIL

To: Elizabeth DiMaggio
From: Joseph Cole
Subject: Media
Date: January 19 7:56 a.m. (CST)

We plan to file our formal complaint tomorrow, as does Stewart. We have thoroughly reviewed all of the discovery evidence and are convinced we have mapped a winning strategy. Attached, by precinct, is a summary of our findings.

Contrary to my initial reaction, Jessica Myers and her team have been a blessing. In fact, without the additional discovery, we could be as many as 50 votes short.

Having the additional manpower has also allowed us to push for an aggressive hearing schedule. As you are aware, we will soon have over 4 million ballots in play and there will be hearings in 110 separate jurisdictions. Even with their help, it becomes a logistical nightmare.

This case will be won or lost in the trenches. The Supreme Court is not structured for an intense, evidentiary-based proceeding and will be relying on the various local judges' determinations.

To that end, now is the time for you and the party, local and national, to begin taking the media fight to Robinson. As with any media-focused judicial proceeding, we need to also win the war of public perception. Any of the PR firms you asked about should be up to the task. Above all else, it is vital to have a loud, vigilant, and consistent voice in the local media. In all cases, there is an audience of one: the local judge assigned by the Supreme Court.

CHAPTER EIGHTEEN

THE BACK BENCH
"If you let it slip, we catch it"
January 24

The Supreme Court of Illinois convened today to begin hearing the matter of *Allen v. Robinson.* The primary agenda item for today's docket was to review process and set a master timetable for the recount. This is the first statewide election contest since the previous methodology was found unconstitutional in 1977 and a new law was passed to correct the deficiencies.

Over the course of the next week, the Supreme Court will entertain procedural motions challenging their recommended implementation of the law. The court is tasked with conducting evidentiary hearings in each of the 110 election jurisdictions. These mini-hearings will be the place where the parties will present evidence as to whether their candidate is entitled to gain votes against either adversary.

In a nutshell, the Supreme Court has chosen a panel of twenty-two currently sitting circuit and appellate court judges to conduct hearings and issue findings. Each of the judges will preside over five such hearings, with each hearing anticipated to last one week (weekends included). Judges will then have a week to review and rule on the evidence before starting their next hearing in sequence. The proposed plan would run hearings for ten weeks, concluding in mid-April.

Most commentators find this schedule to be extremely aggressive. Just based on the averages, each hearing will cover roughly 250 precincts and 40,000 voting records. That is a veritable mountain of votes to consider and digest in only seven days.

The Supreme Court will then review findings from all of these evidentiary hearings, including a closing series of oral arguments. Its final order is targeted to be issued on May 10. Most remember *Bush v. Gore* having been decided in a matter of months. But, with the presidency on the line, the resources were limitless. By comparison, in Minnesota the *Coleman v. Franken* U.S. Senate seat contest took six months to decide.

Regardless, Joseph Cole has signaled that he will ask the court to further expedite by empaneling at least forty judges, and having judges issue their rulings in four days. He estimates this will allow the hearing phase to conclude in late March and the Supreme Court to issue the final order by April 10.

Cole points out that hearings are likely to require ten days, not the seven proposed by the court. If he is correct in his calculation, using the process proposed by the court, final determination would be pushed into late June at best. While that may not set off bells and whistles on Main Street, it could have a cataclysmic impact on Pennsylvania Avenue.

This is a remap year, meaning all legislative districts, state and federal, are redrawn based on the census. Under the Illinois Constitution, passing redistricting legislation creating new maps requires a simple majority vote until May 31 and a supermajority (a 60 percent vote) thereafter. Assuming cooperation from the governor, currently Tom Robinson, the

Democrats and the E Party could pass their favored versions of the maps before Allen (assuming he wins the challenge) would be sworn in and able to veto a plan not likely to be in his party's interest. From the Republican perspective, it therefore becomes imperative that the case be decided as quickly as possible, and in all events in sufficient time for Allen to be the sitting governor when the legislature passes the remap bill.

This also plays to Cole's advantage because, as the worst kept secret of the millennium, he is in league with the Stewart camp and therefore better suited to handle more hearings more quickly than Elaine Richards and her band of merry men.

It's definitely going to take more than one scorecard to track this heavyweight fight.

In other news...

* * * * * *

It wasn't so much what Joseph Cole presented in his *Petition of State Election Contest Before the Supreme Court* as what he did not. He had personally reviewed all of the discovery data from the precincts chosen based on the anonymous note found on his windshield. The outcome of this mysterious correspondence to date? Zippo. Nada. In fact, Cole concluded that if Robinson's team dug deep enough, they might unearth a net gain of five to six votes from those precincts.

Cole was kicking himself. Why had he wasted almost ten percent of his discovery reviewing those precincts when there were other potential discovery hot spots? Acting in a way totally unlike his usual self, he'd allowed the mystery message to cloud his judgment. This case was too close for mistakes and he'd already committed a major blunder.

Had the note been a deliberate ruse? If so, put there by whom? And why? Cole had been up against candidates backed by Speaker Kennedy and Danny Ryan on many occasions; subterfuge was not their style. No need to play penny-ante crap when you own the judges. As for Robinson and the E Party, his research showed them to be cleaner than Caesar's wife.

Or, impossible as it seemed, had he blown it? Was the fraud so subtle that it had escaped not only Cole but his entire team? Had he misinterpreted the message and chosen the wrong precincts in discovery?

* * * * * * *

Nancy Rae Mitchell had long ago stopped attending inaugural festivities in Springfield. She wasn't one for the see-and-be-seen parties and balls. And, although welcomed at many, she was not interested in attending the smaller family-oriented dinner celebrations, either. Further, since her lobbying career required attendance on virtually every day the General Assembly was in session, any extraneous time in Springfield was harsh medicine.

Of late, she had avoided the predominantly procedural and perfunctory first few weeks of each General Assembly, when members are assigned to committees, committee chairmen anointed, and first bills introduced. And since it usually takes a week or two for all bills to be assigned to substantive committees by the powerful Rules Committee, what's the rush?

This year, in particular, none of her clients had any defined legislative agendas. Considerably higher on her newly revised priority list was her budding relationship with Danny Ryan. Nancy Rae did not want to miss out on one moment of bliss before facing the realities of her seasonal duties and commitments.

It was therefore the third week of session when she made her initial appearance downstate. First stop, Representative Sanchez's office.

Juanita, Sanchez's assistant, greeted her with a grin.

"Good morning, Juanita. You look lovely today. How were the holidays?"

"Oh, you know…kids, grandkids, bedlam, chaos…the usual," Juanita said, but she was smiling. Nancy Rae liked Juanita and knew how much she treasured her multi-generational extended family. She continued to make small talk with Juanita as she hung her winter coat and changed from snow boots to Louboutin heels.

"Nice shoes," commented Juanita, eyeing Nancy Rae's recent purchase.

"Caught a great sale at Barney's," said Nancy Rae with a wink. Juanita and she shared a similar shoe fetish and each tried to keep the other in the loop about recent purchases. She angled her head at the inner chamber. "He in yet?"

Juanita shook her head no. "Won't be long, though. He's at the Education Committee meeting. The Speaker is testifying on behalf of HB1. I hear the room's packed. Have a seat. Can I get you something to drink?"

Nancy Rae sat and ruminated. The Capitol was the people's house, comprised of the two legislative chambers, with offices for the statewide constitutional officers, their staff, all senators, a few representatives with seniority, legislative staff, and the press. It also housed meeting rooms, a newsstand, a cafeteria, and an under-utilized chapel. Accordingly, the hoard of lobbyists was left to fend for itself for valuable "hangout" space to deal with mundane needs like coat hanging and supply storing, as well as business needs like the occasional meeting or a copy machine.

Nancy Rae had been hanging out at chez Javier since his first term. This session would be no different, especially since his seniority allowed him to choose one of the nicer, larger, out-of-the-way spaces with a sidecar conference room essentially dedicated to her.

More important, Nancy Rae Mitchell and Javier Sanchez had become an inseparable political force. He sponsored her clients' most important bills and helped defeat those they opposed. In exchange, she saw to it that her clients kept his campaign coffers brimming. The pair regularly chatted and conspired regarding his political future; she either facilitated or ran interference with Danny Ryan and others to keep Javier on track.

As Nancy Rae waited for Javier Sanchez, Juanita Hernandez took a good, long look at her friend. Juanita had been Javier's assistant for his entire tenure. In exchange for lunches, dinners, the occasional use of

Nancy Rae's Chicago condo, as well as theater and sporting tickets for her and her husband, Juanita also functioned as Nancy Rae's unofficial assistant. She couldn't say she knew Nancy Rae well—who could, frankly—but she was no fool. The girl was positively glowing.

"What's going on there, girl?" she said. "You're looking, how should I put it…like the cat that positively devoured the canary whole."

Nancy Rae felt more like a deer caught in headlights.

"Um, you know, nothing, really. What do you mean?"

"You can't fool this old goat," Juanita laughed. "Either you're gettin' some delicious bootie or I'm the Prince of Persia. And that ain't happenin' any time soon."

Nancy Rae knew Juanita was right. The woman had seen her through more ups and downs than the Chicago weather. She laughed, almost relieved to admit her recent…what…escapades? As if that could possibly describe her tryst with Danny Ryan. "Well, it's not from clean living," she said.

Juanita barked a knowing chuckle. "Good for you, Nancy Rae Mitchell." She lowered her voice. "But who is this mystery man?"

Representative Javier Sanchez chose that very moment to return from committee.

"Darn," mumbled Juanita. "Just when things were getting interesting around here."

Javier ignored his assistant, whose outspoken nature was well known around the Capitol.

Nancy Rae also chose to take the convenient distraction as her way out of a tricky conversation.

"Come on in," said Javier. "Good to see you. Glad you could finally grace us with your presence."

"You know Springfield," Nancy Rae said, deliberately avoiding his sharp gaze. "Got here thirty minutes ago and it already feels like forever. How's the session? Anything going?"

"It's slow," Javier conceded, "very slow. If it weren't for the education bill, I could be in Siberia and not be missed. Everything—and I mean everything—is about *the* recount and *the* remap. Otherwise, I predict we can all go on siesta until late May."

"Glad you mentioned it, actually," said Nancy Rae. "I was talking to Danny Ryan about the map the other day. He thinks, um, we think, that with the pick-up in Hispanic population, you should have a few options. Personally, I think pushing your district's boundaries either south or west is preferable to north. You'll be safe with any of those, but veering south or west better positions you for a run at the Hispanic congressional seat, if and when it opens up."

"You're always looking out for me, Rae," Javier acknowledged. "Should I call Danny and set a time?"

Nancy Rae was reminded that there were only two people in the world who ever called her "Rae." Danny Ryan and Javier Sanchez. An interesting observation... or totally irrelevant? She looked up. Javier was waiting for her answer.

"Not quite yet. I'll let you know," she said. "Anything else?"

Sanchez nodded. "I got a call from a constituent asking about a lobbyist."

"For the right money, I'm at their service."

"Sorry, Charlie, not so fast. You don't want this one. Not at any cost. The caller is interested in defeating the education package, and I doubt they could print enough money for you to work against the Speaker."

"Damn straight," said Nancy Rae, curious. "Mind if I ask who this caller is?"

"I don't really know," he said in a bald-faced lie. "A local school council member made the actual call, but I'm pretty sure they were fronting for someone."

"Interesting," Nancy Rae said. "Taking on the Speaker is no day at the beach. By the same token, though, whether it's the teachers union or anyone else looking to perpetuate our miserable education system, I'm sure they're all plotting as we speak."

"So, who would you hire if you were in their shoes?" Javier asked.

Nancy Rae didn't have to consider long. "It's not so much who would be best as much as who would be willing to go against Kennedy. Remember, most of the hired guns, yours truly included, make our living because of real or perceived access to his highness. No reason to be biting that hand. Plus, the votes would have to come from his caucus. It's a given the E Party is solidly in support and, unless I'm missing something, the Republicans will oppose. Not that they don't badly want education reform, but it's clearly a political trick bag for them. My rough math tells me someone will have to find twenty Democratic votes to defeat the bill in the House and ten in the Senate. With help from Leader DiMaggio, that's where I'd make my stand."

Javier waited patiently.

She went on after a moment. "Obviously, you're talking contract lobbyists as opposed to in-house. Other than the unions, any other organization would be nuts to have someone on their payroll front and center against the Speaker. Anyway," she concluded, "I'll kick it around. Any rush?"

"No, no," Javier downplayed. "I can't imagine there is."

* * * * * *

Three days later, Javier Sanchez dialed into his voice mail. "Javier, I'm leaving this message as a follow-up to our discussion earlier this week," came Nancy Rae's lilting yet forceful voice. "There are a few lobbyists who might fit the bill, but I'd have to start with Carla Hilton."

Brilliant, thought Javier. Why hadn't he thought of Carla Hilton? Nancy Rae had come through for him once again. The name of Carla Hilton was on its way to Eddie Cobb within seconds.

The wheels were in motion.

CHAPTER NINETEEN

Carla Hilton had it all and Carla Hilton had nothing. Attractive and intelligent, she possessed an engaging personality and was born to a life of luxury. Sadly, she attracted the wrong men, was too smart by half in a way that was insulting, used her personality to manipulate, and distrusted other's motives regarding her fortune. She worked diligently to maintain her looks, was highly educated, constantly had men at her feet, and knew how to use her wealth to open doors. Sadly, she had just completed her fourth marriage, never settled into a lasting career or a vocation, and was always "searching for meaning" in her life. Everyone who understood the parts wanted to be her, but the sum of the parts was a tormented soul. What better milieu for her to engage in than politics?

Her introduction to politics had been the result of a lascivious relationship with a self-made multi-millionaire taking a run at the U.S. Senate. His advisors cautioned that the most eligible bachelor syndrome was not polling well and that a classy, poised woman by his side, with a hint of marriage about, was required.

She'd played her role to the hilt, but was ultimately relieved with his defeat. Without the senatorial swagger, he held no lasting appeal to her. But her exposure to politics did.

Her introduction to Illinois politics and the American Civil Liberties Union was born of her fourth and longest marriage. After a torrid encounter on a high-end singles cruise, she invited herself to live with him in his Chicago penthouse. He had a wide range of interests and contacts rooted in old money and equally significant connections to the people who mattered. He was fascinating to a fault and she thrived in his universe.

Their marriage had thrust her onto the local philanthropic stage. In a sequence that neither of them could possibly reenact in hindsight, she'd gravitated toward and became ensconced in the ACLU. She had risen to prominence on the board, attended conferences nationwide, chaired committees, and raised money hand over fist.

Over time, it was the issues and the mission that captivated and consumed her. She was particularly taken with the occasional foray into lobbying activities and fought to establish a regular presence for the organization, and she on its behalf, in Springfield. There was no issue too small and the ACLU charter gave her license to insert herself to the detriment of anyone careless enough to underestimate her determination. She coupled her newfound ambition with an outpouring of personal political contributions that would be the envy of the best funded trade associations.

That her avocation slowly but surely drove a wedge between her and her husband was ultimately of no consequence. She was obsessed with her new love and, absent children and the home life he coveted, there was little to hold him. Curiously, they stayed in a marriage of convenience that allowed for discrete third-party entanglements. Surprisingly, they grew to be trusted friends and confidants.

* * * * * *

Eddie Cobb closed the dossier on Carla Hilton. His smug expression, like a hyena savoring its carnage, made his findings evident. For Eddie, only one question remained: How was he to entice the ACLU to take up his cause to defeat the education bill? Well, two questions. Assuming he got the ACLU on his side, how would he get Carla Hilton to lead the charge?

* * * * * *

MEMORANDUM

To: Board of Directors, ACLU, Chicago Chapter

From: Carla Hilton

Subject: HB1: "The Reinventing Education in Illinois Act"

Date: January 25

The Reinventing Education in Illinois Act (the "Act"), House Bill 1, is a marvelous piece of legislation. Were it to pass, I personally think the children of Illinois would benefit greatly. It could then serve as model legislation nationwide. Unfortunately, much of what Governor Robinson refers to as his "Getting to 21" concept violates multiple constitutional principles.

At its core, Getting to 21 is designed to deal with the drop-out problem. In Illinois, approximately 25 percent of high school students drop out, and a large percentage of that population is relegated to a life of poverty, crime, or both. Until age twenty-one, the Act requires they either be enrolled in school—high school, college, vocational school, or one of a list of alternatives, including the seminary—or be working to obtain a high school equivalency *and* be participating in one of a list of activities that includes gainful employment, apprenticeship, internship, military service, or a recognized value service (e.g., the Peace Corps or AmeriCorps). There are exemptions, generally for health related reasons, through a rigorous process that includes countless due process red flags.

Anyone convicted of a felony before age twenty-one is expected to complete his or her high school equivalency as a condition of release. There are, as above, exemptions that won't pass constitutional muster.

Attached is a legal opinion from our outside counsel describing in great detail the state and federal constitutional deficiencies of the bill as filed.

In light of the serious concerns, at next week's board meeting I will make a motion to make the defeat of House Bill 1 our primary legislative target for this session of the General Assembly.

* * * * * * *

THE BACK BENCH
"If you let it slip, we catch it"
January 25

Governor Robinson issued his first executive order today. As with the majority of his predecessors, he also voided various executive orders on the books. In what may prove to be a controversial move, he eliminated a few executive orders that had given preferential employment benefits to union members over nonunion.

Executive Order No. 1 creates a task force for the purpose of conducting a forensic audit of all government agencies as well as all boards and commissions with paid staff or budgets in excess of $1 million.

This is an interesting twist on an old theme. Most incoming governors conduct their due diligence during the transition period with an eye toward a series of press release recriminations of past practices and a lightning-fast start with new agency heads upon inauguration. Robinson, through his Operation Grassroots Democracy, has taken the tortoise route over the hare's and has steadfastly avoided any games of gotcha.

The task force is to be headed by General Smith. In what would appear to be a breach of the state's Purchasing Act, a team of supporting professionals was identified, including accountants and lawyers, to assist in the review.

It's not certain whether the Robinson administration failed to read the fine print of the state's Purchasing Act or if it is deliberately seeking to push the envelope as the E Party has done on so many occasions.

In other news…

* * * * * *

THE BACK BENCH
"If you let it slip, we catch it"
January 25

EXTRA EXTRA EXTRA EXTRA EXTRA EXTRA

As predicted in our earlier edition, it did not take long for the Robinson administration to stumble into its first controversy. Within hours of Robinson's Executive Order No. 1—creating a task force to audit state government—Republican Leader Elizabeth DiMaggio called a press conference to announce that the governor had violated numerous sections of the state's Purchasing Act.

She took the opportunity to chastise the rookie governor for not only violating state law, but also for failing to honor various and sundry campaign pledges to run an open government. As she put it, "Hiring a hit squad of crony accountants and lawyers under cover of night is inconsistent with Governor Robinson's pledge to run an open and honest government."

One gets the sense from the tone of Senator DiMaggio's announcement that she intends to be the magnifying glass for all Robinson missteps. Probably to be expected given the circumstances. Roughing up Robinson, particularly with a claim of having violated statutes, gives an assist to Allen.

In other news...

* * * * * *

E-MAIL
To: Scott Grusin
From: Elizabeth DiMaggio
Sent: January 26 11:46 a.m. (CST)
Subject: Need some back-up

In case you missed it, the Robinson administration made a major blunder and we pounced on it. We received great coverage at the local level, but want to press our advantage. With the hearings about to start, I am hoping you can work some angles to keep this alive both locally and nationally and possibly get a few of the conservative commentators to take a whack on this week's talk shows.

* * * * * *

THE BACK BENCH
"If you let it slip, we catch it"
January 26

EXTRA EXTRA EXTRA EXTRA EXTRA EXTRA

Barbara Jenkins appeared in the press blue room with Robinson administration legal counsel Kellie Morgan and spokesperson Lisa Boudreau this afternoon to address the issues raised by Republican Leader DiMaggio related to Executive Order No. 1.

In an unusual bit of *mea culpa*, they opened with an apology for mishandling the release of the order by not issuing an accompanying statement clarifying the circumstances surrounding the engaging of the accountants and attorneys.

Counsel Morgan carefully reviewed the relevant sections of the Purchasing Act to clarify that the task force was not an entity subject to its jurisdiction and that the professionals were also beyond its scope because they had volunteered their services.

Before the media could go on the offensive, Ms. Boudreau quickly genuflected, while announcing that new professionals would be engaged and that any and all the procedures required under the Purchasing Act would be followed.

Was it a mistake? An admission of guilt? They seemed to take a page out of the old Clinton playbook by responding immediately. If so, they forgot to read the chapter on never admitting guilt and always fighting back. If the law was on their side, why give? Or is *Allen v. Robinson* having a debilitating impact on their thought process?

No doubt, Senator DiMaggio smells blood in the water.

In other news...

CHAPTER TWENTY

For the first time in her life, math genius Barbara Jenkins felt as though she had flunked an exam. For the first time in her life, she felt inadequate and incompetent. She was also hemorrhaging guilt for having let down Governor Robinson and the E Party.

What was she doing serving as chief-of-staff to the governor? What did she know about executive orders or press releases or, for that matter, government or legislation or anything else that was piling up on her plate?

She felt lost, alone, with no one to turn to. Her entire staff was comprised of the brightest from the top-rated schools, with the finest professional pedigrees. They were hard-working, dedicated, and collectively possessed every other puffball skill found on the most eminent resume and curriculum vitae. They were also youthful novices. Why, oh why, hadn't she followed her instincts to add a graybeard or two? She desperately needed a battle-tested political veteran. But who?

An uncharacteristically despondent Barbara Jenkins was sans compass. She cancelled her late afternoon and evening plans. *Get some exercise*, she self-prescribed. *Get some sleep. Get some help*!

She thought of her mother, a woman who had overcome abject poverty and a life of unrelenting crisis management. Where had Mom found the strength to persist? How had she managed to patch the quilt of life that had thrust her daughter to a galaxy far beyond the squalor? How had she managed to greet each day with a boundless reservoir of hope and determination?

If Barbara had one regret she was destined to carry to her grave, it was the fact that her mother had passed before her daughter could ever reciprocate. At moments like this, what Barbara wouldn't give for a ten-minute conversation.

Two and a half hours later, post-cardio, yoga, her first home-cooked meal in a month, and a carafe of her favorite red, she didn't feel much better. And the Blackberry she'd deliberately left behind at the office was calling to her like a persistent smoke signal. Finally, too exhausted to think straight, she collapsed into bed.

When she awoke at the crack of dawn, it was with a thought that lent a jolt of perspective. Hopeful, if not excited, she picked up the phone.

"K.C., it's Barbara. Oh—sorry! I just realized how early it is where you are. I'll just call back later—really? Well, okay, if you're sure. Thanks. Here's the thing, K.C. I need help."

K.C. looked at the clock on the nightstand. Four-thirty Mountain Time. She'd have been better off not looking before she said it was okay to continue the conversation. It wasn't even close to time for liquid stimulation, not even for Atlas, whose early-to-bed, early-to-rise lifestyle she had attempted to adopt so as to spend more time with him. K.C.'s East Coast metabolism, however, was still fighting tooth and nail to hang onto its roots as a much-later-to-rise and much-later-to-sleep animal. At this point, it had not yet adapted to anything more strenuous than the *Aspen Times* and NPR, with the volume on very, very low, before the caffeine kicked in and she could complete her sentences. The urgency in Barbara's voice, however, appeared to be summoning endorphins. K.C. combed back the hair from her forehead and tugged on a robe.

"Just give me a sec to walk to a quiet spot, Barb. Okay, here I am. What's up?"

"K.C., I'm lost. I've got a problem. But it's not the kind I'm trained for, where you have a set of facts and work to find a solution."

"Tell me about it," K.C. said, pushing the button to start the coffee percolating. She might as well make a full pot as she doubted she'd be able to get back to sleep after this call.

Barbara was already regretting her rash decision to call. "No, you know what? I'm really sorry to have bothered you, K.C. Don't worry. I'll figure this out by myself."

"Oh, no, you won't," K.C. said instinctively. "You can't hang up now. We're all in this together. Besides, I just started the coffee. Go on. Tell me everything."

It took over two hours to drag the whole story out of Barbara and give her time to purge herself of the weighty emotional baggage. A half dozen cups later accompanied by a huge slice of homemade coffee cake she could ill afford, K.C. began to feel she had the picture. Barbara's "jolt of insight," as she'd called it, was a good one. They promised to keep in close touch with a steady diet of girl-power conversations in the ensuing days and weeks to help Barbara regain her focus and sense of mission. Strangely enough, though, the call had produced another result. It had built a fire under K.C.

Team E was not off to a dynamic, well-conceived start. The entire cause might soon be in jeopardy. The governor, consistent with his desire to please, was bogged down in a constant stream of dysfunctional, unproductive meetings. Barbara, symptomatic of her mathematical training, had been burying herself in minutia with too little playing chief and too much playing staff. Mark and Lisa were each stretched too thin, with feet in every facet of E Party operations, spending an unhealthy weighting of time and energy in managing the media regarding all things recount. Her beloved husband and his buddy, the General, were too worried about settling their case to free up funding for vouchers not yet submitted.

All in all, K.C. surmised that a colossal train wreck was rapidly approaching.

Without bothering Atlas with her disconcerting overview of the state of affairs, K.C. took it upon herself to task Liz with scheduling a two-day, cancel-everything, come-to-Jesus session with the E Party flock. Liz worked her usual magic. The ever-expanding E Party core leadership team, in conjunction with the non-overlapping newbies from the Robinson administration nucleus, would meet in inconveniently located Bloomington, Illinois, for a weekend of all work and no play.

* * * * * * *

Atlas, accustomed to setting the agenda and leading, was nonplussed by his wife's sudden surge of focused activity. He'd noted her bustling about the house for a while, making calls, trucking her iPad with her from room to room, but, in all honesty, his own self-absorption had made it easy to watch it without much curiosity. Now that the meeting she and Barbara had called was at hand, he willingly and completely deferred to K.C., proud as a peacock and marveling at her managerial and organizational skills.

K.C. made her first priority Barbara Jenkins, whose considerable après-training-wheel stumble required a get-back-on-the-bike approach to stem the damage. K.C. noted that Barb, in turn, had instinctively reached out to Tom.

Barbara Jenkins and Governor Tom Robinson were quite the odd couple, the Felix Unger and Oscar Madison of the party. Where Barbara could diagram the physics of a major league curveball, but was about as coordinated as an octopus on land, Tom could hit a curveball a mile, but balance his checkbook? It was an oft-told joke in their group about how many times he'd let checks bounce because he'd forgotten to make timely deposits or use a calculator to do his subtractions.

Barbara had juggled a teaching career, the thriving foundation she established for children gifted in the arts, and a long list of school and community committee work. To his credit, Tom had also strung together a series of valuable philanthropic activities, including participation in the Commissioner of Baseball's Ambassador Program and the creation of a mentoring program in cooperation with Chicago's South and West Side churches. They had been thrust together in a marriage of convenience, it was true. Chief-of-staff, especially in government, is the one position that requires a vast reservoir of trust, generally developed over years of close contact and battle-tested mutual admiration. The reservoir, in this case, was at best a kiddie pool, given they barely knew each other. Under the circumstances, however, no one short of his athletic trainer and nothing short of his double-play combination would have passed the test.

K.C. had negotiated the *shidduch*, and was darn proud of it. She'd seen the vast potential in meshing the vibrant and compelling intangibles before the couple had seen it themselves. The two were poster children for scout merit badges, with an emphasis on "loyal," "brave," and "reverent." Fortunately, they also had the capacity to laugh at themselves, something that so far had kept them swimming above water.

If the E Party support group couldn't provide the political GPS for these people at the helm, well shame on them.

As K.C. saw it, the first shame-on-them moment had just arrived.

Not unlike Barb, but unbeknownst to her, Tom's on-the-job training was extracting a heavy toll. He was spending far too much time and money in the indigestion and pain relief aisles of his local CVS pharmacy. Bouts of sleeplessness, usually from long road trips; stomach pains, usually from too much spicy food served late night after games; headaches, usually from dryness in hotel rooms; and irritability, usually from the rare, but inevitable, mid-season batting slump—none of these was unusual during his sports career. For whatever reason, naivety, he supposed, he had not expected them recurring here, now, in the role he'd taken on. His metabolism felt like it was being gang tackled every other minute. Most troubling, though, was the fact that his duties to date hadn't yet risen to mole hills, let alone the mountains he knew to be ahead.

As soon as Barbara began describing her recent "meltdown" and how she'd called K.C. "in the middle of the night" to lament, it all clicked for Tom. They had stopped playing to win and had begun playing not to lose.

Fortunately, Tom Robinson knew both the symptoms and the remedies.

* * * * * * *

"Javier, not catching you at a bad time, I hope."

Eddie Cobb generally opened his calls the same way each time, though why he did so was a mystery. The man couldn't care less if he interrupted the person on the other end of the phone or not. Least not when the person he was calling was Javier Sanchez.

"Don't know how you did it, ol' boy," Cobb went on, "but I'm feelin' about as happy as a pig in shit."

What was Cobb on about this time? The man was positively schizophrenic.

Curious, Javier stayed quiet, although it was, in fact, *not* a good time, seeing as he was dining with some of his major contributors. He should have shut off his ringer. His acute case of cell-phoneitis would not allow him to ignore the VIP indicated on the screen. How unfortunate that he could not impress his guests with the identity of his caller.

Smoothly, Javier, pro that he was, extricated from the table all the while racking his brain in search of what he could have done to deserve Eddie Cobb's sudden adulation.

In the relatively quiet hall behind the wall of diners and banquettes, Javier listened carefully. Every seasoned politician masters both the art of taking credit and the art of deflecting blame. Javier had long ago earned an advanced degree in each.

Apparently, Eddie Cobb attributed Carla Hilton's decision to lead the lobbying effort against House Bill 1 to Javier—a welcomed chit. That Eddie was now expecting Javier to parlay his success into a subversive collaborative with that same Carla Hilton would require some clever tap dancing between that narrow yet metaphysically enormous space between the Speaker and Eddie Cobb. Not impossible, of course, and definitely worth the risk.

Javier understood that the chairman was an impatient and impetuous taskmaster. He therefore understood that contacting Carla was a priority. Plus, currying favor with the ACLU and one of its generous benefactors had long been on his to-do list. It seemed Carla Hilton, at least according to Eddie Cobb, was equally eager to meet Javier. Well, he *was* a rising star in Democratic Party politics, both local and national. And, coincidentally, access to the Hispanic caucus was a perceived weakness in Carla's preliminary sketching of the plan to defeat HB1.

The next day, at Javier's pointed direction, Juanita juggled a few appointments and made reservations at Saputo's, an unlikely selection for a meeting place. Javier did not particularly care for Italian and always avoided places such as Saputo's, where lobbyists and legislators seemed to hang from the rafters. For this occasion, however, he would tolerate marinara sauce and the exposure.

There are no secrets in Springfield, particularly when the legislature is in session. Rumors and innuendo travel at the speed of light, and timely, dependable information, particularly with respect to those higher in the pecking order of power, is a currency. To that end, Javier determined that the surest way to avoid suspicion, especially where the Speaker was concerned, was to flaunt his dinner engagement—and his guest.

Carla Hilton was surprised by Representative Javier Sanchez's choice of venue for dinner. She never chased a rumor she didn't start and did not necessarily relish the peppering that a solo sighting with Sanchez would evoke. Yet, scoring dinner with a high-ranking member of leadership was validation that her level of access was expanding. It didn't matter what they were discussing, only that the discussion took place and onlookers would be sure to note that their meal had lasted over three hours.

From their individual perspectives, time had flown. Carla Hilton and Javier Sanchez had previously known little about each other, and each had a fascinating personal history to break the sometimes impenetrable ice of the politically in-the-know. It took time, neither one willing to dip a toe in first, while they footsied around House Bill 1 with appetizers. Why should either of them tip their hand until the signal had been sent—and received—by both parties that they shared common interests in the outcome? Until that Ouija board unleashed its secrets, Carla was reluctant to unveil her strategy; Javier was reluctant to risk the trust of the Speaker.

Those onlookers still lounging about at the end of the meal hoping for a raised tone or a secretive look took note of the body language between the two and declared the evening—whatever it was about—a success.

* * * * * * *

E-MAIL

To: ACLU Chicago Board
From: Carla Hilton
Sent: January 30 11:56 p.m. (CST)
Subject: Update

I had an enlightening conversation over dinner this evening with a high-ranking Democrat regarding HB1. Best of all, this official reached out to me. It would appear that, if handled properly, there could be sufficient votes in the D column to achieve our goal. A very promising development, indeed.

E-MAIL

To: Chairman Cobb
From: Javier Sanchez
Sent: January 31 7:06 a.m. (CST)
Subject: Update

Had a very informative meeting with Ms. Hilton last night. I am convinced we can facilitate her effort to impede the Speaker and governor over House Bill 1. Will contact you over the weekend to discuss strategy.

* * * * * * *

For a group of people historically pampered by rendezvous in venues like New York and Vegas, a weekend-long meeting in Bloomington was a long, rude step down. It was K.C.'s idea, and Barb had agreed: throw an imaginary dart at the map of Central Illinois to send a message about the mindset of the new governor, while simultaneously sending a message to the assembled cast that playful diversions in Aspen and elsewhere were off-limits at this crucial juncture.

From Tom Robinson's perch as governor, it didn't mean the tone had to be somber and pensive. He understood, perhaps too well, the inevitability of distractions and losing streaks. It wasn't uncommon for championship teams to lose their edge after an off-season filled with excessive celebration and public relations tours. Comparison to the E Party after its stunning election victory would not be forcing it. The great sports dynasties also knew to look within to right the ship. So must his party and his administration.

One of Tom's favorite tools for ship righting was the kangaroo court.

In his role as team captain, Tom opened the meeting by announcing that court was in session and that he would be the presiding judge and jury. Each individual there would be called to defend themselves. Tom, and Tom alone, would then pass judgment. To properly set the table for the session, he called himself as the first witness and stepped to the head of the table where he had placed a large wooden chair on a block of wood a few inches high to mimic a courtroom. There was always room for a bit of drama—and humor—he thought, no matter how serious the circumstances.

In the chair, Tom read a lengthy indictment of his failings of late, then issued a harsh sentence. He would pay a fine of five thousand dollars for the crime of acting like a Democratic governor and a second fine of five thousand for acting like a Republican governor. The hearty chuckles of his friends told him that the medicine was taking affect.

Barbara Jenkins was called as the second defendant; K.C. was appointed prosecutor. The indictment included such serious offenses as impersonating a political animal, attempting to make a government omelet without breaking any eggs, and micro-managing without a license. Barbara pleaded *nolo contendere* and was fined one thousand dollars for each offense. Judge Robinson suspended her sentence for time served in Bloomington.

The tone had been set. One by one, the assembled members of the E Party and Robinson administration were called forward, duly humiliated and roasted, and fined amounts that would create a sizeable kitty for distribution to needy charities across Illinois. Fifty thousand for Atlas for taking himself too seriously, attempting to snatch defeat from the jaws of victory by prematurely settling the tax fraud case, and, worst of all, not taking his wife's advice on a variety of issues. Twenty-five thousand for the General for his role as co-conspirator in the tax case settlement discussions and for contemplating retirement. And on it went.

Before it was pushed to the side of the room, the witness stand had been warmed by each member of the E Party, who had received a healthy raking over the coals. While all concerned appreciated the satiric bent of the exercise, there was no masking the underlying truth of the assertions, and over the span of a couple of hours the mood in the room slowly shifted from *please don't call me up to the hot seat* to *maybe I needed that slap in the face* to *how did I not see this coming* to *no more mistakes, butthead.*

Barb and K.C. took the reins after lunch with the goal of moving the discussion from the individual to the Robinson administration and then to the E Party. Consensus built quickly that both organizations had drifted far from their original blueprints. From that meeting of the minds, the next steps flowed like a river in springtime.

Political comedian Zam Zam Berundi presided over the group's entertainment that evening to everyone's delight after the fruitful but draining session. A modern-day Don Rickles, Berundi capped off their day of constructive sarcasm and criticism with his own brand of playful humiliation. With plenty of leading tips from K.C., he had no end of fodder to skewer Atlas, General Smith, and Governor Robinson. Tom, Barb, and K.C. congratulated themselves on anticipating that the side-splitting humor would be a fitting exclamation point for their mission accomplished.

* * * * * * *

E-MAIL
To: Scott Grusin
From: Elizabeth DiMaggio
Sent: February 2 10:09 a.m. (CST)
Subject: Polling

Thank you for all your help. It may not be much to write home about, but for the first time in a long time, our recent tracking polls have detected a weakening in favorability regarding Governor Robinson. Until now, his ratings were ridiculously high and had even notched up a bit following his inauguration address.

After a week of pounding in the media over his staff's Purchasing Act stumble, his numbers have dropped a hair or two in a few categories.

Not sure how much of this is attributable to the media or just the inevitable slowing of inertia. To the extent it's the former, I have asked my staff to design a public relations attack module that we can replicate with all due speed with each and every political blunder. No doubt, the new governor and his staff will present opportunities. We will be ready.

E-MAIL
To: Elaine Richards
From: Atlas
cc: General, K.C., Mark, Lisa
Sent: February 2 4:17 p.m. (MST)
Subject: Playing to win

I am sorry that you were unable to join us in Bloomington, but clearly your attention to the recount hearings is top priority. To that end, we are all anxiously awaiting your next status briefing.

Although I suspect the outcome of our meetings will not bear on your strategic approach, there was a vote to reverse our recent political course of action.

As you well know, in great measure due to the tightening of the vote totals, our decision-making efforts on most fronts have been affected by a desire to move cautiously and avoid errors. This philosophy stems from a perceived need to mitigate any negative public sentiment and perception problems that could spill over to your efforts.

I understand that any mistakes of commission over the next few months will undoubtedly make your life more difficult. But the unanimous conclusion of the assembled group was that we were heading down a path riddled with mistakes of omission. The E Party was not built that way. As Tom put it, we have been playing not to lose. We need to get back to playing to win.

On our related topic of *U.S. v. Stein*, we are now similarly charging ahead. If a settlement cannot be framed to our satisfaction, we will renew the fight. To that end, I have decided to defer completely to K.C., Lauren, and the General. It's time to open the Internet public funding spigot.

Look on the bright side. At least you'll be assured of getting paid!

CHAPTER TWENTY-ONE

Now into his third decade as Speaker of the Illinois House of Representatives, David Kennedy had grown increasingly insular. He was beginning to contemplate the inevitable and, of late, spending considerable effort piecing together an exit strategy. At the appropriate time, he'd simply set the table and sit back to enjoy the food fight.

His frame of mind was partly due to the fact that many of his earliest cronies had literally and figuratively moved away, some from the world of Springfield, and others from politics altogether. Although most were accessible and still exceedingly loyal, it was too difficult to paint an accurate picture of all the angles on a given issue for their opinions to be of benefit, particularly with the recent dynamic of the E Party. If his friends and former associates weren't living it all day-to-day, there wasn't much they could add.

The other factor contributing to his isolation was his internal insistence that he not be perceived as favoring any one potential pretender to the throne. The bevy of wannabes never diminished in size and, while he was quick to nurture with leadership and committee assignments, a healthy distance and balance had to be maintained prudently and consistently.

Three crucial elements of the succession plan were on the table. The centerpiece was redistricting. The Speaker was obsessed with the notion that he must secure the future of the Democratic Party of Illinois through the design of the new legislative map. With a nod to Darwin, he was willing to leave the identity of his successor to the political version of natural selection, but he was unwilling to leave his successor to oversee an uncertain political landscape.

Similarly, the Speaker was committed to turning over the keys with the state's budget in the best condition possible. He did not view this aspect of his plan as an obsession—or compulsion. Fact was, in the previous General Assembly, the E Party had unsuspectingly contributed toward his retirement by driving a level of creativity and discipline to the budget process that had long eluded the two-party system, where each party had become too entrenched in fiscal policy special interests on their respective ends of the liberal-conservative spectrum to bring about the balance the E Party had imposed.

Finally, the Speaker had begun to contemplate his legacy. Neither setting nearly all modern-day records for longevity nor being revered for his intellect and cunning was what he had in mind. To the contrary, if unmoored to substantive triumphs, possessing longevity, intellect, and cunning would only be a curse on his tenure.

Early in Kennedy's speakership, he had envisioned addressing serious social concerns. The failures of the modern two-party system, however, for which he was as much to blame as anyone, had caused him to abandon any hope of directing positive outcomes. Again, surprisingly, it was the third party that had awakened the possibility of education reform, a legacy the Speaker could proudly carry to the grave.

As on many evenings of late, he had asked his assistant, Dawn Eckersley, to arrange a carry-in dinner to facilitate his long hours in the Speaker's chambers, digesting his strategy for the map, the budget, and education reform. In all scenarios, the map was the center of the universe. Votes on all critical issues at the end of the session would hinge on the map. Had the Democratic candidate for governor been elected, and in total control, such consternation would have been irrelevant. But it was not to be, and Kennedy had made a late, decisive call to help seat Tom Robinson in lieu of the Republican, Robert Allen. Now, even that victory might unravel.

Each time Speaker Kennedy mentally ran the traps, he came to the same circuitous conclusion. To achieve the map of his choosing, Robinson either needed to win the election challenge or the election challenge needed to be continued until he could cut a deal with the E

Party that could pass the General Assembly and be signed by Robinson while he was still governor.

The map negotiations depended on Kennedy's ability to deliver the E Party's education package. If the package fell apart, the E Party would have no political will to support his map. To pass the education package, Robinson and the E Party would have to build public support in the face of daunting attacks from unions and others. However, they had not started strong. Too many rookie mistakes.

The Supreme Court would be reading the media tea leaves. If public opinion of Robinson were to suffer greatly in the interim, the justices would be less inclined to interpret the facts and law in his favor on discretionary items. The recount was certain to become a referendum on each judge in their next decennial election, and handing victory to an increasingly unpopular Robinson could become an albatross. Conversely, particularly for those Democratic judges from Cook County, overturning a victory by the state's first Black governor could doom them in either the Democratic primary or the general election. If nothing else, it could ensure having an opponent in each.

This much was clear: It was in the Speaker's interest—and the interest of his party—to help keep Robinson's image strong.

This much was also clear: Elizabeth DiMaggio, and others, would be running the same traps as he was, and concluding, as he was, that weakening Robinson was paramount to their effort. This was borne out by her early and incessant attacks on the audit rollout and other recent missteps. With all their drum banging, they had gone national as well. Why not? If the situation were reversed, he'd be doing the same thing. Allen was not likely to prevail if Robinson and the E Party were not brought down quite a few notches.

This much was very clear: The next few months might be the most challenging in his entire tenure as Speaker. If nothing else, it was time for Speaker David Kennedy to marshal his resources.

* * * * * * *

Intriguing, thought Carla Hilton again as she second-guessed her dinner with Javier Sanchez. First rule of lobbying: get a definitive yes or no from the legislator. If you fall for "strongly considering," "I think I'll be with you," "very interesting concept," or, her personal favorite, "can't see why not," you end up with the equivalent of the fortune cookie routine where every saying concludes with "in bed." When it comes to legislators, anything short of "yes, you have my vote and my total support" really concludes with "until I change my mind," as in "strongly considering…until I change my mind," "I think I'll be with you…until I change my mind" and "can't see why not…until I change my mind." When you're a lobbyist counting votes, a yes means yes, a no means no, and anything else means "until I change my mind."

Had Sanchez really said yes or had she wanted to hear yes when he was really saying "until I change my mind"? He had talked about what he could do to help, he had pointed her in the right direction on some strategic points, and he had suggested avenues to approach other legislators to support her position. But had he mouthed the words, "Yes, you have my vote and my total support"? No.

She had to know. She had to be sure that what he said meant yes. Because Sanchez's yes represented another basic element of lobbying: for every issue you need to find champions. Champions aren't just those legislators who vote in favor of your position. They are those legislators who take the lead, speak strongly in support in caucus meetings, work undecided members one-on-one to influence their decision, and argue strenuously in debate both in committee and on the floor.

If ever there was a time for champions in Carla Hilton's corner, it was now. When the Speaker is the sponsor of a bill you are trying to defeat, you need all the champions you can acquire. Prior to her dinner with Representative Javier Sanchez, Carla had found, count them, exactly zero champions. Not a good start.

But why would Sanchez, a member of leadership with virtually nothing to gain by opposing the Speaker, take a chance on House Bill 1? He could find himself in political Siberia in the blink of an eye. Something just didn't add up.

The math was so fuzzy, Carla began to wonder if she'd been set up. Had the Speaker sent Sanchez to spy on the opposition? No, that didn't make sense either. Speaker David Kennedy would never fear—or lose— a battle to the likes of Carla Hilton and the ACLU. Which left her only one option. She would have to direct her entire strategy on the Senate. The bill could never be stopped, or even slowed, in the House. But in the Senate, well, that would be a new ballgame.

Then again, maybe, just maybe, she was approaching her analysis from the wrong angle. Maybe it didn't matter if Sanchez were a champion because even an all-star team of champions would not stop the Speaker from passing House Bill 1 over to the Senate. But, as chairman of the legislature's Hispanic Caucus, Javier Sanchez had reach to the opposite chamber.

Intriguing, thought Carla for the hundredth time that day. *If* Sanchez had indeed said "yes."

* * * * * * *

"Stone? Carson."

"Hey, stranger, great timing. You're at the top of my call list."

"Yeah, yeah, that's what they all say. But I'll take it. I was beginning to wonder if you'd forgotten about your favorite reporter. What about all these trickles about some confab in Bloomington?"

"The short version? We needed a collective kick in the pants," said Mark.

"So, I take it Atlas and the General rode in on white horses to kick some butt."

"You'd think so, but no. Not quite. Turns out, they needed a good dose of butt-kicking themselves. Hopefully, all of us got what we needed: a new voice."

"Now you got me curious," Nat said, "Look, I have a deadline— and something I want to run by you. Sooner than later. How's Wednesday—brewskis?"

"I'll be there," said Mark.

* * * * * * *

E-MAIL

To: Atlas, General, K.C., Barb, Lisa

From: Mark

Sent: February 6 10:46 p.m. (CST)

Subject: Dinner with Nat

Had a chance to catch up with Nat Carson over dinner. Talked about Bloomington, follow-up to Bloomington, and some introduction to the planning for K.C.'s institute this summer. Should get a good play in his next piece.

Nat also tells me he's getting less than subtle pressure to "balance" his presentation. In his words, to "rough us up a bit." Seems as though our friends at the DNC or RNC or both have lodged complaints with his editors.

Nat feels obligated to slap us around a bit in his next article, but I believe my damage control effort was effective. Should pale in comparison to the venom currently being spewed on the cable talk shows.

Can't say I'm surprised. Serves as a reminder to never underestimate their reach or their tenacity.

* * * * * * *

Note to our readers: The article below is part of a series that *Time* will run at least monthly through the next general election. Nat Carson, editor-in-chief of *The Back Bench*, one of the nation's leading political dailies, will chronicle the activities of the E Party. In addition to these monthly columns, Mr. Carson will further document the E Party's journey in a new and exciting blog, posted at www.time/carsonblog-eparty.com.

K.C. STEIN PUBLIC POLICY INSTITUTE
By: Nat Carson

Despite having had months to prepare, in the most awaited start since Tiger Woods's return from dealing with "personal issues," Governor Tom Robinson's administration broke badly from the gate. The governor's inaugural address was sufficiently inspiring, but his first executive order, issued within days of taking office, has led to a series of attacks from the Republican Party and an admission by his chief-of-staff, Barbara Jenkins, that they may have violated their state's Purchasing Act.

The executive order was itself fairly vanilla, calling for the creation of a forensic audit to scour state government. All in all, not much different from actions taken by most new administrations wishing to demonstrate their best efforts at cobweb sweeping. But, perhaps in haste, they arguably violated state law by improperly engaging the accountants and lawyers tasked with conducting the investigation.

Elizabeth DiMaggio, leader of the Illinois Republican Party and minority leader of the State Senate, seized the opportunity to conduct a whirlwind statewide media campaign to excoriate Governor Robinson and his top aides.

Under normal circumstances, the apology and explanation offered by Ms. Jenkins would have been sufficient. But these are not normal times in Illinois.

According to Julia Dwars-Lennon, a professor at the University of Illinois at Chicago and an expert on Illinois politics, the E Party picked an inauspicious moment to invite controversy. "Considering that they managed to stay above the fray for two election cycles, one would have thought their first pronouncements would have been sufficiently vetted. The last thing they could afford was to have their reputation tarnished so early in the new administration. Although mistakes are inevitable, this one was completely unnecessary. It casts early doubt on their ability to both manage and execute and comes at a time when their public image needs to be maintained at a high level pending the Allen [*Allen v. Robinson*] case."

The Republicans in Illinois are emboldened with the tightening of the election results and can be expected to attack the slightest error or at any sign of weakness. They have very little downside and a huge upside should their candidate for governor be declared the winner in the election challenge.

Members of the Illinois political elite have differing views of the executive order and apology. Yale Griffith from the *Illinois Public Policy Forum* believes the quick apology will serve the E Party well in the long run. "The American public will find this refreshing and honorable. They are generally forgiving, especially in light of honest mistakes, and will come to appreciate an administration that is capable of saying 'I'm sorry.' Too often, our politicians offer false apologies and attempt to use the occasion to deflect blame. Barbara Jenkins's comments were immediate, contrite, and sincere. I think she won a few hearts."

However, Thomas Glennon, former Republican U.S. congressman from Illinois' Third Congressional District, totally disagrees. "The American public appreciates strong leadership. Barbara Jenkins came across as hesitant and weak. Deer-in-headlights material. Those attributes will quickly wear thin."

Although details remain sketchy, the E Party recently held an emergency all-hands-on-deck session in Bloomington, Illinois, to review and rectify the situation. According to a high-ranking E Party official who asked to remain anonymous, "This incident, although unfortunate, has caused us to evaluate our approach to governing and will make the Robinson administration much more efficient and effective."

Our source conceded that the recount has been a major distraction and quoted Governor Robinson as being upset that his young administration has adopted a "playing not to lose" mentality. What remains to be seen is whether they can quickly regroup and change course.

Professor Dwars-Lennon suggests it may not be that easy. "They have two problems as I see it. First, they have a highly inexperienced team. An essential element to effective governing is an appreciation for avoidable mistakes because they are unduly magnified by the public spectrum. Second, as long as the recount remains undecided, it will be difficult for them to attract the seasoned talent they need. An unfortunate catch-22."

However, Congressman Glennon adds that one critical hire could go a long way toward righting their ship. "My advice to them would be to engage a seasoned pro to help them with the budget. Aside from the State of the State address, it is the one knock-it-out-of-the-park turn at bat on which the governor must concentrate. All else between now and then is meaningless prologue."

While avoiding comment on the substance of their meetings in Bloomington, E Party spokeswoman Lisa Boudreau did confirm in an exclusive interview that they are poised to unveil various initiatives, including the launch of the K.C. Stein Public Policy Institute.

Julie "K.C." Stein is the wife of Alex Stein, a self-made billionaire and the person generally attributed with being the founding father of the E Party. She, too, has been a member of the E Party's original kitchen cabinet and is warmly credited with being the "woman's intuition" of the organization.

According to spokeswoman Boudreau, an early element of the E Party master plan has been the creation of a separate and distinct think tank to both develop public policy and to serve as a training ground for future political leaders. Until recently, planning for the institute has been repeatedly relegated to the back burner, given the success and demands of the political operation.

Professor Elliot Saltzburg of the University of Chicago Harris School of Public Policy admits to having been contacted by a member of the steering committee and is very intrigued by the concept. "By virtue of being outside academia, they will be able to draw from a broad and diverse universe of collaborators while not being constrained by the regimentation of a degree program. By concentrating on both policy and training political leaders, this will be a unique exercise in government."

However, Professor Saltzburg also cautions, "This will test notions of whether leaders are born or made out of circumstances. At the U of C, we have a fairly effective system for identifying the students who should excel in achieving their advanced degrees. It's an entirely different thing to predict who might excel at political leadership. It will be interesting to see how the new institute recruits and what goals it defines for success."

When asked about Professor Saltzburg's observations, Lisa Boudreau flashed her best Cool Hand Luke smile and predicted that the institute will exemplify the "out-of-the-box thinking that the E Party is known for."

Their other initiative, more surprising in timing than content, will be the E Party's initial foray at public fundraising for E Party candidates and causes. Until now, funding for the E Party has been somewhat secretive, with apparent ties to a series of trusts created by Alex Stein. It is that very funding mechanism that is under attack by the federal government as part of a pending criminal tax fraud case.

Boudreau denied any link between the sudden change to public funding and rumors that settlement discussions have allegedly broken down. She stated: "We have always expected to seek public funding once the party matured. Given our tremendous electorate success to date, the logical progression is to significantly broaden the scope of our efforts, both in the number of jurisdictions in which we field candidates and in the number of candidates. Any such expansion of our party demands public funding, both for the sheer volume of funds required and for the fact that most jurisdictions have much narrower campaign finance laws than those in which we have participated to date."

When asked to interpret Lisa Boudreau's carefully worded pronouncement, officials in both the Republican and Democratic

Parties reached the same conclusion. It is obvious to them that the next election cycle will see E Party candidates in all fifty states. The bigger question is whether they will run candidates for Congress or even field a candidate for president.

Jennifer Chung of *Fox News* doubts the E Party will run national-level candidates. "They are a savvy bunch and it does not fit what appears to be their overall game plan. If you look at where they have competed to date, there are two constants that stick out. They are currently competing in states with the most favorable campaign finance structures and where they had the best opportunity for entry at the legislative level. Running a national slate, whether for congressional seats or higher, requires a much larger and sophisticated fundraising apparatus. As for opportunity, those tasked with drawing the new congressional maps will clearly be doing so with the E Party in mind. At the end of the day, I believe they will conclude the risks outweigh the benefits in the next election cycle. Time is on their side."

However, Saul Grossman, author of the controversial political best seller, *Throw The Bums Out,* says, "The E Party needs to strike while they have momentum. In the age of the Internet, creating an effective fundraising component does not present the same challenges as the old-boy network, work-the-phones efforts of the past. De la Rosa has already demonstrated that the E Party can compete with the best when it comes to the Internet."

Grossman's mention of "de la Rosa" is a reference to E Party IT genius Lauren Chavez de la Rosa. In another deft move by Alex Stein, he commissioned de la Rosa to create the next generation of Internet-based political campaign protocols. Her various innovative applications have been credited in some circles as being the difference-maker for the E Party.

"I know it's a cliché," said Grossman, "but anyone who underestimates de la Rosa's ability to launch a highly successful

Internet fundraising facility for the E Party does so at his or her peril."

CHAPTER TWENTY-TWO

It was Super Bowl Sunday. From the continuous stream of status symbol cars and stretch limos, one might logically conclude that Eddie Cobb was serving pigskin to a cast of luminaries. Chairman Cobb's parties were legendary, and it was not unusual for his more festive events to run for days and have more attendees than a holiday sale at Walmart.

The traditional Cobb crowd was rabid for football, from the Friday night lights of high school ball to the pros in Dallas and Houston. The beloved Cowboys had faded down the stretch, however, and the Texans had yet to field a championship caliber team. Each had been relegated to the links before the playoffs started.

Hence, this particular gathering was all business. The U.S. Census Bureau had released a critical mass of PL 94-171 population files containing population counts down to the block level, and their release had officially launched the redistricting season. Politically focused junior Rand McNally's across the country had begun a frenzied dash to present their political bosses with scenarios that would either preserve or establish political dynasties for the next decade. Eddie had been cracking the whip over his techno geeks to crank out an executive summary of statistical highlights and possibilities on a state-by-state basis.

Cobb had been strategizing around this day from the moment he'd ascended to the DNC throne. He had already elected his party's choice for president. He was obsessed with combining a re-election of the president with the most scientific, mathematically advanced redistricting modeling that had ever been attempted or devised.

For the past eighteen months, his actuarial team had assembled the most thorough demographic database on the face of the planet. They knew as much about the 230 million potential voters as all the check-out scanners in all the retail stores, all the Internet platforms, from Google to Facebook to LinkedIn to MySpace, and, arguably, all the covert government agency operations put together.

They had all been ensconced at the DNC ranch in preparation for Eddie Cobb's political Super Bowl kick-off—the day his data geeks would initiate coordination with his political gurus to realize his vision for political domination.

Historically, redistricting had been a state-by-state slugfest, each state-based Democratic organization drawing maps to suit its own parochial vision. Tip O'Neill was right that all politics is local, but Eddie also understood and demanded that an over-arching national vision be superimposed. For the first time outside a national convention, he had brought together under one roof all state chairmen and their top advisors. With one exception. In David Kennedy's place was Representative Javier Sanchez.

Sanchez and Cobb had become daily correspondents, generally through late evening telephone and Skype updates. Eddie was proud of his choice of Sanchez, who had quickly gained Eddie's trust by singularly orchestrating the ACLU's involvement in the lobbying campaign against HB1. Eddie made no bones about his insatiable need for updates, but Sanchez had stepped up to the plate with political intelligence regarding Speaker Kennedy and anything E Party. Eventually, Eddie had felt himself willing to reciprocate, more and more receptive to Sanchez's desire to become involved in national-level issues. When they agreed that Eddie's inability to invite Sanchez to the redistricting meeting was regrettable, the two of them had quickly hatched a simple yet elegant plot.

Eddie would personally call the Speaker to extend the invitation to his confab, knowing that Kennedy would never accept the call, let alone the invitation. Javier Sanchez was the highest-ranking member of Kennedy's caucus within national Democratic circles, so it only made sense that Cobb would turn around and extend that invitation to

Sanchez instead. Sanchez, of course, would personally request the Speaker's permission to attend. The Speaker would be daft not to grant such entré—particularly under the condition that Javier act as the Speaker's mole and report back any schemes hatched by the nefarious Eddie Cobb.

Simple. Elegant. And it worked just as it was drawn on the chalkboard.

* * * * * * *

Prior to the preceding general election, Speaker David Kennedy would have said that it was impossible for his disdain for Chairman Eddie Cobb to magnify. Now he saw how wrong he'd been. The only thing the Speaker regretted was that he had not yet conceived of a way to honor his pledge to the General to separate Cobb from his kneecaps. Long a subscriber of the *don't get mad, get even* philosophy of the political brotherhood, as well as the *leave no fingerprints* commandment, Kennedy had to assume that time was on his side and a jerk like Cobb could inevitably find sufficient rope to hang himself. Perhaps Javier Sanchez would provide the fatal tether.

Rejecting Eddie Cobb's invitation to join his redistricting powwow had been a reflex as quick and easy as scratching an itch. It did give the Speaker a moment's pause to consider Cobb's true motivation, but Sanchez's unexpected insertion would satisfy Kennedy's curiosity.

When word arrived from Danny Ryan that the PL94-171 file for Illinois was available, the Speaker found himself full of the renewed energy and discipline that always kicked in with crisis mode management. This was his fourth bout with redistricting and would be his legacy-enabling last. He saw now that, in comparison, the first two had been walks in the park, when technology was only a word, not a full-blown way of life.

The last go-round, the first real computer-waged war with the advent of both geek squads and a statistical barrage of pubescent theories to maximize the design process, was nightmarish. Once that had settled, a nine-month war of litigation in state and federal courts had cost more money than all of the primary and general election campaigns the new map would generate. As difficult as that cycle had been, however, it had ultimately played out with Democrats retaining total control of the state government, at least pre-E Party.

Now, despite a divided legislature, a governor's office in E Party hands, a Supreme Court that would be less inclined to toe the party line in the current environment, and a federal court where the past decade had further eroded some of the principles they had previously relied upon to gerrymander, the Speaker expected to find a new way to maximize Democratic party domination.

* * * * * * *

Fortunately, Scott Grusin had saved Elizabeth DiMaggio from an ulcer that seemed to positively thrive on all the games of intrigue and power-mongering. It was already a month since her conversation with Grusin, who had flown to Chicago to share a meal with her in a quiet spot of her choice. Although he'd make it clear that he would not share the reasons for his optimism, he had agreed to provide all resources necessary to optimize the drawing of the new maps and fund any legal challenges to defeat the assumed collaboration of Kennedy and General Smith. Elizabeth's hope had flared; her ulcer had calmed. She was instructed to utilize any and all measures to delay the map process in Illinois until the governor's race was settled. That was something she could do.

* * * * * * *

When it came to redistricting, the E Party felt relegated to the Sahara Desert, *sans* oasis. In response to Eddie Cobb and Scott Grusin's move to quietly lock up anyone of any perceived talent, the party was left to search for those seasoned political cartographers not yet engaged. A rather obvious Help Wanted sign on appropriate Internet sites and blogs had been posted to address this need. Undermining their efforts was the clear message rippling through the remap community—to the extent there was such a thing—that anyone assisting the E Party's redistricting efforts, with respect to any facet of map design or its legal process, would never again be awarded a contract by either major party. Through sufficient back-channeling, the entire political establishment was now on alert that there was a bounty on the head of anyone who might be foolish enough to violate the decree.

Mark Stone had drawn the E Party's redistricting straw. His morning ritual of intense aerobic exercise and his late-night ritual of imbibing liquid tranquilizer had not in the slightest assuaged his stress over not anticipating that Cobb and Grusin could or would so effectively preempt his talent search. Politics is a young person's game and the events of the first few months were proving too taxing for his middle-age metabolism.

The E Party had played into their opponent's hands by waiting until after the inauguration to staff up. Stone, now one month into his team-building, had exactly zero experienced personnel to show for his endeavors.

Sure, he'd broached his concerns with Atlas and the General in Bloomington. But, with all the other pressing issues—and let's not forget Barbara in semi-meltdown—the topic of redistricting had again been relegated to a downstream focus.

The Census Bureau data had been issued. The competition was already at full throttle.

Mark Stone sensed another looming disaster.

* * * * * *

MEMORANDUM
To: E Party Leadership Distribution
From: Mark
Subject: Redistricting
Date: February 7

All of the U.S. Census Bureau data sets are now available for the redistricting process. In the absence of experienced talent, Lauren has agreed to dedicate an initial working group from her team to begin crunching numbers and drawing both legislative and congressional districts in our targeted states. Although they may not have the level of sophistication required for our purposes, there are a number of surprisingly intricate modeling programs now available on the Internet. At least it's a place to start.

The target date for the initial analysis is one month from now.

As promised, I have cobbled together a brief summary of relevant election laws. (For those wishing greater depth of analysis, please see the most current decennial publication on redistricting law produced by the National Conference of State Legislatures. It is an excellent treatise on the subject. Their website is www.ncsl.org.)

With all due respect, let's call my summary, limited to highlights of federal redistricting law, "Redistricting for Dummies." Attachment A identifies state law outliers with which we will contend in the targeted states.

1. The requirement for apportionment and redistricting emanates from Article I, Section 2 of the U.S. Constitution. Apportionment is essentially the process of determining how the 435 congressional seats are allocated among the states, whereas redistricting refers to the actual drawing of boundaries for election districts, whether federal, state, county, or municipal. It's a fascinating history, but for our purposes, most of current redistricting law was born during the last half of the twentieth century. During that time, the Voting Rights Act of 1965 was passed, the Bureau of the Census within the Department of Commerce was tasked with various statistical authority to support redistricting, and

the U.S. Supreme Court held that district courts have jurisdiction to consider redistricting challenges.

2. Apportionment is achieved through a mathematical formula dating back to 1941 and is not your old-fashioned formula of dividing population by seats. Once the number of congressional districts in each state is determined, in order to uphold the concept of "one person, one vote," standards have also been set to determine how much deviation in population is allowed between districts. The term "ideal population" refers to the number produced by dividing total population by the number of districts. But, because the drawing of districts does not always lend itself to creating districts with equal numbers of people, most redistricting complies with standards that set limits on the range of allowable deviation among districts.

As a general rule, the courts have required the population base for congressional seats in each state to be as statistically tight as possible, but deviation in legislative districts will not create a *prima facie* case unless the overall range exceeds 10 percent.

3. One significant enhancement of "one person, one vote" relates to redistricting with respect to minorities. Section 2 of the Voting Rights Act specifically deals with scenarios to avoid discrimination based on race or color. Section 5 requires any jurisdictions covered by the Act to prescreen any changes to electoral laws with the Department of Justice. However, the Supreme Court very recently held this section unconstitutional so the issue will again be before Congress.

Unfortunately, I would need a law degree from Harvard before attempting to distill the laws governing how minority districts must be drawn. The NCSL materials alone cite over twenty examples of what it calls "major cases about racial and language minorities." Bottom line, any attempt at redistricting that creates a legitimate claim that a minority group has effectively been disenfranchised is asking for long, drawn-out litigation and runs the risk of the court playing Etch A Sketch.

4. Even when taking race into consideration, there are a series of "traditional principles" that have been recognized by the courts (defined in Attachment A). The historical granddaddies are compactness,

contiguity, and affording representation to political subdivisions. My takeaway is that the principles are honored more in the breach.

5. Perhaps most confusing and mischievous of all is that political gerrymandering is recognized as an inherent part of the process. Further, the courts have never been able to signal when they will find that a particular plan has, excuse the pun, crossed the line. So, if a plan doesn't touch the third rail of race and can follow time-honored principles, including compactness and contiguity, there is nothing to prevent blatant, politically driven, map-drawing favoritism.

6. Take everything above and consider that each state has its own set of election laws and standards and that the outcome is mostly dependent upon which party controls the process and which party controls the courts. Show me a state where one party has cashed a trifecta ticket by controlling all three branches of government in the preceding election cycle, and I will show you a state where that party will have a monopoly on government for ten years.

CONCLUSION

Raise your children to be voting rights lawyers and they will never be unemployed. As for the E Party, I am comfortable with our selection of states in which we will be actively engaged in the redistricting process. Also included in Attachment B is my attempt to identify a Tier 2 of those states that should also be considered and why.

CHAPTER TWENTY-THREE

Danny Ryan spent a miserable January buried at headquarters. The Democrats' newly elected General Assembly members were experiencing the culture shock of legislative life and required the usual hand-holding. They were opening their district offices, which required hiring and orienting support staff. These concerns were pretty much status quo. It was finding bills for them to sponsor to justify their political existence that had Danny back to his eighteen-hour-plus pace and crashing on the couch at his bungalow, Sports Center as his nightly lullaby.

Nancy Rae insisted that he stay at her place while she was traveling in Springfield, but the logistics were not worth the hassle without the benefits. She had delayed her initial foray downstate, but was now similarly trapped in her day job world. They were equally despondent at being apart for long stretches, but their geographic dilemma presented no apparent solution.

It was therefore all the more surreal to have the Speaker call with an extraordinary proposition. Given the complexities of the session, the challenges of the remap, and the need to closely monitor the election challenge, he had decided to consolidate as much of his brood as possible. Danny Ryan was to relocate to Springfield for the foreseeable future—at a minimum, until the remap was finalized.

Hallelujah.

* * * * * *

THE BACK BENCH
"If you let it slip, we catch it"
February 8

Finally! This week concludes hearings on procedural motions before the Supreme Court in *Allen v. Robinson*. Although the three-week-long series has resolved many critical process points, the combination of oral arguments and briefs has been the equivalent of watching paint dry. A complete listing of the court's rulings is posted on the blog and will be updated as required.

It is not clear if there is a winner in this particular sequence, although the lawyers' meters have been happily spinning.

Starting Monday, in hearing rooms across the state, evidence will be presented to determine if Republican challenger Robert Allen can gain the 190 votes he needs to become governor of Illinois. Each hearing will last no more than two weeks, pending the granting of continuances by the Supreme Court. There will be over one hundred hearings and this stage will conclude in late April.

It is not known at this point if the lead lawyers— Cole for Allen, Myers for Stewart, or Richards for Robinson—will go head-to-head and, if so, in how many of those hearings. Some have speculated that the lead lawyers will only tackle the most complex hearings based on their comfort factor with the evidence and, in the alternative, take a seat in the press box in order to puppeteer their legal squads.

Let the games begin.

In other news...

* * * * * * *

E-MAIL
To: E Party Leadership Distribution
From: Barbara Jenkins
Sent: February 8 9:19 a.m. (CST)
Subject: Budget Prep

The first draft of the budget address is attached. It's not where it needs to be, and the governor says we need more eyes and more creativity.

Also attached is the executive version of the analysis of the state's dismal fiscal condition prepared by the Speaker's appropriations staff at our request. The General's idea to reach out to the Speaker has been a godsend. In addition, we are meeting with his top fiscal advisors each evening at the governor's mansion.

Per our arrangement, there can be no recommended cuts to education or the state employee pension system without the Speaker's blessings. Everything else is fair game.

Unfortunately, the attached analysis demonstrates a $2-plus billion structural deficit. The changes we drove last session got the state to the point that, for one year only, budgeted revenues match budgeted expenses. Making matters worse, through a history of budget gimmicks, the state owes at least another $1 billion from prior year deficits. Since we're on a cash accounting basis, the state has been juggling its books by, among other things, significantly delaying payments to vendors.

So, the $3 billion question is how to address the deficit and over what period of time. The more aggressive the timeframe, the deeper the cuts must be in the early years. Given the state of the general economy, there will not be sufficient incremental new tax revenues to close the gap, and we all have ruled out tax increases.

Contrary to the Speaker's advice, at the last leaders meeting the governor asked for recommended cuts. It was if he had just thrown a snake on the table. No takers. Yup, it's lonely at the top. The Republicans seem to be enjoying the bind in which we find ourselves. DiMaggio's perpetual smirk speaks volumes.

We are setting aside time for a team call next week. In the meantime, please send through any comments, criticisms, etc.

Thanks.

* * * * * * *

The prospect of a night in the sack with Nancy Rae had Danny Ryan out of his mind with visions that would give *Fifty Shades of Grey* a run for its money. So much so that his drive to Springfield was noted for only one other thing: the expensive ticket he got for doing forty over. Oh, yeah, that and the empty gas tank that had forced him to steer his car off the road and walk to the next truck stop. He was fortunate he hadn't been in so much of a hurry that he'd forgotten to put his sneakers in the car and had been able to trade them for his work shoes and that the truck stop was less than a mile up the road.

When he got to Nancy Rae's, bedraggled and slightly the worse for wear, all she had to say was, "Look what the cat dragged in." They'd fallen into each other's arms, where they stayed for quite a while.

The next day Danny and Nancy Rae settled in to talk. They weren't stupid, of course, nor novices to the world of *Sex in the City*. From that time forward, Danny Ryan and Nancy Rae Mitchell would go to great lengths to camouflage their nocturnal trysts. Not that news of their relationship wouldn't inevitably leak out, but things were always particularly sensitive during the session, and they wanted to be in control of that leak to minimize any political repercussions. Any success achieved by Nancy Rae's clients would become the target of the press corps' constant vigil for scandals, and at least some of her clients would be among those targeted. "Lobbyist Trades Sex for Success" or "Speaker's Lieutenant Takes Working Overtime to a New Level," were just two potential headlines to be avoided at all costs.

* * * * * * *

Representative Javier Sanchez was briefing the Speaker on the events of Super Bowl Sunday. He started with a description of Eddie Cobb's technology database and then moved on to Eddie Cobb's assembled staff. After that he expounded on Eddie Cobb's huge range of support services available to each state's remap team. Finally, he portrayed Eddie Cobb's nationwide vision for maximizing Democratic electoral success.

If Speaker David Kennedy heard Eddie Cobb's name one more time, he felt he could not be responsible for the outcome. Not one to let emotions stand in the way of pursuing excellence, however, he reined himself in, listened politely to Sanchez's tedious monologue, and offered an appropriate tip of the cap to his national chairman. Much as he hated to admit it, he was sufficiently intrigued by the extent and sophistication of Cobb's operation to contact Danny Ryan. There had to be something worth sharing that would enhance their own remapping operation.

What Javier Sanchez kept entirely to himself was that there was a lot more that had gone on at the ranch. Things that the Speaker had no need to know. Copious sessions regarding the alternative Democrat map for Illinois that reflected Cobb's arrangement with Grusin, for example, and planning for the defeat of the E Party's education package in concert with Carla Hilton. And the *pièce de résistance*, Javier's play for Speaker—if and when Allen became governor.

Javier Sanchez had consumed sufficient DNC ranch Kool-Aid to believe what the others had said to him. And it tasted damn good.

* * * * * *

THE BACK BENCH
"If you let it slip, we catch it"
February 11

The initial evidentiary hearings in *Allen v. Robinson* began yesterday with the expected degree of media mayhem.

The national networks each sent a bevy of reporter types and each featured the story as the lead for their prime time evening broadcast. NBC actually has its network anchor stationed in Chicago for the first week. In a bit of a surprise, press credentials have been requested by various international news syndicates. From the conventional newspaper, radio, and TV stuff to the ever-growing unconventional cyberspace world of blogging, tweeting, Facebooking, and YouTubing, Illinois has become the epicenter of the news-seeking world.

Hearings began in three locations: Chicago, suburban Wheaton, and downstate Effingham. *The Back Bench*, in cooperation with *Time* magazine, is covering all three locations and will be streaming live through the magazine's website at www.time.com.

All judges are respected veterans of the Illinois Appellate Court, all reportedly no-nonsense, straight shooters, and, judging by the respective first day's accounts, distinctly focused on delicately balancing the need for precision and speed.

Although the stakes are incalculable, the hearings themselves are about as exciting as waiting for a computer to reboot. In all three courtrooms, attorneys for Allen spent the first day laboriously presenting details regarding each contested vote. The only variation in the three matters was the apparent jurisdictional voting bias. In Chicago, where Robinson originally scored big, Allen's attorneys were predominantly focused on taking away votes. Conversely, in Republican-leaning Wheaton, most of the challenges were attempts to add votes to Allen.

Time's chief legal correspondent, Arthur Young, attended the hearing in Chicago. Based on a scoring system created specifically for these hearings, he concluded that, of the potential 437 votes contested today, 56 were leaning in favor of Allen, 53 in favor of Robinson, and 14 in favor of Stewart. Total scoring for the day based on *The Back Bench/Time* system is a potential net gain of three votes for Allen. However, until the other parties begin to present evidence, there is no way to know the relative merits of Allen's potential pick-ups.

In other news...

CHAPTER TWENTY-FOUR

Bloomington was all of two weeks past and, in a 4G world, at best a fleeting memory. What at the time had appeared to be the *I Ching* of the Robinson administration had proven to be no more than a class reunion. In the subsequent fourteen days, new problems had exploded. Solutions remained few and far between.

If there was any silver lining in their hurricane-force storm cloud, it was that each member of the team had been called upon to summon the leadership qualities that had accorded them such great success in their non-political lives. Now they were taxed with bringing these qualities to this brave new world of governing.

The realization came quickly that, no matter how skillfully and aggressively they played to win, no real victories were to be had, particularly in the short term. For however long or short their tenure and however valiant their efforts, neither the scope of the problems, nor the unrelenting political opposition, nor the unyielding bureaucracy offered hope for success. Their initial legislative session would not be the equivalent of the first lunar landing; it would be more like the political equivalent of the Hippocratic Oath.

Compounding matters, the Robinson administration was facing twin terrors: the constitutional mandate that the governor deliver a State of the State address at the beginning of the annual session of the General Assembly, and Article 50 of the Civil Administrative Code of Illinois—the State Budget Law—which mandates with great specificity that the governor submit a state budget.

Were Tom Robinson a graduate of the University of Political Hackery from which his predecessors had earned their stripes, neither event would present much consternation. A quick review of the state's archives confirmed what they already knew. State of the State addresses had been reduced to political puffery, savory sound bites, and apathetic applause lines. All of which were easily expendable, one-day wonders. Similarly, the budget address had been reduced to a fictional effort bearing little resemblance to the "Generally Accepted Accounting Principles for Governments" that state law demands. More puffery. More applause lines. Yada-yada.

Had the General the sole vote, he would have counseled to cut and run and live to fight another day.

Had K.C. the sole vote, she would have counseled to summon the eloquence and courage for which the Land of Lincoln's namesake is famous.

And so it went. In turn, each member of the E Party leadership counseled either or both Governor Robinson and Barbara Jenkins to adopt a variety of conflicting and inconsistent approaches to the challenges at hand.

After an unproductive series of conference calls and aborted drafts, and in the interest of time and sanity, it was agreed that Barb and K.C. would work with designated staff to fashion an aggressive approach, while the General and Mark would work with other staff to fashion a passive approach. Tom, Atlas, and Lisa would serve as judge and jury. Tom would hold the ultimate veto rights.

The "aggressive approach" squad's motto: Damn the torpedoes; full speed ahead. This team would develop State of the State and budget messages laying out an accurate picture of Illinois government as they knew it to be—in financial and procedural ruin. Why risk precious time awaiting the fate of the judicial gods when every second counted? Having boldly proclaimed the charge before them, Governor Robinson would lay out his comprehensive four-year plan to rectify the core issues.

The "passive approach" squad's mission: Don't rock the boat; proceed with caution. They would craft a message reflecting the political reality of their tenuous hold on the executive branch and the various land mines they needed to navigate through the conclusion of the recount. Why risk potential victories in education reform and making redistricting a fair and open process? Governor Robinson would therefore lay out the safe, and likely ambiguous, plan to facilitate their short-term political and legal challenges.

* * * * * * *

It was arguably the first time Nat Carson had ever truly set the agenda for what would be his next article about the E Party. On most prior occasions, he had been their witting tool whenever they sought a newsworthy boost. And why not? The telling of the tale was always left to Nat's devices. For over two years, he had thoroughly enjoyed being along for the ride. His relationship with Mark Stone had deepened enough to enable a certain bond of trust as well, such that now Nat felt compelled to cut him a break over beers.

"I'm just about done with my next piece for *Time*," he said. "This is your chance to rebut."

Mark looked at Nat over the foam in his beer mug. "Rebut?"

"Well, rebut might not be strong enough, actually," said Nat. "I'll level with you, here, Mark. With everything that's happening, I've decided to review the one hundred days since the election. You know, take measure of Tom Robinson and the E Party from the election forward. Not exactly the usual first–hundred-days-in-office stuff. In this case, the hundred days post-election seems more compelling."

"Not bad," Mark said after a large gulp of local craft lager. "Creative, even. So, if I may be so bold, what's there to rebut?"

"Well, as it turns out, lots, actually. The picture I keep getting is not exactly a day at the beach. Well, depends on the beach. This one's more like a day on Omaha Beach in June 1944." When Mark opened his mouth, Nat held up a hand. "Sorry," he said. "No need to be so obtuse. I'll rewind. First, what's happened to the E Party?"

"Come again?" Mark said without inflection.

"Come on, you know where I'm going with all this. The E Party I know would have seized the opportunity. Would have turned Illinois government on its head by now. All I keep hearing about is a flock of aimless sheep, the more I poke and prod my way to the story. Any chance you'll slap me around a little so I can get my story headed in a different direction?"

"Kind of hard to bid against myself," Mark said wryly. "Anything specific or just the usual unnamed source crap?"

Nat shook his head and called to the waiter for another pitcher and a burger with the works for each of them. "Fair response," he said. "There are definitely more requests for 'off the record' and 'deep background' than maggots at the bottom of the garbage bin." Mark grinned at that. Nat Carson had a way with words that put most other writers to shame. "At the same time, there's enough smoke to make me think a fire's on the way ready to ignite and burn your ass. And burn it to a crisp, too."

Again, he held up his index finger to put Mark off.

"Listen. You and I have been at this E Party stuff for over two years. You guys have been Teflon the whole way along. At some point, something's bound to stick."

Mark put down his beer. "So, what are you suggesting, Nat?"

Nat sighed. The subject matter was uncomfortable even for him, the most jaded of all jaded newshounds. "Look, Mark, there are too many fiction mongers waiting to go viral with even a hint of a good rumor—facts optional. I can walk away for now. But if you want, I can work with you, head this thing off at the pass. Whaddaya say?"

Mark Stone assessed his position. "I'm not sure there is much to say, Nat." Then he smiled. "At least on the record."

* * * * * *

Anthony Manzella: Decorated veteran with a uniquely refined specialty of procurement and base management. Facilitator of transitions for the peacekeepers, most often the United Nations. The person there when someone needed to turn on the lights and, occasionally, turn them off. Anthony Manzella was one of very few who truly understood the toll wars take on a society, in particular relative to the vast reparations necessary to restore the most basic civil functions—and any semblance of human dignity to the vanquished.

Anthony Manzella's stint in Operation Iraqi Freedom had been an eye-opener of unprecedented impact, in no small part because his nation-building role occurred during the four long years preceding his retirement. If you said he'd played an unsung, yet instrumental, role in restoring Iraq's power grid and rehabilitating its water and sewage systems from their eighteenth century heritage, you'd be right.

It was therefore amazing to Anthony that he felt so blindsided by his current predicament. Nothing, *nothing*, in his past, not in all his years of work, had prepared him for the disjointed and dysfunctional bureaucracy he'd been asked to manage in Illinois. It wasn't only that the system was in a state of disrepair reminiscent of a war zone, it was that it was antiquated, particularly with respect to computer and communications technology in a way that undermined its very underpinnings. Most disturbing of all? The inertial forces that resisted with the strength of a herd of wooly mammoths any effort to modernize or introduce efficiencies.

The people of Vietnam, Iraq, and Afghanistan had suffered terrible tragedies, yet embraced the effort to restore and rebuild. The bureaucrats in Illinois had their bloated, vested, tenured pensions, and just didn't give a damn. It didn't help that they were flooded with resentment at the notion that an upstart political party had made their reincarnation among its primary goals, and that some career, all-star military mind had been commissioned to whip them into shape.

* * * * * *

The best business negotiators can read body language, the best poker players can read eyes, and the best lobbyists can read the traffic pattern within the capitol. At any one time, literally hundreds, if not thousands, of legislative and budget deals are in play. It is the place where votes are traded and politics intersects with governing.

The best lobbyists start calculating when they see Lobbyist A talking to Lobbyist B or Lobbyist C talking to Legislator D.

Continuously filtering these interactions through the pros and cons of the session, they adjust the picture for resolution and clarity to assess where the deals are headed.

Carla Hilton's curiosity was aroused. She'd noticed Barbara Jenkins entering the Speaker's office on multiple occasions over the period of a week, and since it was too early in the session for the governor's chief-of-staff to be cutting budget deals and too early for the remap to be in play, Carla knew something was up. Add to that the education lobbyists who were sharing the same door around the same time, and it wasn't rocket science to predict that HB1 was about to move.

Nancy Rae Mitchell had a what-the-hell reaction when she picked up on Representative Javier Sanchez's seemingly frequent contact with one Carla Hilton. It started when Nancy Rae had learned about the pair's dinner at Saputo's, and was heightened when she stopped by the office to meet with Javier one afternoon and found them conferring. Unless they were an item, and Nancy Rae would bet her money on Javier's aversion to such a renowned man-eater, something was going on.

Just yesterday, Javier had stepped out of a meeting with Nancy Rae to take a call from Carla on his cell. Nancy Rae only knew this because his phone had been on the table between them when Carla had called. Man, had Javier jumped to shield her from seeing the screen. Nancy Rae had played dumb, naturally, but it was too late. She knew what she knew. As soon as she got the chance, she called Juanita, who blithely confirmed that Javier and Carla were talking almost daily. Nancy Rae hated to use her friendship like that, but the end in this case surely justified the means.

Barbara Jenkins's curiosity was piqued upon sighting a stunning Black woman along the rail outside the Speaker's office on multiple occasions. Sure, it was common for lobbyists of all ilk to hang around the seat of power like pubescent groupies, but this woman would command attention at the Victoria Secret's runway show. Barbara Jenkins was not steeped in the ways of lobbyists, nor did she give any thought to reading traffic patterns. Yet she could not help wondering why this seemingly misplaced beauty was stationed in Springfield. Such a striking creature obviously maintained—no, commandeered—an impressive sphere of influence.

Barbara's meetings with the Speaker were not only about the business of passing HB1. She remained in awe of his mind's strategic thinking, particularly in combination with his encyclopedic marshaling of the political and legislative process. The whiz kid in her was sponge-like in grasping for the wisdom he imparted in every session.

For the Speaker, HB1 was presenting an interesting screenplay. There was Barbara Jenkins, for instance, whose presence was causing him to feel increasingly energized—almost like his old self. The woman was brilliant, yet apparently without a contentious bone in her body, something rarely, if ever, seen in his guarded world. She was refreshingly hopeful, yet not naïve. Unlike the usual Springfield pedestrians who forced him to erect barriers, Barbara asked questions that pushed his intellectual buttons and aroused his sense that the consideration of his legacy was not misplaced.

Barbara asked one particular question after the close of a recent strategy session that was so out of context that it had demanded his contemplation for days. She had casually inquired if he knew the uncommonly beautiful and blatantly sexy woman who had been hanging around outside his office complex. Speaker David Kennedy, for the first time, chose to evade her question.

*   *   *   *   *   *   *

E-MAIL

To: E Party Leadership Distribution
From: Barbara Jenkins
Sent: February 12 2:23 p.m. (CST)
Subject: HB1 update

As you are aware, at the Speaker's suggestion we have been working to finalize the logistics to pass HB1 on an accelerated schedule.

Over the past week, he has summoned the effected constituencies to his office in an attempt to ferret out their concerns and complaints. In what I assume is a completely uncharacteristic gesture, he has invited me to sit in on *every* conversation. And it has been fascinating!

I never could have anticipated the negotiating dynamic, especially when comparing those groups with whom his tactics are dictatorial compared with those groups with whom he is conciliatory.

I also never could have anticipated the topics under negotiation. It's as if education were of secondary or even tertiary consideration. The unions are singularly focused on pension benefits for teachers to the exclusion of advancing education quality. One gentleman was perturbed when the Speaker would not exclude me from the conversation. He then proceeded to put his price in front of the Speaker, who did not flinch when this man posited that his own pension be doubled or there would be no deal. I'm not sure if the Speaker expected the outburst of unmitigated greed or was simply prepared to acquiesce, as though it was business as usual.

Almost all groups are focused on the new legislative map. Whereas the Speaker has indomitable power over the Democratic Caucus, many of the education constituencies claim control over certain legislators or voting blocks. As you might expect, he knows who's puffing and who's not.

Kennedy discusses each volley with me in striking detail, as if he's deliberately providing me with access to the source code in his mind. Fascinating!

Certain elements of the plan appear overly simplistic, such as getting to sixty votes in the House and thirty in the Senate. By my count, it should be a no-brainer. But he cautions that the dynamic of votes is much harder to lock down in the second chamber, in this case the Senate, assuming the bill passes the House. Although he's consulting with Senate President Welk, he is mindful of which lines he can cross and which he cannot.

There is also the quest for a veto-proof majority in the event Robert Allen becomes governor. Which leads to the Speaker's insistence that we get the bill to Tom as soon as possible to avoid any such risk. Which, in turn, leads to how much and when to trade for votes as the hour glass in his head runs down.

There are times, no matter how momentary, when you can sense the Speaker is performing a multi-dimensional calculation for which he would never be able to articulate the variables under consideration.

E-MAIL

To: E Party Leadership Distribution
From: Barbara Jenkins
Sent: February 13 11:18 p.m. (CST)
Subject: Address to General Assembly

With a grudging appreciation for the process we have undertaken, attached for final review is the draft of the joint State of the State/budget address for tomorrow. Although I am wedded to the outcome, I cannot help but regret that we have built a camel and not a stallion. I think I could not be less disappointed in a course of action in which I am complicit and for which I feel singularly responsible. Let's get through this and move on!

CHAPTER TWENTY-FIVE

THE BACK BENCH
"If you let it slip, we catch it"
February 14

EXTRA EXTRA EXTRA EXTRA EXTRA EXTRA

Oh, somewhere in this favored land the sun is shining
bright;
The band is playing somewhere, and somewhere hearts are
light;
And somewhere men are laughing, and somewhere children
shout;
But there is no joy in Mudville—Mighty Casey has struck
out.

Sorry, you'll have to indulge me. By the time Tom Robinson finished his first State of the State/budget address this afternoon, I couldn't stop myself from revisiting Earnest Lawrence Thayer's classic poem about the local hero who failed to deliver when it mattered most.

Just over a month ago, I gave Governor Robinson credit for his brilliance when, in his inaugural address, he pledged the same "level of commitment" as governor that he had displayed during his Hall of Fame career.

So how is it that in his first meaningful at bat, the best he could do was to hit a few foul balls and head back to the dugout with a "K" on the scorecard?

Upon replay, it was not the worst presentation to have been suffered upon the people of Illinois, but it failed to meet the expectations of this reporter and many others who had high hopes for Illinois under Governor Robinson's leadership.

In what has now become tired material, he spent far too much time on the virtues of education reform and rebuilding an efficient bureaucracy to better serve the state, while spending virtually none on the critical budget or other long-overlooked issues facing the state. In short—long on mush and bereft of solutions. Had this speech been delivered by a Democrat or a Republican, it would still have fallen short of the mark.

In his inaugural address, the governor talked about being a "scared young man" as a rookie in the bigs. Let's hope this episode is more about a scared grown man weighed down by the challenges of a difficult job, intractable issues, and the uncertainty of an election challenge. And that he quickly finds his stroke and his ability to lead.

* * * * * * *

E-MAIL

To: E Party Leadership Distribution
From: Lisa Boudreau
Sent: February 14 3:01 p.m. (CST)
Subject: Tom's speech

Nat's piece in *The Back Bench* did not help, but the story appears contained in Illinois. Thankfully, an uneventful speech, even with us constantly under the microscope, will not compete for national attention with today's other headlines.

Regardless, I have been working damage control all afternoon with the media. This may have to be one of those times when we take some lumps, throw in a few *mea culpas* and move on. Tomorrow's press conference should help.

My guess is that it's a one-day play unless the Republicans can find something to spin. To that end, I think we did an excellent job of scrubbing for attackable sound bites.

* * * * * * *

As they each listened to Governor Robinson deliver his speech, Speaker Kennedy and Republican Leader DiMaggio put the finishing touches on their respective remarks to the press. Each had received the compulsory advanced copy early that morning, but, as seasoned veterans, had withheld final judgment pending the delivery and reaction from the audience in the gallery.

Kennedy would walk that fine line between partisan nitpicking and expressions of willingness to work with the new governor on his agenda. The Speaker well understood that the target audience for the speech had been two distinct courts—the court of public opinion and the Supreme Court of Illinois. To that end, Kennedy viewed the speech as both inspired and suitably vanilla. The only ones to take offense would be the true believers on the political extremes, and they would not matter again until the next election.

Senator Elizabeth DiMaggio and her public relations contingent had read and re-read the speech in the allotted timeframe with the goal of unleashing a nationwide multi-media attack. They'd been convinced that Robinson would announce a bold agenda that would create multiple opportunities for them to drive his negatives through the spin cycle.

To their collective chagrin, the speech proved to be fastidiously and unspectacularly brilliant. Worse yet, it was sufficiently laden with Republican themes that they would pin themselves in a corner if their attacks were any less than laser strikes. With the press, unless those laser strikes were spoon-fed, they would be too risky to chance. The E-Party had done it again. Much like Kennedy, Elizabeth DiMaggio had no choice but to walk that fine line between partisan nitpicking and expressions of willingness to work with the governor on his agenda. On this day, in the battle for the hearts and minds of the Illinois Supreme Court, Robinson had not struck out. He had hit a home run.

* * * * * *

THE BACK BENCH
"If you let it slip, we catch it"
February 16

Just one day after his siesta-inducing State of the State address, Governor Robinson held a press conference with Speaker Kennedy and Senate President Welk to announce that HB1, the Reinventing Education in Illinois Act, would be fast-tracked. Neither would commit to a definitive timetable, but, given the rules of procedure and the current schedule for session days, three weeks is not out of the question.

Kennedy's enthusiasm for HB1 was manifest. Not only is he the House sponsor, but he used the occasion of his remarks at the legislature's swearing-in ceremony to make HB1 the centerpiece of the General Assembly's Spring Session. Having President Welk now on board is the lynchpin, particularly as to the accelerated timetable.

Key union officials and educational leaders from across the state appeared with the governor and the Speaker on the podium.

In perhaps the ultimate political one-upmanship, Governor Robinson reminded the press that both Jeff

Stewart and Robert Allen had signed pledges of support during the gubernatorial campaign.

If there is anyone who can show cause for why the Illinois Legislature should not pass HB1, speak now or forever hold your peace.

In other news...

* * * * * * *

Carla Hilton was no wuss, but when she learned of the plan to accelerate passage of HB1, her first reaction was panic. After that she quickly dialed straight to hysteria, and then plummeted back to panic. Within the hour, she had managed to ratchet down the panic to consternation, but it had taken an appropriate amount of alcohol and quite a few of the cigarettes she kept only for emergencies. Now, all that was left was to kick herself with self-directed anger for having lost her cool.

After another hour or so of agonizing self-pity, she picked herself up off the metaphorical floor. It was time for reorganization and recalculation.

One: Carla always knew the game would play out in the Senate. To win, she needed the Republicans to hold rank and she needed to add "no" votes from Democratic minority Senators. Two: She had already launched her Hispanic outreach through Javier Sanchez and had devised one-on-one messaging strategies for members of the Black Caucus. Three: Once she had an accurate count, she could always backfill for votes from the tried-and-true pool of ACLU loyalist Senators. As most of them were also ultra-liberal education wonks, she would draw upon that reservoir only when necessary. Four: Time was now the enemy. Welk needed to be slowed down. She needed a strategy.

She arrived at Javier's office to find Juanita on break and another woman she didn't recognize manning her post. Carla requested an audience with the representative and politely waited to be announced. The woman, smiling in a way that implied she knew something Carla did not, made the call, then stepped out from behind the desk to introduce herself to Carla Hilton.

"Nancy Rae Mitchell," she said.

Carla tried to hide her embarrassment at believing for even a minute that Nancy Rae Mitchell was someone's admin, and apologized. Nancy Rae gracefully poo-pooed Carla's faux pas. They both knew where they stood. Why bring it out into the light? Besides, with a community as insular as that of Springfield lobbyists, it was unusual that the two of them had never been formally introduced before.

They politely, if a bit stiffly, talked shop as they waited for Javier to surface. Carla seethed inside knowing that Nancy Rae's ties to Danny and the Speaker severely compromised her mission. Everything was fair game. Everything could and would be used against her.

She made a snap decision, getting up from the couch where they had settled.

"Oh, shoot," she adlibbed. "I just remembered. I have a meeting. How could I have forgotten? But it's been such a pleasure meeting you, Nancy Rae. Would you mind... would you have Javier—Representative Sanchez—give me a call?"

Javier, huh?

Nancy Rae just nodded and smiled.

* * * * * * *

"What in the hell is going on here?"

Eddie Cobb wasn't holding back. "What do you mean, HB1 is on a downhill run?"

Javier had prepared himself for such a tirade. Still, he held the phone away from his ear and winced at the static. "I'm telling you everything I know," he said, knowing it sounded lame.

"Then get more," Eddie screamed. "And get it fast. That asshole Speaker of yours... I have a good mind to..."

The phone went dead.

* * * * * * *

"Carla, it's Javier. Sorry it took me a while to get back to you. What can I do for you?"

As if he didn't know already.

In her mind's eye, Carla was still seeing Nancy Rae Mitchell's shit-eating grin. And feeling ill. "I assume you heard today's news, Javier. About Welk's also moving quickly on HB1?"

"Of course," said Javier, as if things like this happened every day. "And I've been giving it some thought. Options we might employ to slow things down."

Carla felt herself relax. Slightly. "Oh. Good. I was hoping you'd say that. Can you get to Welk?"

"Well, I don't know," Javier said, a little taken aback by Carla's lack of tact. "I'm not sure I'm ready to show my hand in this matter quite yet."

"Oh," Carla said again, not sure what to say to that equivocation. "Then what *do* you suggest?"

"I was thinking about a full-scale public relations campaign. A full-blown attack-style campaign designed to take some air out of their balloon. At a minimum, it would create doubt in the minds of the senators. Remember, until that happens, all of this is Kumbaya."

"Public relation campaigns cost money," Carla said shortly, not pleased with Javier's first "option." "And the one you're describing will cost *lots* of money—millions—particularly to get it moving sufficiently fast enough to create the appropriate negative buzz. Where's that kind of money going to come from?"

"Let's assume I can find some benefactors," Javier said, unwilling to be undermined. "Do you think your ACLU cronies would accept contributions if the campaign were launched in the organization's name?"

"Doubtful," Carla sighed, "but I'm willing to make the pitch if you can prove the funds will be there."

"Give me forty-eight hours," Javier said.

* * * * * * *

"Sanchez!"

"Eddie? Why are you calling now? I thought we agreed to talk later tonight. I have a dinner starting any minute…"

"Let 'em wait," Cobb sputtered. "If we don't get our arms around this education thing, we might as well pull the plug on the entire plan. If Robinson delivers on his education plan, there will be no stopping him *or* his cousin the Speaker. But if you can't connect those dots, maybe I've got me the wrong partner."

There was a silence as big as the Grand Canyon as Cobb congratulated himself on cracking the whip and Sanchez bit his tongue to keep from telling Eddie Cobb what he could do with his "entire plan."

When Eddie felt enough time had passed that he'd made his point, he picked up the ball. "So, gimme everything you've got."

Javier regrouped, as Cobb expected him to. It would not serve him to argue with the drama queen of politics. "I bounced some ideas off some of my best sources," he said tightly. "Their thinking revolves around two themes. One, the Speaker is trying to shore up Tom Robinson's image in the wake of his lackluster performance to date. Two, the Speaker may have cut a deal with the E Party on the map, but has to deliver on his end first."

"Exactly!" said Eddie. "My money's on door number two. Although I wouldn't mind slamming both shut asap. What do your sources say about that?"

"Well," began Javier. He heard the hesitancy in his voice and hated himself for it. "As *I* see it, there are a few choices. First—and I have already broached this with Carla Hilton—the ACLU launches a public relations attack campaign. Second, we, or I should say you, work the unions at the national level to have them slow down their Illinois brethren. Third, someone gets to Welk with an offer he can't refuse. I can play the Hispanic Caucus card," he added, "but I would prefer to save that for later."

Eddie smiled. This Sanchez was one sharp cookie.

"Let's walk this through, then," he said. "Precisely what did Ms. Hilton say?"

"That she'd go to her board, but only once she knows the money is there."

"An appropriate ask on her part," Eddie said begrudgingly. "You think this broad can deliver?"

"Honestly, I have no idea," managed Javier. "But under the circumstances, who else would even consider a kamikaze mission against the Speaker?"

"Fortunately, there are plenty of rich ACLU nut cases involved with the Democratic National Committee. How much do you think we're talking, there, Sanchez?"

"Frankly, *Eddie*," Javier said, "I was hoping you would know the answer to that one. And now, if you don't mind, I'm late for dinner. This will have to wait. I'll call you later."

Shocked by Javier's sudden disconnect, Eddie relit his cigar and considered the call. Funding for the ACLU would be a snap. Nothing like a little flag burning to excite the faithful. As for the unions, there was no apparent downside. He wasn't asking them to jump in front of the train, just slow it down. As for Welk, well, that might take some doing.

Sanchez was smart.

Hopefully not too smart for his own good.

CHAPTER TWENTY-SIX

THE BACK BENCH
"If you let it slip, we catch it"
February 18

The first round of hearings in *Allen v. Robinson* has concluded without much in the way of news or excitement.

The second round is now underway in Chicago, Waukegan, and Murphysboro and, understandably, the fanfare has been ratcheted down. The national newsies have moved on, leaving behind the B teams and unemployed freelancers looking for movie deals.

Self-crowned political handicappers seem to be in agreement that the vote totals do not appear to have been significantly nudged either way. Of course, much more will be known when the judges submit their findings to the Supreme Court one week from now.

In other news...

* * * * * *

E-MAIL

To: Atlas

From: Liz

Sent: February 20 1:14 p.m. (CST)

Subject: Don Colletti

Your old union buddy, Don Colletti, called for your number in Aspen. Said if you're too busy, he could talk to the General. I hope I wasn't rude, but I was a bit surprised he didn't already have any of your numbers. Thought I had better check first.

* * * * * * *

E-MAIL

To: Liz

From: Atlas

Sent: February 20 12:18 p.m. (MST)

Subject: Don Colletti

Thanks, Liz. Knowing Don, the numbers are all on matchbook covers in a drawer somewhere. He's a dinosaur. I doubt he has a cell, let alone a smart phone. Please set the call as soon as possible. Try to add the General. Better yet, see if Don has time to spend a few days in Aspen. Tell him the snow is unbelievable.

* * * * * * *

"How long has it been?" asked Atlas of his old pal Don Colletti.

"Too long, too long," Don said. "I still need to meet your bride. The woman who finally snagged you has to be either a saint or a nincompoop to put up with all your *mishegas*."

"Don't be using your Italian Yiddish on me," Atlas threatened. "And I'm not crazy. ...okay, maybe a little. But what about you? I read you're retiring. I never thought I'd see that happen. Then again, being a national level union big shot is pretty much like being retired anyway."

"Yeah, okay, but if I'm retired, who saved you and that bullshit political party last year when you were about to tank?"

"Tank?" Atlas shot back. "Us? The General and I were just giving you a chance to get into our good graces. Speaking of which, why don't you get your ass out here for a few days?"

The two old friends traded stories and barbs for almost an hour before Don got around to his business. "I'm calling to give you a heads-up. Even though I'm not much into the day-to-day stuff, I still hear things. It could be nothing, of course. Thing is, you, Tom, and the General must be stirring the pot up there in Illinois. Someone high up at the DNC is asking us at national to intercede with the locals to head off some disaster in the making. Thought if you could enlighten me, I could work the traps on my end."

"That's interesting," Atlas said, "because if you ask me, we haven't been stirring much of anything, let alone the pot. With the election challenge hanging over our heads, it's been more like walking on eggshells."

"Well, I suppose it might not be you," said Don slowly. "All I know is that in a recent meeting, one of our Midwest liaisons said we've been asked to make some calls regarding an education bill that's moving too quickly. I assumed that meant the E Party."

"Now, that helps," Atlas acknowledged, his pulse picking up despite himself. "They're talking about our education reform package. It's almost two years in the making and should pass this session. In fact, Speaker Kennedy is on board and recently got the Senate president to put it on the fast track. My understanding right now is that the unions are all on board and their representatives stood in support at a recent press conference. Tom's chief-of-staff, a sharp gal named Barbara Jenkins, has been working with Kennedy for months to iron out the rough edges."

"Hmm. I see what you mean," said Don, "particularly when you mention Kennedy. Great friend to the unions, that man. Well, like I said, I'll work some traps on this one, good buddy, and get back to you."

* * * * * * *

<u>**E-MAIL**</u>
To: Atlas, General
From: Barbara Jenkins
Sent: February 21 7:14 a.m. (CST)
Subject: Don Colletti follow-up

I passed along your friend Colletti's information to the Speaker, who called late last night to discuss. When's a good time to talk?

* * * * * * *

"Barb, I've got the General on a conference line."

"Hi, Atlas, General. Glad we could connect so quickly."

"Is Tom joining in, too?" they asked.

"He's at a legislative dinner with the Conference of Women Legislators. I was supposed to attend, but we traded places when Liz scheduled the call. I'm heading over as soon as we're finished. At the Speaker's recommendation, we're both reaching out to build some legislative relationships."

"How's that going?" asked Atlas

"Hard to say. I don't have to tell you that Tom is a natural in social settings, but these dinners usually end up as an extension of what he calls the 'squeaky wheel' chats. That's wearing thin on him. Everyone has a wish list. His view of the world is team building. Around here, it's all me, me, me.

"I try to deflect as much as possible, but most people insist on talking directly to the governor. The worst part is that there's not much we can do. As you might imagine, it's mostly about jobs or funding for some wonderful project, and we have a moratorium on hiring and new programs. But I don't have to tell you..."

"He needs a good bodyguard," the General said disgustedly. "When I was in the field, I gave the job of saying no to the meanest S.O.B. in the platoon that I could find. Kept me from having to listen to the whiners."

"So you're saying I'm not a mean S.O.B.?" Barb asked.

"It's all part of the learning curve, my dear," the General said, "all part of the curve. I'm sure there's hope for you yet. But seriously, Barb, eventually you'll learn both how to say no and how to make it stick."

"Speaking of learning curves," Barbara said, "I feel like a freshman at the Speaker's school of legislation. How does the cliché go? He's forgotten more than I'll ever know. Not sure exactly why he's helping, but I remain in awe of his genius."

"I'm curious," said Atlas. "What's his take on Colletti's info?"

"According to the Speaker, there is an effort taking shape to thwart the passage of HB1. He's not certain of all the conspirators, so he wants to let it play out a little to see if he can confirm his suspicions. He's sure Eddie Cobb's fingerprints are somewhere, but says even Cobb would need people on the ground in Springfield."

"I'm one hundred percent in agreement with that assessment," said the General. "That M.F. Cobb's name sure shows up a lot. No one's ever been successful with air cover alone. You always need infantry. What's the strategy?"

"President Welk is working the vote count now. We need sixteen out of twenty-five Democrats in the Senate and he's about halfway there. I sat in on most of the Speaker's arm-twisting sessions. Welk operates differently, to say the least. Much more democratic, with a little 'd.' The Speaker says there are about a dozen Democrats Cobb could pick off, so he'll have his sources on alert. I think he wants to find out who's been corrupted in order to set his trap … so he can catch Cobb in the act."

* * * * * *

THE BACK BENCH
"If you let it slip, we catch it"
February 23

EXTRA EXTRA EXTRA EXTRA EXTRA EXTRA

The first set of findings in *Allen v. Robinson* was posted on the Supreme Court's website about an hour ago. Each is well in excess of 1,000 pages, inclusive of attachments containing digests of the evidence presented.

Consistent with the protocols set by the Supremes, contested votes are grouped in one of four categories: challenge accepted, challenge denied, recommend accept, and recommend deny. The "accepted" and "denied" categories are to be based on conclusive findings of fact. In the event the evidence is not conclusive, the judge is to weigh in favor of one of the "recommended" categories.

A quick glance at the rulings suggests that the preponderance of the findings are categorized as accepted or denied. Unfortunately and unexpectedly, there is no way to determine which candidate has advanced based on this initial sample. That will not be revealed until vote proportionality is factored.

What is vote proportionality, you ask?

As it turns out, the great majority of challenges do not tie back to a known vote. For example, most of the accepted challenges from the Chicago hearing relate to undercounts. In this case, a vote is removed from the count, but there is no way to know for whom that vote was cast. Therefore, each candidate's total is reduced by the percentage of votes they won in that precinct.

For example, if there were 100 votes in a precinct where the totals were 40 votes or 40% for Robinson, 35 votes or 35% for Allen, and 25 votes or 25% for Stewart, tossing aside one vote means Robinson loses four-tenths of a vote, Allen 3.5 and Stewart 2.5. When applied, Robinson is left with 39.6 votes, Allen 34.65, and Stewart 24.75 votes.

Sufficiently confused?

What it means is that all of the findings have to now be processed against the totals by precinct. That will not be done until the Supreme Court has reviewed each series of findings to reach the final decision. Although I am certain there are computer geeks running preliminary results to create tomorrow's headlines.

In other news...

THE BACK BENCH
"If you let it slip, we catch it"
February 24

Sure enough, at least a dozen websites appeared overnight with an instant analysis of the initial set of findings in *Allen v. Robinson*. A list of the sites I was able to locate is posted on the blog. Surprisingly, there is a wider disparity than I would have thought. The basis for the disparity relates to how the "recommend" categories are valued.

For whatever it's worth, Robinson's projected lead ranges from a high of 192.7 to a low of 186.9. For those readers wondering how there can be a .7 vote or a .9 vote, I have posted a detailed explanation of the proportional reduction system on the blog.

Still confused? Me, too!

In other news...

* * * * * * *

Eddie Cobb hated losing. He hated it even more than he hated not being in control. And apparently that's what he was—out of control—and that's what he was doing—losing. For all his scheming and beyond-the-scenes maneuvering and all the money and political capital he had invested to date, Eddie Cobb, Chairman of the National Democratic Committee, was losing.

And big.

The initial round of findings in *Allen v. Robinson* was disappointing. Certain projections even had Robinson gaining votes in Republican strongholds.

Speaker Kennedy was pushing hard to give the E Party a boost as big as the f—ing Texas sky to public perception by passing the education package. To make matters worse, the ACLU was putting up resistance to supporting the PR campaign required to arrest momentum.

As recently as forty-eight hours ago, Eddie Cobb had been coaxing at least one national union organization to pressure their Illinois local to oppose the bill. Then his "guy" had called to report that the local would not risk "antagonizing" Speaker Kennedy at this time. Eddie seethed with the injustice of it.

His Illinois remap team should have had its initial cut on his desk a week ago. For reasons beyond his understanding of the variables, it was proving difficult to create a map sufficiently weighted to Republicans and Hispanics that Sanchez could leverage into the speakership.

Sanchez wasn't doing such a piss-poor job. On the other hand, he wasn't getting the job done. But if not Sanchez, who? Eddie, who ordinarily took as few steps as possible to save energy, paced his office, a constant cloud of cigar smoke in tow. How far removed was he from every critical decision point? How long before control slipped through his fingers? Eddie Cobb was used to getting everything he wanted, when he wanted, and how he wanted.

* * * * * * *

E-MAIL

To: Atlas, General
From: Barbara Jenkins
Sent: February 24 9:30 p.m. (MST)
Subject: Don Colletti follow-up

The Speaker called earlier this evening. He was demonstrably pleased to report that his sources had worked with Colletti to repel the attempt to disrupt the union coalition support of HB1. He also felt comfortable that, in his words, "no fingerprints were left." To that end, he asks that you find the appropriate way and time to thank Colletti for alerting us to the problem.

CHAPTER TWENTY-SEVEN

Speaker Kennedy had temporarily put his Eddie Cobb DON'T GET MAD, GET EVEN file on the back burner. Cobb, though brilliantly devious and unabashedly ruthless, was also inevitably careless. Therefore, even though the Speaker had made a commitment to the General that he would "take care" of Cobb, and intended to honor that commitment, he would sit back, at least for a while, and be ready when Eddie Cobb took his first misstep.

While Chairman Cobb's attempt to disrupt the Speaker's union coalition had been summarily avoided, it had also served as a reminder that Mr. Ruthless was re-engaged in Illinois politics. It was this reminder that prodded the Speaker to summon Danny Ryan, who was directed to put all loyalists on the alert for anything that the chairman and his henchmen might be pursuing.

* * * * * *

Despite having her initial entreaty regarding the PR campaign abruptly dismissed by the ACLU Board, Carla Hilton would not be rebuffed. In hindsight, it had been sloppy to ask the chair to call an emergency session of the board without having thought through the operational details. And equally sloppy not to have done a better job lobbying her board member friends in advance. Carla had been unprofessionally rash, and she regretted it.

There was an enormous amount at stake—defeating HB1 primarily, but she also wanted to prove herself to Javier Sanchez. On a track to higher office and perhaps Democratic Party stardom, that man was fascinating in ways she had only begun to discover. With each encounter, she found herself increasingly taken with his charisma. Honestly? He appealed to her inner cougar.

Javier Sanchez's laid-back persona was endearing. Not at first, of course. At first it had been irritating as hell. But now, for whatever reason, his calm reassurances were allowing her to placate her own demons. Carla looked forward to spending more time with him on this campaign they'd cooked up.

Yes, she'd probably be forced to spend a *lot* more time with that handsome Javier Sanchez.

For his part, Javier was not correctly reading the emotional signals Carla had begun emitting, but he was gaining an increasing appreciation for her creativity and sophistication. These were skills he did not regularly encounter in the punch-'em-in-the-face world of Illinois politics, yet ones that Javier sensed could greatly aid in his quest for higher ground. She had already earned him praise from Eddie Cobb—inadvertently—but what difference did it make? Praise from Eddie Cobb was a rare thing indeed. Finding ways to tap the potential she presented was becoming a high priority.

* * * * * *

The only reaction Eddie Cobb had ever received from sulking was a good swipe upside the head from his daddy, which had pretty much cured him of the habit at a young age. Much better to savor some fancy, aged bourbon, get a good night's rest, and then rewind, and rewind some more, until the path to resurrecting his failed scheme *du jour* presented itself.

Eddie was a master at compartmentalization. Adept at reducing the most complex issues to the simplest denominator—and at separating overlapping concerns the way magicians separated conjoined rings. The *Allen* case could wait. As far as the local unions' deference to Speaker Kennedy, they would be properly admonished and punished when Sanchez became Speaker, Allen became governor, or both.

HB1 remained Eddie's immediate focus. If those namby-pamby eunuchs at the Illinois Chapter of the ACLU didn't have the balls to launch a negative public relations campaign with the money Eddie had so efficiently corralled, then he would find another way.

That's when he saw it. The answer. Laid out right there in front of him like the devil's own staff. Eddie smiled and reached for his Rolodex for one of the numbers he chose not to keep on his phone for obvious reasons. He'd kill two albatrosses with one stone. Or, in this case, with one phrase: Super PAC.

* * * * * *

"Governor. How did the speech go tonight?"

"Best part of my day, boss," Tom said. "It's amazing, Atlas. I'm getting anywhere from ten to twenty requests a day for these things. On top of the forty to fifty meeting requests, that is. I finally had to insist that any event I accepted had to involve the causes most dear to me. For example, I asked Barb and the Speaker to identify education groups that are interested in hearing my HB1 pitch—with a focus on Getting to 21, of course."

"And tonight?"

"Parent-teacher association group in Rockford. Flew up late afternoon and just got back. I was impressed. It was a very engaged audience. Every once in a while it feels good to end my day on a high note."

"I hear you," said Atlas. "And that's good. Because you've seemed kind of off since Bloomington. You know, not your usual self. Then when the General and I talked to Barb the other day, well, I just thought I should check in, see how you're doing."

"With anyone else I might be annoyed at being the subject of the conversation," said Tom, "but one thing I know about Barb is that she has my back…along with the rest of you."

There was a pause. Atlas let Tom talk.

"It's hard to believe she and I didn't hit it off at the beginning. Now I know it was the circumstances, not a compatibility issue. She's shifted to a new gear or two since Bloomington. I think we all have. But the woman's got energy. I mean serious energy. Reminds me of those rookie phenoms who manage to play hard all day and party hard all night. Pure adrenaline. Only in Barb's case, it's work hard all day and then work hard all night. I don't know how she does it."

"Same way you do, I suspect, Tom," said Atlas. "And, speaking of adrenaline, how's yours?"

"Mine?" Tom laughed. "I think every last ounce of mine was left on the ball fields. My pace—and schedule—now is more of the Ronnie Reagan variety."

"I know what you mean," Atlas said, "but what about the rest of you? You feeling okay about everything these days?"

Tom sighed. "I won't lie to you, Atlas. This is one tough job. And that's if they let you do it. Once you realize that no one is trying to solve problems, that it's all about avoiding blame, well, it gets old, you know? One of the things I always liked about baseball—most sports for that matter—is the simplicity. Most of it comes down to see the ball, hit the ball. Here, no one wants to see the ball *or* hit the ball. Most of 'em don't even want to get in the game."

Atlas was listening carefully.

"Take this meeting we had the other day regarding construction delays for major road repairs in Chicago. Things aren't just delayed, mind you, but way over budget. We had contractors, unions, local officials, and people from the Department of Transportation in the same room together and the meeting ran almost two hours. Two hours! And still, none of them could agree on the problem, let alone the solution. You couldn't get a straight answer to the simplest questions. One big exercise in CYA."

Atlas made a few supportive noises, but Tom was on a roll.

"Anyway, about halfway through, I'd had it. I turned to Tony Manzella and told him to go bust a few heads and report back. I don't know how much time you've spent with Tony, but I get the feeling he's busted more than a few heads in his day. Turns out, the project was under-engineered and underbid from day one. And everyone knew it. But that's par for the course. Bids get let for X dollars even though everyone knows it should have been two times X or whatever. The scope of work gets underestimated as well. They wait till they can find an excuse to claim there was some unexpected problem and then ask Uncle to issue a change order to bail them out.

"Only, Manzella won't bail them out. And I'm not bailing them out. So they're stuck trying to figure out who's gonna take the financial hit. In the meantime, the job is at a standstill, the papers and TV stations have caught wind and are sniffing around for gotcha stories, and I'm stuck in bullshit meetings up to my eyeballs with guys hoping to wear us down with excuses."

There was a long silence and then Tom gave a huge exhausted sigh.

"What can I say, good friend? Multiply that times ten or so meetings a day. You look back at the end of the day or week and nothing's moved. *Nothing.* It's as though the meeting itself was the point, not what could come out of it. They go back to wherever they go, tell their people whatever it is they tell 'em, and wait for another meeting. At least until government wears down and puts more skin in the game.

"Honestly? I find the whole thing disgusting. We're roughly a month and a half into this and haven't solved one real problem yet. In the meantime, thousands of discontent commuters are dealing with road construction, or whatever other government dysfunction is bogging down the system, every day, just wasting people's time and lives."

He sighed again. "Frankly? I can't see doing this for four years."

Atlas held his tongue. What had he had gotten his old buddy into?

* * * * * *

THE BACK BENCH
"If you let it slip, we catch it"
February 27

True to their word, HB1 flew out of the House today, just under two weeks after the joint Robinson-Kennedy-Welk press conference announcing the fast tracking.

Debate in the House was spirited and surprisingly one-sided. Even more surprising was the final vote: 118-0.

You read that correctly. All Democrats, all E Partiers, AND all Republicans voted in favor.

What gives, you ask? Let's just say it's a clear case of first chamber syndrome. The art of voting for a bill knowing that it will face scrutiny in the second chamber where *that* vote is the one that determines if the bill goes to the governor.

Not unlike the parent who gives in to the kid on a fairly obvious "no" question only to add "go ask your mother/father," knowing the second parent will put on the kibosh.

How many times has a tough bill passed overwhelmingly in the first House only to die or be bludgeoned to death with amendments in the second House?

Otherwise, there's no explanation for the Republican vote. Last thing they want to see happen is Governor Robinson's number one agenda item becoming law during the recount. But even though it has to also pass the Senate, all Republican state representatives now have photo-op and bragging rights, having advanced the cause of educating the little darlings.

Gotta love government.

In other news…

CHAPTER TWENTY-EIGHT

Through the convenience of e-mail, text, and Twitter, Carla Hilton and Javier Sanchez were clinched in a furious collaboration to either defeat HB1 or significantly delay its passage.

Defeat was a math exercise. The bill could be stopped in the Senate Education Committee or stopped on third reading before the full Senate. Six "no" votes would defeat HB1 in committee and thirty would do the trick on the floor. Unfortunately, "stopped" and "defeated" are relative terms. The Senate's procedural rules do not restrict committee votes to one attempt. Even in defeat, a bill can rise from the ashes as many times as the committee chair is willing to move the question.

Carla and Javier viewed the committee as a place to buy a few precious days or weeks through procedural motions. With the eleven-member committee comprised of six Democrats, three E-Partiers, and two Republicans, it would take four Democrats to vote no in consort with the two Republicans to block a "due pass" motion. Even if they found six allies, they both knew all too well that, at the next meeting of the committee, President Welk would use his considerable discretion to remove and replace those uncooperative committee members with new ones who were certain to vote "aye."

Fortunately, Senator Gonzalez was one of the Democrats on the committee. Gonzalez was Javier's senator and a trusted friend. In a pinch, he might be persuaded to vote no. But, as a lighter lift, he could easily be counted on to assist in delaying tactics, no questions asked.

The floor vote is an entirely different matter. One vote—up or down. If successfully defeated, the legislation could always reappear as an amendment to another germane bill, but that would take much longer and, by then, hopefully, time would be on their side in the recount.

Given the political makeup of the Senate, they needed a total of ten Democrats to marry the twenty Republicans in order to reach the magic number of thirty "no" votes. For that matter, the Democrat sympathizers could vote "present" and have the same impact.

Although Carla and Javier were proving to be remarkably compatible in their strategic approach, their one divergence was in how to find the ten votes needed. Javier was certain that all necessary co-conspirators could be found among the Democrats, especially considering the eight Hispanics he was hoping to control. Carla was convinced that they also needed to mine the E-Party for votes. But, with her intuition up against Javier's amigos, she ultimately conceded that finding all Democrats was the preferred course. Her pushback was to finesse Javier to agree on an expansion of their target list to at least twelve Democrats in the event he could not corral the entire Senate Hispanic Caucus.

The great unknown was how quickly President Welk would attempt to pass the bill. If he was willing to ask the Senate to waive all posting and notice requirements, it could be on the governor's desk in three legislative days. Without waivers, the over/under was maybe two weeks.

Absent Carla's ability to persuade her board to reconsider its decision and launch a PR campaign against HB1, it would take a minor miracle to kill the bill. At best, they could expect elementary delaying tactics, which would not be sufficient.

What Carla Hilton and Javier Sanchez had going—more than anything else, it turned out—was that odd and compelling synergy of two competitive individuals who feed off each other, as if in training for a marathon. Javier had Eddie Cobb's stick constantly tapping down his back as well as the carrot of the Speakership. Carla had the stick of her commitment to the cause—while her carrot was her lust for the affections of Representative Javier Sanchez.

Within forty-eight hours of the passing of HB1 by the Illinois House of Representatives, the clerk of the House officially sent the enrolled version to the Senate, where the first reading occurred during perfunctory session.

During that same time period, Carla and Javier had locked in their strategy. Javier would work the Hispanic Caucus for no and/or present votes on third reading, while working with Senator Gonzalez to slow things down in committee. Carla would work the four additional senators on their wish list.

* * * * * *

In redistricting years past, Danny Ryan would have presented his first draft of the redistricting map to the Speaker within weeks of the census data report release. Once population and demographic shifts between the previous and current census were understood and corroborated, the design of the districts was not too difficult, with the emphasis placed on protecting all sitting members with districts likely to contain at least 55 percent likely Democratic voters and with as much geographic overlap with their current districts as possible.

Each census had its own nuance. The previous census had seen the city hold relatively flat, while the suburbs grew in population and downstate lost. The challenge of this particular census was that Chicago had lost population. The bulk of the diminishment was in Black legislative districts. At the same time, the Hispanic population had increased significantly. Accordingly, protecting the sitting Black legislators would have to come at the expense of not adding Hispanic seats. Reconciling this population shift would not be easy.

Redistricting for sitting white Democratic representatives and senators could be accomplished seamlessly between city and suburbs. As Danny often consoled himself with crude redistricting humor, at least all the white guys looked alike. Conversely, not all Democratic districts looked alike statistically. To get to the minimum 55 percent magic number of likely Democratic voters required to create safe districts, the Black and Hispanic districts could only tolerate a minimum component of white suburban voters. In almost all cases, it meant the

Blacks and Hispanics needed districts with at least 60 percent likely Democratic voters, of which no more than 30 percent could be white.

The saving grace to this year's exercise was that the E Party had obliterated their majority by eroding the number of Democrats in the House to fifty-four. Had this been ten years ago, he would have found it virtually impossible to save all sixty-seven of the then sitting members of the House Democratic Caucus. The challenge in this case was creating a sufficient number of new seats from which they could find the six needed to recapture the majority. If he drew six new safe seats, a loss of any one would doom their hopes for a majority. If he drew more than six, they would have to dilute the pool of likely Democratic voters in each district. It required sacrificing quality for quantity: safe districts for relatively safe districts.

Because of the inherent difficulty, Danny presented the Speaker with a half dozen different models, each predicated on a list of priorities Kennedy had carefully prescribed for him.

Given that Danny Ryan found the Speaker's priorities challenging, he would have cowered at the Illinois instruction manual for Eddie Cobb's geek squad. Consistent with all states, Cobb's Illinois analysts were tasked with maximizing maps using sequencing of more than thirty variables from fields such as income, mortgage debt, education, career, family status, heritage, voting history, religion, and sexual orientation.

Given that Danny Ryan found the Speaker's priorities unnecessarily complicated in ferreting out the penultimate Democratic strategy, he would have been numbed by Eddie Cobb-induced variations designed to achieve majority control in the House by leveraging Republican seats with Hispanic Democrats. Sixty seats comprised of forty to forty-five Republicans and fifteen to twenty Hispanics. In addition to maximizing a path to sixty seats, Cobb's geeks had been instructed to devise a path that would set off alarm bells in every Democratic precinct.

While Danny Ryan had advanced his cause from simple math to calculus, and while Cobb's team had advanced to nuclear physics, Mark Stone's E-Party remap team was still working its way through the training manual. It wasn't that the formulas to design maps were problematic. Lauren de la Rosa's team could balance as many variables as there were angels on the head of a pin. Instead, and essentially for the first time, the challenge was to define and identify the quintessential E-Party voter.

Whereas the Democrats and Republicans knew their voters' historic tendencies and voting records, the E Party had never conducted a contested primary vote. All of their candidates had been handpicked by Atlas, the General, and Mark Stone, based on footwork in the communities, personal interviews, and well-honed instincts. The Democrats and Republicans had been holding primaries and caucuses and conventions for over a century and could draw from lists upon lists of contributors, volunteers, friends of friends' lists, and voting records.

Not only was the E Party without lists, the lists it needed to produce were proved in the negative. They had to identify anyone not on a Democratic list or a Republican list and, to the extent possible, guess which of the remaining potential voters were predisposed to vote with them.

* * * * * * *

E-MAIL
To: Carla
From: Javier
Sent: March 2 9:56 p.m. (CST)
Subject: Committee vote

Spoke with Senator Gonzalez today. He has agreed to approach Chairman Benjamin to ask for additional hearing dates to take testimony on HB1. It should all appear somewhat innocuous to the chairman. As predicted, it did not require my having to offer anything to Gonzalez by way of explanation. Wonder how they will react when Carla Hilton of the ACLU indicates a desire to testify in opposition?

* * * * * * *

THE BACK BENCH
"If you let it slip, we catch it"
March 4

The Senate Education Committee met today to take testimony on HB1, the Reinventing Education in Illinois Act. Consistent with the hearings in the House, it was essentially a love fest. Educators, parent groups, unions, and experts from a list longer than my arm drooled all over the issue for over five hours.

In what was a bit of a surprise, Chairman Benjamin did not call for a vote. Rather, the hearings were continued to the call of the chair. Unless the Senate adds session days this week, the continued hearing will have to wait until next week.

Not exactly the fast track we expected.

In other news...

* * * * * *

Upon learning that Representative Javier Sanchez had bought one additional week at a minimum, a thoroughly giddy Eddie Cobb gave orders to unleash his PR campaign. Unless he had totally miscalculated, before Chairman Benjamin could next gavel his committee to order, HB1 would be littered with media-induced shrapnel.

CHAPTER TWENTY-NINE

THE BACK BENCH
"If you let it slip, we catch it"
March 6

The airwaves in Chicago were bombarded last evening with a series of political ads on both television and radio expressing varying degrees of contempt for HB1. Sources indicate that coverage will gradually be increased to statewide saturation and that the attacks will extend to print and social media as well.

These are not your typical political attack ads. Taking a page from the E Party playbook, they are thoughtful, clear, and hard-hitting. All of them can be found on *The Back Bench* blog.

The first ad to debut suggests that HB1 violates both the Illinois State Constitution and the U.S. Constitution in various respects. It is set as a takeoff on the original constitutional convention wherein a rather obvious George Washington, Benjamin Franklin, and James Madison decry the bill's limitations on personal freedoms.

The second suggests that the act would expose children of illegal aliens to deportation. Although a touch too soap-operaish, it raises a compelling question that Governor Robinson will have to face in the Latino community.

The third is not necessarily a direct hit on HB1. It points out that our military is already inundated with underqualified applicants and suggests that the requirements imposed by the Getting to 21 section of the law will degrade the quality of our armed forces through back-door conscription if HB1 and other related legislation is passed.

Who is behind this campaign, you ask? Curiously, each ad is identified with a different Super PAC. In order: Friends of the Constitution, Citizens for Open Immigration, and the Coalition to Keep our Military Strong. However, they are apparently the collective residual of a well-timed and well-orchestrated campaign.

In other news ...

* * * * * * *

"Mark? Nat. I hope this isn't a bad time, considering you and I are probably on the same mission right now."

"Tell me about it," Mark said. "Any idea who's behind the attacks?"

"No idea," said Nat. "I've got all my sources working on it and the boys at *Time* have jumped in as well. But it's tough to crack the shells on those Super PAC nuts."

Mark groaned. "Yeah, I know. We've got nothing here either."

"What about the Speaker?" Nat went fishing.

"We discussed it," Mark said. "We're a thousand percent certain he's been alerted. That man has sources you and I can only dream about. I'll call you when I have something."

* * * * * * *

The knocking at the door was unusually loud and unusually late.

Startled from his SportsCenter cat nap, Javier Sanchez took a quick look around until he spotted that day's laundry-bound shirt to cover up. Annoyed at the intrusion, he cracked the door, expecting to tell whoever it was to bugger off until the next day's office hours. When he saw who it was, he wasn't sure how he felt.

Carla Hilton avoided Javier's eyes as she burst into the apartment, but there was nothing about his scantily clad body that did not scream "come hither" to every one of her senses. Feeling decidedly at a disadvantage, she moved straight to his living room sofa, then let go with an extended, agitated rant. Would he notice the slight sheen she perceived appearing on her forehead or the fact that she couldn't look him in the eye?

Javier was trying to grasp the situation. His brain, having checked out for the evening hours earlier, was feeding him very little constructive information to help him piece together the threads of Carla's diatribe. It didn't help that he was standing there like an idiot in his boxer shorts. Or that Carla's dress was riding up one thigh like a beacon.

He gave himself a mental slap. He considered getting on some pants, but he'd learned early on that you didn't interrupt a woman on a rant.

Based strictly on volume and histrionics, Javier deduced that he had somehow done something unspeakable. He had placed Carla's career in jeopardy. Carla and he could no longer conspire on HB1. Carla would never trust him again.

Javier's Springfield routine did not necessitate keeping sustenance on hand beyond instant coffee and a weekly assortment of healthier muffins and the like from the local organic food market, although he didn't really think caffeine and sugar would help the situation. Eventually, not sure how he'd managed it, he and Carla were sitting in chairs at his kitchen table, a glass of not too old pinot in front of Carla and a hot Starbucks instant coffee in front of him. Javier had forgotten to shut off the TV. It continued to murmur disconcertingly in the background, but he didn't want to put any distance between himself and the woman across from him. The *Tonight Show* had long ended. Pretty soon *Hogan's Heroes* reruns would start. Was it possible they'd have pieced together the day's apparent calamity by then?

"Are you telling me you had nothing to do with the Super PAC PR campaign?" Carla hissed. "Because I find that hard to believe."

Javier wasn't a natural-born liar, but he *was* a politician. "I had nothing to do with it, Carla. Nothing." Plausible deniability was what mattered here, not that the name of Eddie Cobb was flashing like a neon sign in his mind. "I had no idea they'd attack the ACLU for its assumed role with respect to that group—what did you call it—Friends of the Constitution." That part was true, at least. He'd been on the floor and in meetings until late in the day. He'd planned to check his messages after "resting his eyes."

"And I had no idea you spent the entire day—"

"—and night!" interjected Carla.

"—and night," Javier acknowledged, "under siege from the press, your board, and major contributors."

Javier found Carla an interesting mix. A calloused lobbyist, she could be cold as ice. But when things got tough, she apparently turned into an emotional babbler. Next time he'd recommend his usual solution: Ambien and alcohol.

By the time Javier had soothed Carla's frayed nerves and they'd reworked their short-term plan, *I Love Lucy* had transitioned to *The Andy Griffith Show*, they'd finished off his store of breakfast items, and Carla had transitioned to black coffee.

Suddenly there was nothing more to say. Javier's eyes strayed to Carla's chest. The top two buttons of her dress had come undone.

It was the undoing of one Representative Javier Sanchez.

* * * * * * *

"Mark," said Nat Carson. "I wasn't expecting to circle back so soon, but I suddenly find myself on a deadline. I could use some help."

Mark gave the go-ahead.

"Here's the deal. I'm moving up my monthly article to focus on this attack campaign on your education bill. The brass here smells a big story and they want to gain the upper hand asap.

"I'm looking at all the angles. What I'm hoping is that you can get me access to Governor Robinson, maybe even with the Speaker. This is on a seventy-two-hour-or-bust deadline. Next week's cover, if I play it right."

"Sorry I don't have more for you, Nat. What I can tell you is that we're not much further along than we were. We're still guessing at the five W's on this one. Of course, the H is simple. Someone has access to a war chest. I'm not sure I can do much about the man behind the curtain, but I'll push for access to the governor. I'll get back to you."

* * * * * * *

The attack ads had created a Code Red within the Robinson administration. Word of a rushed piece in *Time* was only intensifying the urgency. If HB1 crashed and burned, everything would be at risk. All of which, following a protracted all-hands phone conference debate, made their decision fairly easy. There was nothing to lose by putting the governor square and center to Nat Carson's national audience and then follow up with their own PR and media response.

General Smith had filed the lone dissenting opinion, cautioning against rushing into battle against an unknown enemy with unknown resources.

* * * * * * *

Speaker David Kennedy sensed his position in the center of the bull's eye. Robinson and the E Party were worthy secondary targets, but it was the Speaker who would suffer untold collateral damage if either were mortally wounded.

It was time to force the enemy's hand. The behind-the-scenes efforts to reverse union support for HB1 had all but confirmed the existence of powerful, influential adversaries. Eventually they would have to engage on his turf, but it was up to him to make sure they played by his timetable. Announcing the fast-tracking of HB1 had, as anticipated, forced that engagement.

It was the scope, immediacy, quality, and ferocity of the attack that had caught him off guard. Its scope told him that national level resources were at work. Its immediacy told him that the product was a well-choreographed plan. Its quality told him that a team of knowledgeable, experienced consultants was plotting his demise. Its ferocity reconfirmed that Eddie Cobb was at its epicenter.

His first call went to Danny Ryan. His second to General Smith, and his third to Barbara Jenkins. Others were placed to Senate President Welk, Russell Washington, in his capacity as head of the Black Caucus, and Javier Sanchez, in his capacity as head of the Hispanic Caucus.

They—whoever "they" were—would play by his rules or he'd be damned.

* * * * * * *

Note to our readers: The article below is part of a series that *Time* will run at least monthly through the next general election. Nat Carson, editor-in-chief of *The Back Bench*, one of the nation's leading political dailies, will chronicle the activities of the E Party. In addition to these monthly columns, Mr. Carson will further document the E Party's journey in a new and exciting blog, posted at *www.time/carsonblog-eparty.com*.

REVENGE OF THE SUPER PAC
By: Nat Carson

There are many who believe historians will ultimately draw a big red circle around 2010 as the year that forever changed the political landscape in America. For the significant majority, the opinion is that it will not have been for the better.

On January 21, 2010, the United States Supreme Court knocked the world on its politically correct derriere with the opinion in *Citizens United v. Federal Election Commission* (the "FEC"). The Citizens United decision was sandwiched between lesser known but compelling decisions in *Emily's List v. FEC* (issued September 2009) and *SpeechNOW.org v. FEC* (issued March 2010), along with a series of important FEC advisory opinions (see accompanying chart detailing these decisions).

The legacy of this year-long legal plague was, in general, a significant expansion of funding for political campaigns and, in particular, the rise of the "Super PAC." Super PACs can raise enormous sums outside the regimen of campaign finance limitations on individuals and "ordinary" PACs and have very few constraints on spending. In theory, they are not allowed to coordinate with candidates or campaigns, but the lines of separation between Super PACs and the candidates and campaigns more closely resemble tissue paper than the Great Wall of China.

Prior to 2010, there had been building, albeit limited, momentum to find solutions to the perceived evils of excessive campaign contributions. Whether from the creation of the FEC in 1974 to the Federal Election Campaign Act in 1982 and the Bipartisan Campaign Reform Act (also known as McCain/Feingold) in 2002, many had tried and all had failed. Yet, activists believed that they were at least headed in the right direction.

However, the one-two punch of the First Amendment and the collective creativity of those who will not be denied political capital has always been a formidable duo. With *Citizens United* on the books, unless and until the balance of influence on the U.S. Supreme Court is rearranged, the debate has been settled.

With the advent of Super PACs, any willing billionaire or mere multimillionaire can independently embark on a single-issue terrorist campaign in the time it takes to write a seven-figure check and to invent a fluffy, harmonious title for their mission such as "Friends of the Pure and Righteous" or "The Committee for Everything Patriotic and Virtuous."

Until very recently, the battle of the Super PAC titans had been waged during presidential and congressional campaign seasons. There is very little evidence of Super PACs' engaging in state or municipal level politics. Similarly, they have not been aggressively used in issue-based campaigns, although such use occurred increasingly during the last general election cycle, particularly among the pro-life vs. pro-choice camps.

However, all that appears to be changing.

Within the past few weeks, three Super PACs began running attack-style ads against proposed legislation in Illinois related to education reform. The fact that the ads all commenced on the same day has given rise to speculation that this is a well-organized and well-funded collaboration. The fact that the legislation in question is the centerpiece of the E Party's legislative agenda in Illinois gives further credence to the conspiracy theories.

"Repulsive" was the terse response from Pierce Lazare, president of Preserving Democracy, a citizens watchdog group in Chicago. "This is precisely the repulsive behavior the United States Supreme Court invited with the *Citizens United* decision. National-level politics have become the province of the über wealthy and now it is spilling over to the states."

Professor Emeritus Paul Reardon of the Political Science Department at Northwestern University disagrees with Lazare regarding the use of Super PACs in state and local affairs. "I believe this will prove to be an isolated instance. On the surface, the recent Super PAC attacks in Illinois are directed at the defeat of a parochial legislative issue. However, the stakes are considerably higher. The E Party has all but announced its intention to run a national slate in the near future. No doubt the Democratic Party and the Republican Party, whether acting alone or in consort, will go to great lengths to prevent them from succeeding. To that end, this is carpet bombing in a much larger war.

"In addition," he adds, "the legislation in question is the pet cause of Governor Tom Robinson. Casting aspersions on the merits of the legislation has a direct impact on the public's perception of his ability to govern. Weakening Robinson is another way to weaken the E Party."

Debra Saviano, author of the *Weekly Saviano Report*, has a slightly different slant. According to her, "It's all about the election challenge. If you notice, the focus of the attack campaign is on Governor Robinson's Getting to 21 program. None of the negativity is focused on the other substantive education reforms contained within the legislation. In essence, this becomes a direct attack on Robinson and is an extension of the vitriol that has been spewing from the Democrat and Republican news commentators since the election challenge was filed."

The E Party, in typical fashion, immediately posted an Internet response on all of their affiliated websites and shortly thereafter added a video of Governor Robinson offering a personal response. In addition, E Party spokeswoman Lisa Boudreau issued a lengthy treatise to the press. Coverage to date has been well reported across media outlets in Illinois. But, as Mr. Lazare points out, "The E Party response, while spot-on with respect to the point of attack, may not be sufficient. Their base of followers has been educated and mollified. The attack pieces, however, are targeted at Black, Hispanic, and Republican voters. The E Party will need to respond in kind to reach these groups. Until that time, the opponents of HB1 rule the airwaves, exactly where the battle must be fought."

But can they?

The principal benefactor of the E Party was originally Alex "Atlas" Stein. Although Mr. Stein is believed to remain an active party strategist and cheerleader behind the scenes, his personal wealth is frozen pending the outcome of tax fraud charges launched by the Justice Department. Without access to the E

Party's primary funding source, they recently launched a web campaign to raise funds. Those funds, however, are dedicated to championing Robinson's case in the election challenge, *Allen v. Robinson.*

Howard Crosby, a leading expert on Internet-based fundraising, cautions that "the public's appetite, particularly in these difficult economic times, may be limited. Although the concept of a third party has engendered much enthusiasm, the electorate is a fickle group with short memories. Because the issue in question is unique to Illinois, it will be difficult to draw support from across the country."

In a rather interesting development, neither the National Democratic Committee nor its Republican counterpart would comment on this developing story. Debra Saviano suggests the two major parties "may find themselves between the proverbial rock and a hard place. Since the parties and the Super PACs are prevented from working together, they could be concerned that their comments could be taken out of context. However, their failure to comment and to distance themselves from the ad campaigns begins to have the look and feel of a cover-up."

CHAPTER THIRTY

THE BACK BENCH
"If you let it slip, we catch it"
March 15

In a classic demonstration of in-your-face politics, the Senate Education Committee passed HB1 yesterday afternoon.

Contrary to speculation that the Super PAC-funded multi-media campaign might retard the announced fast track plan, the bill passed along party line votes with Democrat and E Party committee members' voting to send the measure to the full Senate and with Republicans' voting present.

Also contrary to speculation, President Welk did not need any committee substitutions to gain votes. All minority members of the committee were in attendance and all voted "aye." Obviously, President Welk and Speaker Kennedy worked those votes very hard. Passing the bill from committee through temporary substitutions and without minority votes would signal weakness and that has never been the Speaker's MO.

However, sources indicate that at least three of the African Americans and two Hispanics on the committee have informed leadership that their committee votes will be reversed on the floor if the growing public outrage in their districts is not quelled.

Although the bill easily passed out of committee, there was an element of drama supplied in the form of testimony by lobbyist Carla Hilton of the ACLU. Ms. Hilton was joined by ACLU constitutional scholar Elliot Fuchs. Together, they spoke passionately and eloquently regarding their beliefs that HB1 is constitutionally flawed. With the help of softball questioning from the Republicans on the committee, the ACLU tag team scored points, particularly with the press.

The Speaker's press spokesperson, Sally Mayfield, used the ACLU testimony to further fan speculation that the group is partially responsible for the Super PAC media campaign. In what may signal the precursor of the E Party's response, Lt. Gov. Barbara Jenkins took the ACLU to task for attempting to thwart legislation designed to improve the education system in Illinois. If nothing else, it was a signal from the Speaker to the Democrats in the Senate that he remains committed to passage of the bill.

In other news...

* * * * * * *

Carla Hilton and Javier Sanchez were now spending every waking second consumed by their drive to defeat HB1 and the passion they had recently ignited. Whether preparing for the committee hearing or continually refining the strategy to defeat HB1 in the Senate, any excuse to meet was also an invitation for unabated sex, particularly with the addition of a new sofa to his legislative office.

Javier's brain had yet to engage. He could no more stop this speeding bullet than he could change his ancestral heritage, even if he'd wanted to. Nothing, not his wife at home, his training, or his previous experience with women, had prepared him for living out repressed fantasies. He had no intention of going back to a world of beige.

When Carla wasn't gazing into the face and exploring the body of her new hot Latin lover, she was thinking about when next she would be. His thigh over hers, his arms pinning hers to the bed, the afterglow of political pillow talk. There was nothing better.

* * * * * * *

A thousand miles southwest of Springfield, Chairman Eddie Cobb was experiencing his own orgasmic state, this one prompted by mental masturbation post-success of his Super PAC onslaught.

Following the *Citizens United* decision, Eddie had gently nudged three top lieutenants off the DNC payroll with sufficiently lucrative severance packages to weather the transition and engender eternal loyalty. In this case, transition meant setting up a series of Super PACs and other DNC off-balance sheet entities designed to wreak political havoc on Republicans, E Partiers, and any other perceived enemy in need of pummeling. The result of Eddie's foresight into the possibilities of *Citizens United* was now an intricate web of Super PACs with untold funding sources. All within Eddie's domain, and all totally legal.

Once the simple brilliance of the plan was upon him, it took all of two phone calls and all of six or seven minutes, pleasantries included, to set everything into motion. One call went to his former chief-of-staff, now current CEO of the Pursuit of Liberty Super PAC; the other went to Scott Grusin, who, in turn, set his Republican Super PAC counterparts in motion.

Thank you, U.S. Supreme Court.

* * * * * * *

Life was anything but orgasmic for Nancy Rae Mitchell and Danny Ryan. The Speaker had placed Danny on a 24/7 hamster wheel with instructions to finalize redistricting maps designed to lock in the Senate votes needed to pass HB1. Nancy Rae had to sit back and watch as Danny resorted, over a few short days, to his former political zombie self. It was one of the things she had feared the most, and now it was happening.

* * * * * * *

While the time-wasting, sound-bite-chasing world of self-important media and politicos contemplated the impact of Super PACology on Tom Robinson, the E Party, and HB1, the Speaker set the spotlight of his mind's eye on his fast-track agenda. Once he secured the thirty votes needed in the Senate to pass the bill, nothing else mattered.

As soon as he and President Welk were assured the tote board in the Senate chambers would show thirty green lights, all Cobb's Super PAC horses and all Cobb's Super PAC men would not be able to put the pieces back together again. The only question was if Governor Robinson would sign the bill into law the day it hit his desk or take a forty-eight hour victory lap to garner sufficient kudos and media driven adoration.

Unfortunately, the Super PACs' barrage had made locating thirty votes an unanticipated and unwelcome challenge. The Black and Hispanic Senators had been called to task by myriad Super PAC induced robocalls and e-mail banks. If there's anything that gets the attention of elected officials, it's having their somnambulant constituents aroused and whining.

Kennedy and Welk could currently count twenty-one aye votes from their Caucasian block and the E Party Caucus. They needed nine minority votes, and pronto. If Cobb, Grusin, and their billionaire buddies broke through with messaging to upset the core of twenty-one, locating additional votes would become impossible in the context of their accelerated timetable.

The only way to lock in the nine needed votes was through creative map drawing. But Danny Ryan's team had not found the formula. They could find ways to draw safe districts for eight Blacks or seven Latinos. There were myriad compromise solutions to garner twelve to thirteen votes, but that would leave up to three to four Blacks and/or two to three Hispanics at risk in their next election. At this stage of the session, there was no way to squeeze votes to salvage HB1 unless rock-solid legislative districts were the bait.

Squeezing always worked in late May when there was an endgame dynamic. Under state law, a supermajority vote would be required starting June 1, therefore, the Democratic majority would be faced with the dilemma of either adjourning with a less than perfect remap or having the remap held hostage to Republican votes. Kennedy knew how to use his persuasive powers and wouldn't hold back. He'd prevailed each and every time in the past. Nevertheless, the Ides of March was upon them and it was too early in the session for the squeeze play to work.

The Speaker had tasked Danny Ryan, Russell Washington, and Javier Sanchez with finding nine votes. Ryan would produce maps. Ryan and Washington or Ryan and Sanchez would then meet one-on-one with the respective caucus members in search of votes. Danny Ryan's team would tweak the maps in response to his meeting notes.

And the merry-go-round kept spinning.

* * * * * *

Nancy Rae was horny, lonely, and cranky.

Where was the active, footloose and fancy-free Nancy Rae Mitchell—the Nancy Rae she'd grown to trust and love? The one who wined, dined, and caroused into the wee hours during sessions? Where was the Nancy Rae who didn't mind being alone at the end of those tough partying days? She didn't know, but at some point that Nancy Rae had been effectively decommissioned.

It was time to pick up the pieces and pick up the pace. There might not be anything she could do about the horny factor, but she could sure as heck cure the loneliness with some well-planned visits to the Capitol.

At least, that was the plan.

Nancy Rae trudged over to the Capitol no less than four times over the course of the subsequent week. For her efforts, she was rebuffed each time—gently, admittedly—by Juanita. Nancy Rae didn't take well to being rebuffed, however gently it was managed.

This got her to thinking.

Danny had told her that Javier Sanchez was ensconced in negotiations over votes for HB1. That made perfect sense. But while Danny was shuttling off to the map room to work on revisions, Javier should still be available to talk shop with his best buddy. The first few days, Nancy Rae smoldered. The second few, she smoked. After a week, her suspicions raged.

Why was Representative Javier Sanchez dodging her?

* * * * * * *

Strangely enough, Speaker David Kennedy had never actually met, or even directly spoken with, Atlas. With the startling and disconcerting events of the preceding ten days, however, the Speaker suddenly found himself boarding a private jet bound for Aspen, Colorado. Unless they could devise a winning strategy and implement it quickly, HB1, the map, the election challenge, and even his speakership could be headed straight for the guillotine.

An unfamiliar sense of wonderment crept up Kennedy's spine as his hired limo wound its way up to Stein's Red Mountain enclave. Brilliant, accomplished, and a world-renowned politician, David Kennedy had seen many things in his life. What he was seeing now simply took his breath away. At that moment, taking in the glistening Aspen powder draping the Rockies, he stopped regretting the long flight, the discomfort of air travel, and the creaking in his bones. He was shocked to realize that he'd never even seen the Rockies before. "Well, we meet at last, Mr. Stein," said the Speaker, holding out his hand. "I may be premature in my opinion, but based on my ten minute transport from the airport, were I to live here, I doubt that I would ever leave."

Atlas smiled. Anyone who appreciated his Rockies was okay in his book. "Mr. Speaker, you're not premature. In fact, just nine minutes behind schedule. Welcome."

His bags deposited by the door where they would be tended to by house staff, the Speaker was led into the dining room where Tom Robinson, Barbara Jenkins, General Smith, Julie Kersten "K.C." Stein,

Mark Stone, Lisa Boudreau, Elaine Richards, and Avery Watkins were already gathered for lunch. They would talk and eat at the same time, an approach that worked for everyone.

Unlike the Speaker, Avery Watkins was both a frequent visitor to Aspen and an avid skier. As such, he had arrived a few days ahead to enjoy some spring skiing. Avery always said that nothing beat the exhilaration of charging down Ajax Mountain wearing shorts and a T-shirt on a thirty-six inch base on a fifty-degree day.

A veteran of a number of campaigns with the Speaker and an avid groupie of E Party leadership as well as all things that challenged and provoked the evolution of the American democracy, Avery Watkins was also the William Jefferson Clinton distinguished professor of political science from the University of California, Berkeley.

He and Speaker Kennedy had spent their childhoods within miles of each other on Chicago's South Side. Yet, for all intents and purposes, they'd grown up in different worlds. Kennedy had been reared by the politically-rarified Chicago elite in the area of Bridgeport; Watkins by the gang-riddled Englewood ghetto. Kennedy belonged to the inner circle of Chicago's Irish Catholic aristocracy; Watkins was orphaned and then raised by a series of more or less well-intentioned relatives.

It was Avery Watkins' basketball skills that sent him to college; his drive and intellectual curiosity that brought him the rest of the way. He didn't let it bother him that his success was in some part due to Lyndon Johnson's Great Society, affirmative action, and U.C. Berkeley's need to build a diversified faculty. The thing that distinguished Professor Watkins was his well-known ability to turn lemons to lemonade, which just happened to be the title of his first book.

It was a fluke that David Kennedy had stumbled onto *Lemons to Lemonade* during an unexpected layover at O'Hare and that he'd been sufficiently intrigued to devour its contents before arriving at his destination. As soon as he next spoke to his assistant, Dawn Eckersley, he'd tasked her with gathering all Professor Watkins' additional works. Soon, David Kennedy was an unabashed admirer.

The study in contrasts continued.

Kennedy tended to problem solve from the top down; Watkins took theoretical lemons and designed solution paths for political and social problems from the bottom up. Kennedy dealt in the day-to-day world of politics; Watkins in the what-if world of society's most pressing issues.

As the demographics of Chicago, Illinois, and of the Democratic Party began to shift, Kennedy recognized that he needed to bring additional perspectives to his strategies. His correspondence with Watkins as secret pen pals had spanned decades. Their relationship was virtually unknown to all but Dawn Eckersley and Andrea Sommers, Avery's counterpart. They met occasionally, talked often, and worked together whenever Kennedy's strategic planning required, or whenever Watkin's next book or next class could benefit from Kennedy's unique and brilliant perspective on government.

On any number of prior occasions Kennedy had considered introducing Watkins to the E Party. This time, he hadn't hesitated. The complexities of the moment demanded Avery's presence.

Atlas made the introductions. "We are honored that you've been able to join us on short notice, Mr. Speaker—and that you've included Professor Watkins."

A blurry fifteen hours later, upon entering his tastefully appointed lodgings at the Stein compound, replete with all things Ralph Lauren, the Speaker was shocked to learn that he and the General had concluded the evening just short of 3 a.m. Kennedy was used to long, grudging days of non-stop meetings and schmoozing, but on quick reflection, the events of the preceding day would create a lasting impression—partly thanks to the gifted Scotch the General had been pouring for the past few hours. Kennedy allowed himself a reaffirming nod and smiled one of his rare smiles.

The next day, the Speaker woke up and looked around. He was startled to discover he wasn't in his house in Chicago. He gingerly swung his feet over the side of the bed and slid them into the slippers that had been thoughtfully provided. His head pounded a bit from alcohol consumption, but other than that he appeared to be no worse for wear. He hadn't slept so well in years.

That General Smith is something else, he thought. Aside from Smith's capacity to put away copious amounts of liquor, the man's no bullshit, let's get to a handshake approach was refreshing. The Speaker slowly moved into the bathroom, thinking about Barbara Jenkins, for whom he had already developed respect and admiration for her keen, engaging intellect as well as her youthful exuberance for problem solving and her dedication to cause. He still held in abatement a firm opinion of Governor Robinson, but there was no denying the former star's professional accomplishments on the diamond, not to mention his handling of the situational demands in his run for governor.

Nor did the rest of the E Party team disappoint. This relatively small contingent's ability to turn the political world on its ear might be partially due to luck and timing, but even more so to intellect, perseverance, and dedication. Their divergent opinions and personalities were intriguing, as was their ability to rapidly seize upon a unified course of action, particularly when under pressure. He had to hand it to Atlas. He had cultivated and fostered a vision with an impressive strength of purpose.

As he brushed his teeth and combed his hair, such as it was at this stage in life, the Speaker thought again about how much Avery Watkins had brought to the table. He'd rolled up his sleeves and been knee-deep in alligators before the second course of lunch had been served. Surely, his next book would be devoted to the E Party revolution. In an interesting turn-around, Avery was the one who'd challenged the wavering conviction of Robinson and crew to hold onto the Getting to 21 component of HB1 in response to the Super PAC media onslaught. Kennedy had watched in admiration as the scene played out: Avery delivering the right medicine at the right moment; the others rapt, clearly wanting to be convinced, as the Speaker himself did, that risking it all on principle was the appropriate course for them to take.

The Speaker returned to his bedroom to find his clothes had been beautifully ironed and set out for him. He almost gave another point to Atlas, then thought better of it. If he could trust his instinct, and the Speaker always trusted his instinct, this was the doing of his lovely bride K.C. He slipped on the shirt, enjoying its crispness.

The team had asked questions and offered suggestions that were all consistently probing. In this case, about how to find thirty votes in the Senate. They well understood the push-pull of map design, but whether out of ignorance or courtesy, they had deferred entirely to his redesign of the districts in question. Not unexpectedly, they'd remained steadfast in their insistence that the drawing of districts outside Cook County remain as open and impartial as possible. And he would have been disappointed if they hadn't. Such mathematical gymnastics could be dealt with at a later date.

All in all, the Speaker was remarkably satisfied with the outcome. Tom Robinson, teaming with Lisa Boudreau, K.C., and convert Watkins, would launch an aggressive three-pronged PR campaign to confront the Super PACs, the centerpiece of which would be an old-fashioned whirlwind on the ground, with a stump speech blitz in Chicago churches and schools in support of the guiding principles of HB1 in general and Getting to 21 in particular.

Barbara Jenkins would reach out to her buddy and Grammy Award winner Billy Shakespeare to see if he'd be willing to lend a new rap to the cause. Atlas, the General, and Elaine Richards had a counterattack on the tax case in the works, one that would press for either a settlement or, at a minimum, the continuing public perception of the defendants as victims. Although not tied directly to HB1, the case had festered too long and could easily become the next target of the Super PACs. As he made his way to his airport limo sometime later, the Speaker kept hearing the John Denver song, the one that talked about "coming home to a place he'd never been before."

* * * * * *

THE BACK BENCH
"If you let it slip, we catch it"
March 18

The recount reached the halfway point this week. After a frenetic pace to the opening rounds of hearings, the past month has been as exciting as watching cement cure. The lawyers have locked on their standard operating procedures and, despite the rotating panel of judges, the production of evidence, cross-examination, and rulings on motions resemble the movie *Groundhog Day*.

Inevitably, the news coverage and initial Internet chatter frenzy have given way to an *Ozzie and Harriett*-like monotone as well.

Although there remain a few active blogs, and the tweets from the politico groups have a constant drone about them at #ILGOVRECOUNT, there has not been much excitement on the viral front either.

Among those attempting to handicap the results to date, even the most optimistic evaluations in Allen's favor have him falling far short. Because of the proportional reduction rule, the roughly 400 definitively-tainted votes have allowed Allen to gain only a net of 26 votes of the 189 he needs.

Again, that's from the most optimistic estimate. If you take the average of the more credible analytics, neither Allen nor Robinson has moved the needle. The *Time* analysis with which I am associated has Robinson plus-seven votes through midpoint.

All of the legal teams have been embargoed from the press. The court has set a series of biweekly press availabilities, the next of which is in five days. But, to date, they have all been snore fests as the parties remain tight-lipped about their strategies moving forward.

In other news…

CHAPTER THIRTY-ONE

The Super PAC campaign was producing spectacular results. The recount was not. This made Eddie Cobb feel uncomfortably bipolar.

His sponsored daily polling regaled him with each day's finding, which confirmed that the target audiences were growing increasingly irate with the content of HB1 and equally disappointed with the performance of Governor Robinson. Almost 26 percent of those polled now knew about HB1. Fifty-four percent of them had an "unfavorable" impression. Although the negatives for Robinson were not commensurate, the most recent sample rated his negatives at 21 percent, reflecting a significant increase since the start of the attacks. Conversely, Robinson's positives had fallen to an almost human 57 percent. The PACs had begun running a second generation of attack ads.

Cobb was expecting the erosion to continue at a sufficiently steady pace. However, the attack campaign was of no benefit if it did not translate to the recount. If Robinson held his margins, there would be no opening for any judicial subjectivity. To that end, the daily reports from the hearings were driving Eddie Cobb's blood pressure to new heights.

Each passing day saw Eddie weighing the pros and cons of going all in. If things did not change dramatically in the ensuing rounds of hearings, he would have no choice. The date circled on the calendar was April 4, just seventeen days out.

* * * * * * *

While Eddie Cobb was riding a mental roller coaster, Javier Sanchez was riding a rocket ship, screwing Speaker Kennedy by day and Carla Hilton by night.

From the moment Kennedy had called to solicit Javier's help in obtaining Hispanic votes for HB1, Javier felt as if he were living inside a John Le Carré novel, sequence after sequence, as the ultimate double agent. As far as he could tell, Speaker Kennedy and Danny Ryan were clueless that Javier's "interests" lay outside their camp. Why else would they continue to entrust him with their strategies, daily adjustments, and updates relative to all negotiations?

In turn, Javier continued to feed their data and map revisions to Chairman Cobb, whose team instantly analyzed the update and guided Javier through his orchestrations with each Latino legislator's response, to which Ryan would be forced to again recalibrate. Cobb's team seized on the Speaker's dilemma of avoiding conflict between Blacks and Hispanics. Each new proposal inflamed the jealousies among the targeted Senators.

Javier Sanchez stayed focused on all these proceedings while he weighed if and when it would be advantageous to cut his own deal with the Speaker. The Allen trial was clearly not going in the direction Eddie Cobb—the self-righteous sonnova-you-know-what—had prophesized. For Javier, it should be child's play. Who else had the know-how to play on the emotions of the other Latinos? Who else could deliver at will the required number of votes for HB1 to Speaker Kennedy? Rather than follow Chairman Cobb down a path to oblivion, Javier would deliver the Latino vote and exact his price. "Majority Leader Sanchez" had a nice ring to it, and, as Kennedy's anointed number two, he would be almost assured of being the Speaker's successor.

From the minute he awoke in the morning until he and Carla reached for each other at night, it was a non-stop cerebral adventure, and Javier Sanchez was flying high. Best of all, he was positioned to win either way.

Reminded of Carla and their torrid affair, Javier took in a breath. They had long ago ceased to promote the pretense that intellectualizing around the defeat of HB1 was the main course and sex only an aperitif.

He didn't mind being in the role of pupil to her daily lesson plans, which included sex tools and more formations than a Bill Belichik offense. He also knew that Carla liked his youthful exuberance, as well as his married status, which she always said served her needs "just fine, thank you."

Javier was good with it all.

* * * * * * *

Insight into the Speaker's inner sanctum was every lobbyist's dream, and it was no different for Carla Hilton. The more Javier filled her with facts and figures, times and dates, and a glimpse at process to which few, if any, had access, the more addicted she became.

In her line of work, one's standing in the political food chain is as much a function of perception as it is reality. The two most important credentials are access and the ability to influence outcomes. In each case, as the ACLU's lobbyist, Carla had a reasonable degree of both. The difference was that she had begun to assign a much higher value to leveraging perception over reality in a world where perceived access and perceived influence are as powerful as the real deal. Given the unmitigated success of the Super PACs' campaign, it was time to stop publicly denying the role of the ACLU and start privately taking ownership.

Over the course of a few days, Carla made it her business to visit each of the senators on Javier's list, the Black and Latino senators who were also being targeted by the Speaker for votes to support HB1. In each meeting, Carla strongly hinted, in the way that only lobbyists can, that she had the ability to turn more and more screws to enrage their constituents. Oh, and not just their current constituents. No, it would be much worse than that. They would have to sit by and watch as the media campaign drove public perception so low as to put their seats at risk, regardless of the districts they might draw under the new map.

Each senator had his or her own personal vulnerability, and Javier was feeding her plenty of inside baseball about that, too. Senator Hernandez, for example, didn't stop to wonder how Carla Hilton knew about his various affairs. His only concern was how much she knew.

Senator Williams didn't stop to ask how Carla Hilton knew about the risk of foreclosure she was facing. Her only question was how much Carla knew. Senator Alvarez simply gazed into Carla Hilton's eyes with a hatred she had rarely encountered when she calmly cited his D.U.I. that had been quietly put to bed. And so it went with Senators Gonzalez, Del Rio, Diaz, Rivera, Rodriguez, Rubio, Thomas, Jones, Smith, and Green.

In politics as well as in bed, Carla Hilton was familiar with domination. In fact, it was one of her specialties. From her perch atop a mountain that most of her brethren could only imagine, she was playing her hand like the pro she was. If there was blood in the water, Carla Hilton was the great white, circling ever closer to her prey.

She would defeat HB1 and, along with it, the almighty Speaker.

It was the stuff of legends and she was making it happen.

* * * * * * *

THE BACK BENCH
"If you let it slip, we catch it"
March 20

EXTRA EXTRA EXTRA EXTRA EXTRA EXTRA

In a somewhat hastily called press conference, Governor Robinson made his first public appearance since the anti-HB1 media barrage was launched.

In a compelling and appropriately emotional fashion, he renounced the attacks and, one by one, refuted the content of each. Once his defense was concluded, he introduced Professor Avery Watkins of the University of California, Berkeley, to advance the cause of HB1.

For those unfamiliar with Dr. Watkins, he is a bit of a cult hero in the Black community based on his literature on the plight of the ordinary man and his ability and obligation to overcome obstacles on the path to success. Watkins has long been a proponent of the link between education and its ability to, as he is famous for saying, "throw a lifeline to anyone willing to catch it."

Dr. Watkins said that he will be collaborating with the governor to deliver the message that Illinois desperately needs to pass HB1, particularly to benefit minorities.

It is not clear how and when Dr. Watkins formed an alliance with Governor Robinson, but they outlined a message and a program dedicated to the passage of HB1. Among other things, they pledged to take their fight "to the streets," where they hope to defeat the "cowardly messengers of doom, spewing lies, and regressive ideas to the families and children of Illinois."

In other news…

THE BACK BENCH
"If you let it slip, we catch it"
March 21

The E Party today launched a media response to the Super PAC attack campaign against the Reinventing Education in Illinois Act. In an accompanying press release, they indicated that they will leave no stone unturned in their effort to improve the education system in Illinois.

Consistent with past E Party efforts, their media campaign is well-reasoned and well-presented advocacy, and frames the debate rather concisely. The E Party is selling hope, arguing that the people of Illinois can rehabilitate a failed system and, in doing so, provide their children with the tools needed for success.

The Super PACs are selling fear, arguing to minorities that HB1 will relegate their children to third-world status, while throwing red meat to conservative Republicans that HB1 will trample on the Constitution.

Also consistent with past E Party efforts, the media campaign has been joined with a series of web and social media applications.

In other news...

* * * * * * *

This time Eddie Cobb was ready. He had studied the E Party playbook and, for the most part, had anticipated their moves.

His defensive alignment was brilliant.

• Ready a contingent of talking heads to unleash vituperatives on network and cable television. In league with Scott Grusin, Eddie had the attack dogs from *Fox* on his side for the first time in his political life. Since all political talk shows lean either left or right, no outlet was available for the E Party to compete with this barrage of well-crafted sound bites.

• Ready and launch an Internet response. Eddie's geeks might not possess the equivalent of Lauren de la Rosa's ingenuity, but all they needed was close to break-even. He also had the advantage of human capacity. Again, with assistance from Grusin, they had a staggering ability to out-tweet the E Party. In the tweeting war of words, limited by 140 characters per message, quantity would surely drown out quality.

• Ready and launch ground forces. Robinson was formidable in schools and churches. Professor Watkins had been a brilliant addition to their cache. But the Democrats and Republicans were well stocked with education experts capable of creating an adequate level of doubt on the stump.

• Ready and release a series of "studies" by "eminent authorities" to further bolster the alleged deficiencies of HB1.

The *pièce de résistance*? Representative Javier Sanchez was feeding him Speaker David Kennedy's strategy on a daily basis. Kennedy would eventually find the pressure points to win the vote on HB1 in the Senate, but if Cobb could extend the clock into May, Kennedy would be earning a pyrrhic victory. By then, Governor Tom Robinson would be a fleeting asterisk in the history books and Governor Allen would be in command.

* * * * * * *

Nancy Rae Mitchell could be deterred for a while, but she would not be avoided. She did not grow up in the system without learning a few tricks of her own.

If Representative Javier Sanchez was too "busy" to schedule time to see her, she would simply make it a lot more difficult to ignore her by inserting herself into his day at a time when he *couldn't* ignore her. Juanita was obviously uncomfortable telling Nancy Rae that her boss was, once again, otherwise disposed, and Nancy Rae again felt badly about putting the woman in this position. But, Nancy Rae had a very annoying itch to scratch.

It was late in the day when Javier finally arrived. He hid his surprise well when he saw Nancy Rae waiting patiently, but sent an annoyed glance at Juanita, who suddenly found a reason to dig for something in the bottom drawer of her desk. Then, as if nothing were amiss, he smiled and led Nancy Rae into his inner sanctum, where he politely apologized for his "sporadic and frenetic schedule of late," at the same time pressing his intercom button and asking Juanita to bring in the "urgent paperwork" that required his attention.

When Juanita came in, glaring at Nancy Rae, Javier signed the paperwork without even looking at it. His irritation was front and center, but Nancy Rae had to give it to him. Anyone else who knew him less would not have suspected anything was amiss. The man was that good.

As Nancy Rae returned niceties, she assessed his demeanor. The only way to describe it was that of a man on a mission. Just as she was about to talk shop, however, his cell phone rang. Instead of doing the situationally correct thing and pressing "ignore," the Representative held a finger up, spoke into the phone, and then covered it with his hand. "Sorry," he said smoothly, "I've got to take this. We'll have to catch up at another time."

He had turned his chair around and was already talking to whoever it was when Nancy Rae, after a moment or two of unmitigated disbelief, left the room.

With effort, Nancy Rae pushed her reactive burst of anger aside to think about it. Danny was in with the Speaker, so she could easily find out if they had called, although that didn't feel right. Javier's wife rarely called him—and even if the call was from her, he would not have summarily dismissed Nancy Rae to talk to her. Perhaps one of the Latino senators needed to have his or her hand held? Nancy Rae said a distracted goodbye to Juanita, who was humming a tune and refused to meet her eyes, and headed to her favorite liquor store.

Three hours later Nancy Rae pulled up to the impressively average apartment building. Javier's apartment was on the third floor. She got out of her car, locked the door, and went in through the unattended lobby. In another minute she was at his door, a bottle of his favorite Argentinian Shiraz in her hand.

She knocked. She waited.

No answer.

Nancy Rae could have sworn she'd spotted his car in the lot. She walked back to check. Sure enough, there it was, parked on an angle to keep other vehicles from getting too close. She walked around the side of the building feeling like a cat burglar and hoping no one would get suspicious and call the cops. There was light around the edges of the curtains. He could be in the shower or watching television. Maybe that was why he hadn't heard her knocking.

CHAPTER THIRTY-TWO

Note to our readers: The article below is part of a series that *Time* will run at least monthly through the next general election. Nat Carson, editor-in-chief of *The Back Bench*, one of the nation's leading political dailies, will chronicle the activities of the E Party. In addition to these monthly columns, Mr. Carson will further document the E Party's journey in a new and exciting blog, posted at www.time/carsonblog-eparty.com.

OUR KIDS DESERVE BETTER
By: Nat Carson

Who'da thunk it? A state level education bill drawing attention as if it were the reincarnation of Obamacare.

When was the last time any state level legislation found itself being debated on the national talk shows?

When was the last time a bill before the Illinois Legislature was the subject of editorials in the *New York Times,* the *Washington Post,* and the *L.A. Times?*

When was the last time that national experts on education were walking the halls of Springfield?

I think we all know the answer. When was the last time a third party was on the cusp of national prominence?

After weeks of pounding from newly invented Super PACs with euphemistic names and slick attack messages, the E Party has begun to respond. Governor Robinson has been aggressively campaigning to save his pet project, appearing in as many as ten churches and schools each day. He has also enlisted a talented group of surrogates that includes Avery Watkins, Billy Shakespeare, and an all-star team of highly regarded athletes, with careers both past and present.

Although there is a level of substance and depth that clearly exceeds customary political sound bites and rhetoric, they have also launched a campaign around the slogan "Our Kids Deserve Better."

Allison Ronen, a nationally renowned expert on political messaging and polling, thinks the E Party effort may be too little, too late. "When the American voters make up their minds, it is very difficult to get them to reconsider. Polling shows that the E Party's education proposal, particularly the Getting to 21 component, has been mortally wounded. Whoever is behind the Super PAC campaign knows how the game is played. Notice how quickly they reacted to the E Party's media response—and have no intention of allowing them to regain lost ground."

Thomas Eagleson from the national education think tank "Education for a Better America" agrees in part, but thinks the E Party will benefit in the long run. "If there is one issue that continuously resonates with the public, it's education. Every generation wants the next to have a better life and the key to that better life is education. In fact, if the Democrats and Republicans continue to sit on their hands, they will forfeit the education issue to the E Party. Other than the economy, there is no more compelling issue in politics on a sustained basis."

Which begs the question: Where are the Republicans and the Democrats? Are they so tied to the Super PACs that they dare not incur their wrath? Or, as usual, do they need to test the political winds until they know the safe direction to set their sails? Perhaps both.

"Our political parties are fearful of polling and of staking out risky positions," says Donna Kramer of MSNBC.com. "Even worse, when it comes to education, most elected officials have no idea how to improve the system so they wallow in their indecision. Now that the issue is being elevated to national prominence, it will be interesting to see if the president or Congress steps up, but don't count on it."

In our last column on this issue, neither political party in or outside of Illinois would comment on the record. We again reached out. The Republican Party of Illinois issued a vanilla statement (see below) stressing the importance of education, but cautioning against the concerns raised with regard to HB1. The Democratic Party of Illinois also stressed the importance of education in their remarks (see below) saying, "Speaker David Kennedy is a cosponsor of HB1 and has pledged to pass this legislation as quickly as possible."

"Speaker Kennedy has himself in a bit of a spot on this one," said longtime Illinois political observer Sophia Saladino. "From his actions, he has cast himself with the E Party as a foil to the Republicans. To keep his position as Speaker required E Party votes and that had to come at a cost. Many think the price of those votes is passage of HB1. His speakership is also anchored with the unions, and the teachers union is among the most powerful. It's a very difficult balancing act. There also has to be tension building with the DNC. There is a comfort factor in the two-party system and DNC Chairman Eddie Cobb is a man who surely sees the risks of a successful third party entrant."

The DNC declined to be interviewed or issue a statement. Perhaps Saladino is onto something.

* * * * * * *

"Nat, Mark. Sorry I missed you. Just wanted to thank you for your assistance with the recent article. The Cobb stuff at the end was appropriately muted, but, if the Speaker is right, it'll give the Chairman some pause to know he's being watched."

* * * * * * *

Chairman Eddie Cobb was a happy cowboy riding high. His plan was driving E Party and Tom Robinson negatives, impeding the Speaker's quest for votes, and buying precious time. Sure, he was mildly perturbed to be called out in *Time*, but overall, things were proceeding *en pointe*, as they say. The unexpected access to the inner workings of the Speaker's approach to remapping was a doozy of a bonus. Javier was sure pulling his weight.

Yes, indeedy.

* * * * * * *

The E Party had taken a big hit, but had righted the ship. It had responded late, but done it effectively.

Polling indicated they had stopped the bleeding. From where Atlas and other leaders sat, it was a welcome reprieve for Tom Robinson to be preaching on a stump while mentally embargoed from Springfield.

* * * * * * *

Speaker Kennedy felt uncharacteristically outflanked. He'd bet on speed, but was caught up in a marathon. He'd taken on a partner who insisted on principle over practicality. Looking ahead on the chess board, he saw nothing but a well-defended position. The Speaker needed to catch a break. The few bullets he had left in the chamber had better hit their target.

* * * * * * *

Nancy Rae's hunch was correct. At the time Representative Sanchez had rudely dismissed her several days earlier to take a call, Danny and the Speaker had been in negotiations with Senator

Washington and a contingent of Black senators. One option down. How many more to go?

Armed with her gift of Shiraz, Nancy Rae had placed herself at his doorstep three successive evenings. The second time, she could swear she heard voices inside before she rang the bell, and then knocked with emphasis. It could have been the television, but why would it be on if he weren't home? Last night she'd found a dark apartment and no sign of his car in the parking lot. She'd actually hung around like some derelict for hours to see if he'd show. At midnight, discouraged, tired, cold, and thoroughly pissed off, she'd gone home, opened the Shiraz herself, and had a good stiff drink.

Poor Danny. When he'd finally arrived home after yet another hamster-wheel day, she'd been waiting for him. She'd shot him question after question until he'd put his hands up and retreated into the bathroom to take a shower. His libido recovered, which was nice, but he fell asleep so fast you'd think he'd never slept a wink in his life.

Back in the living room, Nancy Rae scrunched her nose up, drummed her fingers on the sofa, and considered her options. Tailing Javier was out of the question.

Well, unless it became essential.

Until then, she wasn't above snooping around his office.

Nancy Rae drank more Shiraz and fumed.

* * * * * *

THE BACK BENCH
"If you let it slip, we catch it"
March 29

With another few weeks of hearings in *Allen v. Robinson* complete, the scorekeepers are forming a consensus that attorney Cole and candidate Allen are running out of votes and time.

To date, most of Allen's victories have come from historically Democratic precincts. Of the remaining precincts to be vetted, less than 35 percent are in decidedly Democratic areas.

Conversely, of the remaining precincts, roughly 65 percent are in predominantly Republican districts, where Robinson's team have landed their best punches so far.

In other news...

* * * * * *

Neither Joseph Cole nor Elizabeth DiMaggio nor Scott Grusin nor Eddie Cobb nor Javier Sanchez nor Robert Allen nor any other politician hoping for an Allen victory needed to read *The Back Bench* to learn where the recount was headed. Simple math said that there were roughly 500,000 votes still in the queue. Of those, a net of at least 500 changed votes was needed to overcome Robinson's lead. Since all the hearings to date had uncovered less than half that amount on a percentage basis, the odds were dwindling.

Joseph Cole remained vigilant, controlled, and hopeful. DiMaggio, Grusin, and Allen vacillated between positive and anxious, depending on whether they had talked last with Cole or each other. Sanchez remained hopeful that Cobb would find a way to make him Speaker, but had formulated an alternative strategy to deliver votes to assure Kennedy that HB1 would pass the Senate.

Eddie Cobb had kicked the can down the road for too many days. One by one, his circles on the calendar had been scratched out and pushed out a few days at a time. His nuclear option was a last resort, but it was looking more and more likely. For a man who'd easily made every deal with the devil he was willing to offer, pushing this particular button was proving oddly dicey.

* * * * * *

With the Easter/Passover recess upon them, Speaker Kennedy surprised his staff by spontaneously declaring a week off for everyone. Never let it be said that he needed it himself, but the truth was he was physically exhausted and emotionally spent. Still, for a man who rarely enjoyed a day off, a week was a lifetime.

The recount hearings were also recessed for the holidays. Most participants regrouped with family and loved ones.

For Danny Ryan and Nancy Rae, an entire week without constant interruptions and in each other's company was a godsend. He did not resist when she proposed a rematch in Cabo, complete with unlimited margaritas and recuperative sex.

Javier Sanchez and Carla Hilton were among those who retreated to family. He told Carla, who agreed, albeit reluctantly and suspiciously, that the pace they'd been going was unsustainable and a break would be good for them both.

Eddie Cobb wanted to get away. To blow off steam in Vegas with hookers, whiskey, and poker. To ride hard on the ranch and have his favorite local concubines ride him hard and put him down wet. He wanted to fly to the Caribbean, relax poolside, and demand whatever struck his fancy. Unfortunately, his current fixation left little time for anything other than the decision he had to make that was coming down the pike as fast as a racehorse on steroids.

* * * * * * *

The last thing Nancy Rae did before she left with Danny for Las Ventanas was to sneak into Representative Sanchez's office. She'd waited impatiently in the ladies room until she'd seen Juanita leave for lunch, then manufactured a fake delivery to Sanchez that took him into the outer office. While he was out there with the "delivery boy" Nancy Rae had hired to keep him busy for as long as he could, Nancy Rae ran in through the back door—her position lent her unrestricted access and no one would have suspected her since she was there all the time—and swept up Javier's cell phone. With shaking fingers, she'd scrolled through his calls. Besides numerous calls to "unknown," the one number that stood out in flashing neon was to—and from—the ACLU Chicago.

* * * * * * *

The week sped by for Speaker Kennedy. An observant man, he'd downshifted as much as he ever could to reflect during the days leading to Easter, then had quickly begun ramping up for the eight-week journey to the legislature's scheduled adjournment.

Like an obsessive-compulsive football coach preparing for the playoffs, he spent hours on end mentally reviewing the tape of the session to date. He went as far back as the days before the last general election to review his thinking, his goals, and his plans. Always looking for flaws, always looking for strategic advantages, and always focused on the endgame. As he rewound and rewound, the Speaker found himself in somewhat unfamiliar territory as he searched to uncover and correct a series of tactical blunders.

The E Party's response to the Super PACs was late, but proving effective. From his polling, the Speaker knew they had suffered significant negative shifts in public sentiment. Fortunately, Robinson and the party remained above the magic 50 percent approval rating bogey. HB1 had also taken a beating. Yet, with the recent messaging from Robinson, Watkins, and Shakespeare, the public's mood had initially stabilized and, of late, swung a bit in the right direction.

Given this stabilization, the biggest question was whether to continue efforts to pass HB1 on an accelerated path or revert to an endgame strategy where all critical political issues either live or die under the pressure cooker environment in which a budget must be passed and a map must be codified before adjournment.

The Speaker's brain kept arriving at the same conclusion, yet his stomach was gnawing on him.

What was he missing?

CHAPTER THIRTY-THREE

THE BACK BENCH
"If you let it slip, we catch it"
April 7

In an off-the-wall development, the Illinois State Board of Elections has petitioned the Illinois Supreme Court to revise the hearing schedule in the Allen recount case. Apparently, evidence for next week's hearings in Chicago, Rock Island, and Decatur had been collected and stored in a segregated area of their warehouse and a sprinkler malfunction caused a large quantity of ballots and equipment to be soaked. The Board has informed the court that they need a week to dry the ballots and test the equipment.

There is no way to predict how the court or the parties will respond. The overall proceedings are currently on schedule, so a one-week delay may not be viewed as critical. However, the Allen team has always been under pressure, not only to win but to win before Robinson can work with Speaker Kennedy to pass the remap.

Unfortunately for him, Allen's efforts to date are not encouraging. His legal team has not uncovered the votes needed to win. Perhaps a week's delay will give them time to regroup and find a nugget or two.

In other news...

* * * * * *

Filed under the category of "you can run but you can't hide," the light bulb had gone off in Nancy Rae's head. Now she knew exactly where she was guaranteed to find Representative Sanchez. She'd thoroughly enjoyed her time away with Danny, but a significant slice of her psyche had continued trolling the information she'd recouped from Sanchez's cell phone. Luckily, Danny was too tired some of the time and too sexually spent the rest of the time to notice her absentmindedness. Danny Ryan was not remotely religious, but Easter was an exception. When they returned, he would be attending services at Chicago's Holy Name Cathedral. She would go as well.

Holy Name is the church where the cardinal presides over the Easter mass. Accordingly, there is always a seat saved for the mayor of Chicago. Because the mayor was sure to attend, so too would countless local Catholic officials seeking to be publically seen with him on the ten o'clock news.

Representative Javier Sanchez was no different. He'd pointedly made a twofer out of it: observing Easter midnight mass with his family and attending the political show-and-tell. What could be better? Inside Holy Name, Nancy Rae Mitchell and Representative Javier Sanchez nodded courteously to each other across pews. They even exchanged a few minutes of pleasantries on the steps outside the church following services. Nancy Rae had a hard time not gagging at her own solicitous pleasantries, but she must have played her cards right—or Easter had made Javier feel guilty about dodging her—because he had magnanimously agreed to a "second lunch" after he had dined with his family. They agreed to meet in the Pilsen area on the city's West Side, where one of Nancy Rae's favorite Mexican joints was a stone's throw from Javier's campaign office.

A few hours and many delicious veggie enchiladas later, they were still sitting there. Nancy Rae congratulated herself on keeping Javier in her sight this long. Strangely enough, he seemed to be enjoying himself. They'd always liked each other's company, but she'd have thought he'd be less…relaxed. The guy was one heck of an actor. When it became apparent their meeting would soon come to an end, Nancy Rae steered the conversation to HB1, finding votes, and, of course, the remap, then sat back to observe his reaction. Would he have the good grace to squirm?

Although Javier's mysterious behavior and lack of availability had become something of an obsession, Nancy Rae was also concerned about the Representative's long-term political future and the outcome of the current session. His chance to curry favor with the Speaker over HB1 and to solidify his leadership within the Hispanic Caucus by drawing districts to protect his flock for the decade to come was a welcomed daily double. From where she sat, he was positioned to cash the winning ticket.

Javier sat up straighter in his chair. So far he'd been able to steer the conversation on topics other than HB1 or remapping. Nancy Rae's counsel would probably be invaluable there as well—his success to date was admittedly partly a function of their teamwork—but going that direction would be like shooting himself in the foot, especially given her closeness to Danny Ryan. Fortunately, time was growing short quickly.

Frustrated at Javier's by now obvious obfuscation, Nancy Rae decided that the direct approach was needed.

"So, I trust your constituent has been happy with Carla Hilton," she said blithely.

Javier, in the process of taking a small sip from his glass of cerveza, choked a bit. "Carla Hilton?" he repeated.

"Yeah, you remember Carla," said Nancy Rae. "You asked me to recommend a lobbyist way back at the start of the session—you know, for some constituent concerned about the education bill. I left you a message recommending her."

"Oh, right … Carla Hilton. I'd totally forgotten about that. Now that you mention it, though, I passed the name along, never heard back."

"That's funny," said Nancy Rae, whose antennae were now screaming. "Someone told me they saw you and Carla dining at Saputo's around that time. I naturally assumed you were following up on my suggestion. You know, conducting an interview. When she later testified before the Senate Committee I figured you had been involved."

Javier knew that Nancy Rae's wheels were spinning. His own were gyrating out of control. He was trapped. There was no place good to take this conversation.

"Would you excuse me for a second," he said, and left the table with his hand over his stomach.

Nancy Rae was tempted to follow him into the men's room, push him up against the wall and demand information like in the movies. She had seen the man inhale jalapenos like popcorn on many occasions, so it couldn't have been the enchiladas.

Five long minutes went by, then another five. Suddenly, Javier reappeared, cell phone affixed to his ear and two twenties in his hand that were dropped on the table as he pointed to his cell.

"Sorry," he mouthed, "gotta deal with this." And he sprinted for the door. Nancy Rae glowered at his back. *Coward!*

* * * * * *

Nancy Rae was unable to fully connect the dots. During dinner that evening with Danny, she mentioned Javier's unusual behavior of late and their aborted conversation at lunch. Danny's thoughts were already on the next day's remap meetings so he gave the discussion short shrift. But when the Speaker made an innocuous comment about Representative Sanchez at their early morning meeting, Danny impulsively found himself relaying Nancy Rae's vignette.

Danny noticed the Speaker momentarily tweak his facial expression in the way the newspapers found so fascinating and offered a profound "hmm."

Later that evening, after splicing Danny's comments about Javier into his rewind wheel, the Speaker revised and finalized his end of session strategy and made two calls to set things in motion. One to Danny with new instructions and one to the General to explain his intended divergence from the course of action agreed upon while in Aspen.

* * * * * * *

<u>**E-MAIL**</u>

To:　　　E Party Leadership Distribution
From:　　Mark
Sent:　　April 8 7:56 a.m. (CST)
Subject:　Breakfast with Nat

Had a very interesting breakfast with Nat Carson today, whose sources have apparently been combing for information related to the Super PACs. Without naming names, he said all signs point to some very wealthy and very loyal donors to both Republicans and Democrats, all directly linked to the inner circles of the DNC and the RNC. Same incestuous pattern for their key staffs and political consultants. I asked specifically about Cobb, but all I got was a shrug.

According to Nat, these donors have spent in excess of $7 million to date and their resources are limitless.

Nat has also done some polling and reports that we've taken some major hits. Fortunately, he also said the numbers stabilized somewhat as soon as we began to punch back. Lesson learned.

We should talk more tonight about Nat's research and insights so we all know what we're up against.

* * * * * * *

"Eddie!" Cobb shot back excitedly when Javier got the conversation off on the wrong foot.

"I had a very interesting conversation today," said Javier, ignoring Cobb's correction. "And an even more interesting meeting."

"Go on."

"The Speaker called me to his office around noon. Just the two of us."

"The Speaker, huh? What did he want?"

"He thanked me for my help of late. Said he'd given the matter considerable thought over the break and has determined that the

political climate does not lend itself to passing HB1 at this time. It's
being put on the back burner. The remap will remain his sole priority for
this session."

Javier didn't add that the Speaker had clearly expressed how much
he'd look forward to working with the representative "as needed" in the
future. Why share the wealth?

"*Excelente*, Javier, *Excelente*. Music to my ears," said Eddie.
"Anything else? What did our illustrious Speaker have to say about his
other plans...his timing?"

"Not much, actually," said Javier. "We spent another ten minutes or
so on some party matters. He advised me that he and Senate President
Welk were calling a joint House, Senate Democratic Caucus for the
afternoon. He suggested I make a little three musketeers appeal."

"Three musketeers?" Eddie questioned. Had he missed something?

"Oh, you know," Javier downplayed. "One for all, all for one—that
kind of thing. Not that it'll head off the inevitable incestuous fighting
over the drawing of the new districts. And then the Speaker and the
president finished nailing HB1 into its coffin."

There was again quiet as Eddie Cobb processed the news.

Javier barreled on. "What they said was that since it hadn't passed
before Easter, it would only be a nuisance and a distraction moving
forward. They'd focus on the map and the budget from here on out, the
map taking top priority."

"Hallelujia," proclaimed Cobb. "So, when can I get you down here?
High time we looked at the Sanchez for Speaker version of the map,
don'tcha think?"

"Ready when you are," Javier said. The tightrope upon which he
was so carefully balanced had become increasingly slippery. The
Speaker was using him in unexpectedly new and exciting roles, and
Robinson was looking better every day, both in the polls and in the
recount. At the same time, as Javier well knew, hesitate with Eddie Cobb
and your head could roll before you noticed it was gone.

* * * * * *

In the days following his aborted luncheon with Nancy Rae, Javier had plenty of time to rue his handling of the situation. Nancy Rae was perceptive and persistent and, for whatever reason, hot on his trail. Conveniently enough, the Speaker's revised end of session strategy had given him the opening he needed. He'd simply placate Nancy Rae with one-on-one time on session days, feeding her whatever information he could to distract and diffuse.

Javier had never been particularly rambunctious in the bedroom before, but with Carla Hilton things were different, and he was unwilling to sacrifice the pleasure their games offered. Periodically he sent his gaze in the direction of his wife and family, to whom he was certainly devoted in all, well, in most senses of the word. But what used to be comfortable home cooking in the sex department now tasted like frozen dinners compared to Trattoria Carla. It would be worth the crash dieting when the time eventually came, which it inevitably would at the end of the session.

Somehow, Nancy Rae's pursuit of Javier Sanchez's adventures had lost its urgency. Their regular tête-à-têtes assured her that he was sufficiently focused on the map and his political future. The subject of Carla Hilton and the ACLU connection was bothersome, but, then again, given all the other cards on the table, it might not be worth the hassle. Danny certainly hadn't thought much of her "wild" speculations. And frankly, she hated Shiraz.

CHAPTER THIRTY-FOUR

THE BACK BENCH
"If you let it slip, we catch it"
April 9

The return from the Easter/Passover recess traditionally signals the home stretch in any session of the Illinois General Assembly. With the holidays being a tad early this year, we have roughly eight weeks left to the scheduled adjournment on May 31.

This year's session has been a surprising snore to date. Bogged down by the recount, the Robinson administration has failed to demonstrate any leadership. The Speaker declared HB1 to be the session's legislative centerpiece and, once it passed the House, worked with President Welk to put it on a fast track. However, the big bad wolves of the Super PACs have apparently brought that effort to a standstill.

Alas, we find ourselves at that place in most sessions where the budget takes center stage. And, more important, at that place in every decennial session where the legislative remap consumes every sitting legislator's every waking moment.

Whether E Party leaders have the appetite for the budget fight, the map fight, or both remains to be seen. Governor Robinson was sorely lacking in particulars when he gave the budget address. If, as many suggest, he was stalling to avoid controversy in the face of the recount, he may soon have the signal he needs to charge ahead.

With an ever-shrinking pile of ballots remaining to be contested and an ever-shrinking number of hearings on those ballots, it is believed that neither the Allen attorneys nor the Stewart attorneys have yet significantly dented Robinson's 189-vote lead. As we approach the bottom of that ballot pile, if the lead continues to hold, the E Party Eagles can be expected to start strutting their feathers.

As to the remap, it remains to be seen how Speaker Kennedy and Leader DiMaggio will play their hands. Kennedy is accustomed to designing maps that guarantee the sixty safe seats he needs to stay Speaker. DiMaggio's Republicans have seen their numbers enter freefall in the face of the E Party's ascension. If DiMaggio isn't careful, she and her troops will get mapped into Iowa. Never to be heard from again.

In other news…

THE BACK BENCH
"If you let it slip, we catch it"
April 10

Attorneys for the State Board of Elections are due to appear before the Supreme Court today to report on the status of the ballots and other evidence soaked in the recent sprinkler malfunction. Too bad the name "Watergate" is already taken.

There is growing speculation that the board's original estimate of a one-week delay will prove insufficient. Following one of the more comical hearings in the Supreme Court's annuls, the court ruled that ballots could not be removed from their sealed cases to expedite the drying process and asked the board to report back after one week regarding status. In order to facilitate the drying process, the court did, however, allow the board to set the thermostats higher in the storage area and to run fans to increase air circulation.

Under intense scrutiny from all involved legal teams, one container of ballots from a random precinct was to have been opened yesterday to determine if they had dried sufficiently for those ballots to be placed in the hearing queue. Under a rigid gag order from the court, there hasn't been so much as a crumb of a rumor as to the results of the unveiling.

The court also refused to delay the hearings and merely revised the schedule.

In other news…

* * * * * * *

"Leader DiMaggio, Joseph Cole. I'm afraid I have discouraging news."

Elizabeth rubbed her tired eyes. "What now?"

"The ballots that were unsealed yesterday have not dried sufficiently. I'd say they are at least another week away at best, more likely two or three. If we can't convince the court to change course, we will have blown the calendar. The case won't be resolved within the timeframe you need."

Elizabeth DiMaggio listened, the pounding in her head increasing by the second, as her attorney reviewed the options available. None seemed to offer much hope. Their case was going badly from a numerical perspective and Allen wasn't any closer to being seated as governor before the map was drawn, passed, and sent to that office for signature. Allen's governorship was priority one. Seating him in time to veto Kennedy's redistricting creation was no less than 1-A. Then again, with Allen behind in the count, priority 1-A was appearing as ephemeral as a puffy white cloud in a cartoon sky.

"Leader DiMaggio? Are you still there?" Cole asked.

"Yes, yes, still here. So, what's the plan?"

"I think we have to roll the dice," Cole said in disgust. "At the last hearing, the court refused to consider any creative options to facilitate the drying process. With time becoming the enemy, we need to get aggressive."

"Um, am I missing something?" Elizabeth said, annoyed.

"Well, aggressive moves, such as opening the cases to separate the ballots for drying, risks ruining the ballots. Have you ever tried to separate two wet sheets of paper stuck together? They're sure to tear or at least blur the ink. Et cetera. If that happens, the ballots will be useless for any recount. Any ballots removed from the recount only further lesson our chances of succeeding.

"I realize," Cole continued before Elizabeth could respond, "that the recount has not yet produced the numbers we had hoped for. Statistically speaking, however, we are still talking about a razor-thin margin. With a break or two, anything can happen.

"I still remain hopeful that the court will be persuaded to use our alternative methodology for proportional adjustment. That alone would be worth close to a hundred votes, and in my opinion, enough to make a difference in the outcome. That's why, by the time we go into court this afternoon, I need to know how aggressive to get on expediting the drying of the ballots."

As if Elizabeth could take a crash course on drying soaking wet ballots, all of which had begun to look like a metaphor for the future of her political career.

* * * * * *

THE BACK BENCH
"If you let it slip, we catch it"
April 12

EXTRA EXTRA EXTRA EXTRA EXTRA EXTRA

In another bizarre episode, the Supreme Court today heard testimony regarding the now famous soaked ballots. In all, there are approximately 20,000 potentially tainted ballots in fifty to sixty sealed containers, representing about 15 percent of those remaining to be scrutinized in the recount. It may not seem like many, but at this point, to the Allen team, every vote is essential.

The Board of Elections had been instructed to unseal one random container to determine the extent of progress in drying out the ballots, but reported that not much progress had been made in the week to date. They also brought in a few experts to discuss potential options to accelerate the pace. Who knew there were experts in the field of drying out wet ballots?

The board brought in two scientists, who, it turns out, work for companies that produce paper towels. Four hours of testimony and cross-examination on absorbency was alternatively comical and excruciating.

The board also presented a demonstration on a technique they were proposing, which includes using box cutters to create strategically placed slots in the ballot containers to increase airflow.

At the end of the proceedings, the court again revised the hearing schedule to accelerate examination of the remaining dry ballots, while moving the wet ballots to the last week of scheduled hearings, eighteen days from now. The court also approved the box-cutting procedure after the attorneys argued for almost two hours over endless minutia.

In other news…

* * * * * *

After much rumination, Javier concluded that another trip to Texas was out of the question. Fooling the Speaker once? Maybe. Twice? Not so much. Nancy Rae and/or Carla? An insane proposition. Eddie Cobb, though, was easy. Javier's need to stay close to base made sense. Instead, they compromised by agreeing that Cobb would send a team to Illinois on weekends that would work out of the suburban offices of a Cobb compatriot where video conferencing was available to tap into the computer network at the Texas HQ.

Javier had never before been privy to the inner workings of map design and was fascinated with the speed and sophistication of the modeling. Each tweak of a line that defined a hypothetical legislative district instantly reset a legend on the screen on the technician's laptop and updated a set of twenty variables used to simulate election outcomes. The modeling also continuously adjusted for voting history and projected turnout. Cobb's computer modeling would ultimately be tested against phone polling to the hypothetical district to measure a range of issues and candidate preferences.

At a cost exceeding $100 million, no mapping operation had ever analyzed so much scientific data. No mapping operation had ever matched its modeling with real-time phone polls. The Chairman's people had also done an extensive analysis of voters from two prior election cycles and had developed sophisticated scenarios to measure likely E Party voters. Given that the characteristics of the quintessential E Party voter, such as voter registration or exit polling, had not been captured by the Democrats or Republicans in any known database, this was the most delicate part of the operation.

Try as they might, Cobb's team had been unsuccessful in hacking into the E Party's computer operations. Lauren de la Rosa's team, in combination with the General's retired military surveillance experts, had anticipated and thwarted all efforts to date.

For Javier to be elected Speaker, he needed a map designed to produce roughly forty-eight to fifty solid Republican seats and at least twelve solid Hispanic seats. Since the Republicans held over fifty seats prior to the establishment of the E Party, drawing safe Republican seats was relatively easy. Unfortunately, the Hispanic population of Illinois did not support twelve safe Hispanic House seats. Javier knew this from the data he had seen from Danny Ryan over the preceding few weeks of chasing votes for HB1. For all their data, the best scenario developed by Cobb's team could only get them to nine.

The situation was tense, but workable. Team Cobb was as aware as Javier Sanchez that Speaker Kennedy was feeling challenged in designing the sixty safe Democratic House seats he needed to be re-elected Speaker. He'd twice been elected with the help of the E Party, but there were no guarantees moving forward, especially if he failed to pass HB1.

Javier firmly believed he was well situated to attract up to four votes from downstate representatives under the right circumstances. It would take a roll of the dice and the production of a series of simulations, whereby Javier could offer districts to downstate Democrats that were electorally superior to those being proposed by the Speaker.

In order to maximize the number of potential Democratic seats, the Speaker would have to convince many sitting members to accept new districts with no more than 52 or 53 percent Democratic-leaning voters. This was a far cry from the 55 to 60 percent most demanded. Since Javier did not carry the same burden, drawing four to six downstate Democratic districts with the magic of 60 percent protected Democratic voters would be easily accomplished.

After just two working weekends and a bit of eleventh-hour back-and-forth, Representative Sanchez and Chairman Cobb gave each other a video conference thumbs-up in lieu of a handshake.

Eddie Cobb was also convinced he could procure the blessing of Scott Grusin and Elizabeth DiMaggio, who their modeling assured would be elected president of the Senate.

Yet, as they all knew too well, unless Allen became governor, this was an exercise in futility. The Cobb-Sanchez-DiMaggio maps would never be called for a vote.

* * * * * * *

E-MAIL

To: E Party Leadership Distribution
From: Elaine Richards
Sent: April 14 2:01 p.m. (CST)
Subject: Recount Date

It is essential that I update all of you on recent developments from the water-damaged ballots. Please contact my assistant at your earliest convenience with your availability for a conference call between now and 6 p.m. today Chicago time.

* * * * * * *

THE BACK BENCH
"If you let it slip, we catch it"
April 14

EXTRA EXTRA EXTRA EXTRA EXTRA EXTRA

The Illinois State Board of Elections has filed a Motion for an emergency hearing before the Supreme Court. Speculation is rampant that it relates to the water-logged ballots. An unnamed source has been quoted as saying "All hell is gonna break loose."

At this point in the recount process, most observers believe that the estimated 20,000 soaked ballots are all that stand between Robinson and victory. Even the most ardent Allen supporters contend that he remains at least one hundred votes from victory.

You do the math. If Allen has gained less than one hundred votes from the millions counted to date, how can he ever hope to gain more than that from those few remaining?

In other news...

CHAPTER THIRTY-FIVE

No one could remember Elaine Richards calling a meeting, let alone on fewer than four hours' notice. Coupled with the buzz created by the late afternoon, extra edition of *The Back Bench*, she quickly attracted a critical mass.

"Ladies and gentlemen," said Elaine without preamble, "there appear to be irregularities with the remaining ballots. While it is premature to know the full extent or the cause, we are aware that at least one percent of those from Chicago precincts are definitely tainted."

There was an audible murmur from those listening. "When did you find out?" asked the General.

"According to the process designed by the court," Elaine said solemnly, "they unsealed a few of the containers holding wet ballots early this morning. In virtually all of the randomly selected containers, the ballots had dried sufficiently to be counted. In one container, though, a number of ballots appeared to carry a pinkish hue—indicating a demonstrable difference from the other ballots."

"Were you there at the time?" Atlas asked.

"Yes, along with all lead counsels and representatives of the court and the board. The first three opened containers produced dry ballots with some noticeable water damage. However, a quick sampling suggested they could be easily surveyed and that any deterioration had not affected the clarity needed to determine the voter's intent.

"In the next container, there was obvious bleeding of some sort. Multiple ballots bore the pinkish hue I mentioned. These ballots were not continuous in the ballot sequence, but spread throughout the deck.

"All present agreed to immediately cease the exercise and report to the full court. As I trust you are aware, the board filed an emergency motion that will be heard tomorrow."

"Tomorrow?" the General barked. "How will that give you time to prepare?"

"Actually, there is little to be prepared for," Elaine corrected. "Until we have the facts, there's not much to discuss. Tomorrow's proceeding will have more to do with the court's intention regarding next steps. There are a couple of options. They could order a scientific investigation or, depending on how many ballots are affected, simply order the recount to proceed as planned, knowing the respective legal teams will file procedural motions at some point.

"I wanted you to be made aware as soon as possible. This could be a momentary blip—or the result of some fraud that could take the recount in any direction. Either way, I suspect there will be a flurry of media activity, and I wanted us to have the chance to strategize."

"What do you recommend?" Barb and K.C. asked simultaneously.

"As your attorney, my preference is to refuse comment while the case is in progress. This is an incredibly visible political matter. Still, we may not have that luxury, particularly if any of the other parties open themselves to comment."

"If you don't mind," Lisa Boudreau chimed in, "I'd like to do some quick checking, see what's breaking. Maybe sleep on it. Can we pick this up early tomorrow before the hearing? In the meantime, I suggest any press inquiries be deferred to Elaine and that she withhold comment."

There was an instant chorus of "agreed" and the morning call was scheduled.

Similar briefings that evening were held in various locales. In each case, the attorneys easily prevailed on the politicians to hold their powder. However, such voluntary embargoes were not likely to have much tenacity. The press would no doubt be swirling in search of stories with any hint of credibility and the politicians are never short on eagerness to put their names and faces in front of the camera.

Bottom line, it was sheer speculation and guesswork until the court sorted things out. Only one person was capable of providing the truth, and Eddie Cobb had no interest in ever allowing the facts to see the light of day.

* * * * * * *

THE BACK BENCH
"If you let it slip, we catch it"
April 15

The Supreme Court officially learned yesterday what the Twitter world has been buzzing about for over twenty-four hours. There appear to be questionable ballots in at least one remaining precinct. But until more is known, it's a buzz without a sting.

The hearing itself was particularly brief. All of the litigants, as well as the board and the court's monitor, in the matter of the water-logged ballots, unanimously stipulated to the facts.

On its own motion, the court recessed immediately to consider its options.

In other news…

THE BACK BENCH
"If you let it slip, we catch it"
April 16

EXTRA EXTRA EXTRA EXTRA EXTRA EXTRA

It took the Court less than twenty-four hours to issue its ruling regarding the course of action for the potentially tainted ballots.

The recount hearings are to proceed as scheduled, which means they will conclude in eleven days. The court will then review all findings and consider any motions in two weeks.

With respect to the tainted ballots, after they have been vetted in the hearings, they are to be identified and marked by the board. A forensic examination will then be conducted by experts appointed by the court to determine why they have taken on their suspicious pinkish hue.

In other news...

THE BACK BENCH
"If you let it slip, we catch it"
April 27

After almost three months of hand-to-hand combat over nearly four million ballots cast in the November election, the last recount hearing was held yesterday in Quincy, Illinois. As this last hearing was relatively tame in terms of contested ballots, the judge's findings are expected to be released within a few days. Once that occurs, the action shifts to the Illinois Supreme Court.

Pursuant to statute, the Supreme Court has fifteen days to issue its final ruling.

During that time, experts expect three to four days of hearings on a series of process questions, none of which are expected to significantly alter the outcome of the recount.

Barring unforeseen procedural or factual shifts, Thomas Robinson Jr. is expected to be declared governor of Illinois.

Of course, the 800-pound gorilla in the room remains approximately 1,000 suspect ballots from what is now being called "Floodgate." The court has engaged scientific experts to examine these questionable ballots in an effort to determine why they changed color after having been drenched during a malfunction in the State Board's sprinkler system.

The experts are scheduled to report in five days, and the court is expected to hold up to three days of hearings to determine if the tainted ballots will receive unique consideration in the recount.

In other news…

* * * * * * *

E-MAIL
To: Senator DiMaggio, Robert Allen
From: Joseph Cole
Sent: April 30 11:15 a.m. (CST)
Subject: Pink votes/endgame

As you requested, attached is a memorandum detailing our findings and legal arguments as we head to the Supreme Court hearings next week.

A review of the preliminary rulings from the statewide hearings leaves us anywhere from 57 to 261 votes short. As you are aware, there is a series of ballots in each precinct that remain open to interpretation. There are a few "best case" scenarios that put Allen over the top, but they require almost every open decision to run in our favor.

Notwithstanding, we will prosecute the remaining issues with all due vigor unless you determine there is a benefit to conceding at any time. Conversely, we will work to slow the process if you determine there is an advantage to doing so.

Obviously, the question of the "pink" ballots is the wild card. Our experts tell us that, absent tampering of some sort, there is no scientific basis for approximately 1,000 ballots (out of approximately 20,000 that were waterlogged) to change color after exposure to the same elements of water and heat, particularly given that all ballots appear to have been shipped, stored, and monitored under identical circumstances.

There are other facts suggesting foul play:

1. The tainted ballots were randomly distributed through the sealed containers. Had they been lumped at the top or the bottom of their respective containers, there might be an argument that they were somehow exposed to differing conditions of water content, heat, light, and ventilation.

2. All of the pink ballots were from precincts in which Robinson scored a particularly high percentage of votes and which were all very late in reporting.

3. Every last pink ballot was cast in favor of Robinson!

While science suggests the possibility of tampering, it will be difficult to prove how and when this occurred. Similarly, in the event of foul play of some sort, it is not clear how the court will rule. Should it strip all these votes from Robinson, Allen wins easily. Should it apply a proportional reduction, the result will be contingent on where the tally falls between the 57 to 261 vote spread. In that event, our analysis shows Allen wins if that spread ends up being 118 ballots or less.

* * * * * *

Joseph Cole's e-mail to Senator DiMaggio and candidate Robert Allen had originally contained two additional facts. These undisclosed facts could influence the outcome of the case, but in favor of Robinson.

The pink voting ballots had been discovered in containers from precincts matching the description in the mystery note on his car windshield. It aggravated him no end that he had never solved the riddle of the note. Now, he was haunted by the possibility of having failed his client.

That failure was compounded by the fact that the original Allen complaint did not allege fraud. It was the eleventh hour. There was no certainty the court would allow the complaint to be amended, particularly if the alleged fraud should have been caught during discovery.

But *was* there fraud in this case? Cole asked himself that question for the millionth time. A scribbled note on a windshield, some pink ballots resulting from water damage? Neither was conclusive of anything. Yet the case and his career were both resting on them.

* * * * * *

Speaker David Kennedy's sixth sense had switched on like a light bulb the minute he learned a sprinkler malfunction had caused ballots to become soaked and potentially uncountable. He was further alarmed when the circumstances surrounding the event suggested either gross stupidity or foul play. When he was told about the pink ballots, there was no end to his simultaneous disbelief and dismay.

While the media, pundits, commentators, and lawyers worried about process and ballots, the Speaker's interests remained fixated on the remap. If Robinson were not elected governor because a few ballots turned pink, so be it. However, if the findings indicated fraud and the perpetrator of that fraud was linked to Robinson, directly or indirectly, the consequences could be irreversible, especially in the short run and especially during the last few weeks prior to scheduled adjournment.

The Speaker needed answers and he needed them immediately. Particularly given his sixth sense that the entire episode reeked of one Chairman Eddie Cobb.

* * * * * *

The tentacles of Speaker Kennedy's operation reached into every nook and cranny of state government. When confronted with matters of any delicacy in the past, Kennedy had always been able to craft a series of inter-connected human dots to reach his target. In most cases, the purpose of the exercise had been to deliver a message without fingerprints. This was the first time that he found himself in the position where the information being retrieved might one day be the subject of criminal proceedings.

Great precision was required. There could be no hint of tampering with evidence or allegedly culpable acts. Maximum security and confidentiality were essential. Employing his usual and uncanny complex examination of the variables and personalities, the Speaker set in motion a series of Godfather-style inquiries.

CHAPTER THIRTY-SIX

Harlan Cleary was seriously flawed.

People would recall that his deviant tendencies and deficient IQ were apparent by the second grade. They would point out the way he had been passed along by a series of teachers who could not fathom having him repeat their class. Given Harlan's exit from their immediate lives, they might not have been aware that his ensuing sentencing to community service following a juvenile conviction for assault had saved him from spending the majority of his adult life in solitary confinement.

Fortunately for Harlan Clearly—very fortunately, indeed—his assigned community service had been a series of repetitive, mundane tasks at which Harlan had excelled. Such successful compliance had quickly caught the eye of a Democratic precinct captain.

In an election year, replete with unlimited mindless tasks, things like stuffing flyers in mailboxes, posting yard signs, and—the precinct captain's least personal favorite—running countless personal errands to curry favor with constituents—needed such unerring dedication, if not to the greater cause, than to a personal one. The precinct captain didn't care which one it was.

Harlan Cleary listened to the precinct captain with awe. It seemed Harlan was finally getting some of the appreciation he deserved. He took to the proffered praise like a kid to Christmas, outperforming all those who felt they were above such monotonous, petty duties.

For the first time in Harlan Cleary's life, he felt appreciated. Taking to politics with its cult-like demands of true believers and never-ending thirst for dedicated followers, Harlan was rewarded for many of the same behaviors he'd been so severely berated for ever since he could remember. The party encouraged Harlan's devotion to duty and his willingness to take on and complete the things no one else would do. The Party also discovered that Harlan, for all his character flaws and limitations, was like a puppy dog, loyal and dedicated to a fault to those who had earned his trust, specifically including Speaker David Kennedy, Danny Ryan, and the Democratic Party of Cook County.

The ultimate reward bestowed upon loyalists of the party is election or appointment to seats of power. Next in line is lifetime employment, with a secure pension at the end of the rainbow. The Speaker's lieutenants started Harlan in the bowels of the State Board of Elections.

Over time, Cleary inched up the ranks. Eventually, his name appeared on the door of a very nice, if very small, dark office: "Harlan Cleary, Storage."

Someone else might view Cleary's job as inconsequential, but Harlan knew better. Harlan oversaw every division that collected, organized, and stored ballots and other election memorabilia.

Some people might say that for a man of his dedication, albeit somewhat limited talents, this was Harlan Cleary's Peter Principle dream job. It was therefore not surprising that Harlan Cleary would respond to the call of duty.

* * * * * * *

E-MAIL
To: E Party Leadership Distribution
From: Mark
Sent: April 30 10:00 p.m. (CST)
Subject: Redistricting legislation

Following months of trial and error, our remap team has developed a computer model that creates an equitable redistricting formula. It is based on variables used in those other states that rely upon computer-generated models as opposed to politically generated models.

Attached for your review is a report that outlines the variables and their weighting. By way of example, we have over-weighted for symmetrical districts that avoid the amoeba-like shapes of many current districts. We have also over-weighted to keep cities, towns, and villages wholly intact.

As you will recall from earlier communications on this topic, our models reflect and are somewhat constrained by the various federal and state voting rights acts, particularly with respect to requirements necessary to protect minorities.

While this model satisfies the theoretical approach we approved, from the practical perspective it will totally disrupt the alignment of the current legislature. Of the 118 sitting Representatives, over half would be pitted against each other based upon their current residences. There would also be in excess of thirty open seats created in which no incumbent currently resides. In the Senate, just short of half would be pitted against each other with a slightly smaller percentage of open seats.

From our current E Party delegation, four house and two senate members would face each other, while four house and three senate members would face currently elected Republicans or Democrats.

Finally, our report indicates potential results, by party, based on current registration. To that end, I doubt that the Speaker, Ms. DiMaggio, or their minions, will be happy. They have historically attempted to carve districts where the outcome is easily predicted. By definition, the rebalancing in our model avoids that level of certainty in over 70 percent of the newly designed districts.

* * * * * * *

When the Speaker's grapevine reached Storage, Harlan Cleary whistled loud and long, appreciating both the source and urgency of the matter. As director of the unit, sooner or later he would have to be questioned by authorities relative to the sprinkler malfunction. Relieved that the summons had been issued by his leader and not the court, like any good soldier he instantly responded.

Like most of the thousands of patronage employees the Speaker had buried in jobs throughout Illinois government, Harlan Cleary was known, if remotely, to Kennedy for his dedicated work for the party. Other than the polite shake of the hand in the greeting line of his annual holiday party for campaign staff, he had had no personal contact with the man. The Speaker also abhorred meetings if he hadn't set the agenda, or at least well understood the content and context in advance.

Harlan was somewhat surprised to find the Speaker's general counsel also in attendance. Anyone who knew the Speaker could have told Harlan Cleary that no meeting with Speaker Kennedy, other than one of the most purely personal nature, was ever conducted without a third party present to corroborate the facts, should the need ever arise.

The Speaker, who rarely interrupted with questions when more could generally be learned by honed listening skills, took one look at Harlan Cleary, sized him up, and changed course again. And so it went. By the time Harlan left the meeting an hour and a half later, he was dehydrated and shaken after the Speaker's machine gun interrogation.

The Speaker and his counsel immediately adjourned to counsel's office to evaluate the consequences—both criminal and political—of the shocking and incriminating tale they had just been told by Harlan, who had expressed unremittent pride at the multiple risks he'd taken on the Speaker's behalf.

* * * * * *

The return trip to Springfield was the longest three and a half hours of Danny Ryan's life. He had given a fleeting thought to holding over in Chicago, but the drive time would afford him the opportunity to think. And he needed to be with Nancy Rae.

The Speaker's admonishment still reverberated in Danny's frontal lobe. "Discuss this with no one, Danny. And I mean *no one*."

But Nancy Rae wasn't "no one." She was his partner, lover, and soul mate. But for a band of gold on her left hand, she would have spousal immunity. If he couldn't trust Nancy Rae with this dire situation, well, fuck it.

He still couldn't believe it. Harlan Cleary, director of Storage, for chrissakes, had named him, Danny Ryan, a co-conspirator in a felony. One for which he had no doubt the Speaker would insist he take the fall, should it come to that. And it might.

"You are on paid leave until further notice," the Speaker had told him. "You are to have no contact with any member of staff or the political organization. You are not to use your state cell phone. You are not to use the party's e-mail. Am I making myself clear?"

If there was one saving grace, it was that that bastard Cleary's story did not square, and the Speaker knew it. There was no plausible explanation for Danny to have been involved in Floodgate. On the other hand, it smacked of a plot from an Eddie Cobb made-for-TV movie.

Notwithstanding, the Speaker also had to assume Harlan Cleary would ultimately be compelled to tell his story under oath. Cleary's testimony would certainly link his longstanding lieutenant to a web of felonious election fraud. Once that happened, Danny and the Speaker both knew Kennedy's political career would have the half-life of a candle on a three-year-old's birthday cake.

By the time Danny reached Springfield, he had replayed the conversation with the Speaker and his counsel hundreds of times. They'd settled very little, but one thing was clear. Nancy Rae was not "no one." The Speaker would eventually learn that Nancy Rae had been present in all three precincts in which the crime had been perpetrated. He would determine that she was either directly involved or her presence would directly link Danny.

Either way, they were both equally culpable and equally expendable.

In other words, they were both screwed.

* * * * * * *

Chairman Eddie Cobb was contemplating how to best play his cards. In the no-limit poker game of politics, if he played the hand correctly, he had a chance to extract maximum damage with carefully placed wagers through to the river.

Eddie had long held the Harlan Clearly and Danny Ryan cards in his hand. But the pink coloration of the copycat ballots had given him an unexpected, unbeatable combination on the flop. He had also, oh so fortuitously, been dealt a Speaker card, an Allen card, and a remap card—the equivalent of a royal flush.

Given the circumstances of the recount, the Speaker held all the Robinson cards and would be slow playing the field.

Characteristic of his lifelong style of play, Eddie would up the ante. He crafted a careful message for his Sunday morning talk show hit squad and his weekly talk radio assassins, and then turned them loose.

* * * * * * *

THE BACK BENCH
"If you let it slip, we catch it"
May 2

In a rather startling display of political subterfuge, a whisper campaign of sorts has been accusing Speaker Kennedy of election fraud in the Robinson/Allen recount.

Charges by "unconfirmed sources" were cited on weekend television shows and have been repeated on talk radio and Internet chatter throughout the week, suggesting evidence of massive vote fraud and the need for a full-blown investigation by federal authorities.

Any charges of fraud are strictly a matter of Illinois state law, but that fact is of no consequence to Main Street. The drumbeat is seen as an attempt to put added pressure on the Illinois Supreme Court. The court will be risking a huge hit to its reputation if it upholds the apparent Robinson victory without launching a full investigation of the Floodgate ballots. However, a full-blown investigation will cause months and months of further delay. Whoever has decided to link the Speaker to Floodgate obviously wants or needs that delay to occur.

Speculation is also rampant that a desperate Robert Allen, acting through Senator DiMaggio, is at the bottom of it all. Allen needs the court to find fraud to give him any hope of victory. As for DiMaggio, weakening the Speaker as the legislature heads to vote on the budget and the remap would be a welcomed twofer.

It's a dangerous game. If Allen's alleged role were to be confirmed, it could be a matter of "case closed" in short order. If the Speaker can substantiate DiMaggio's alleged participation, there will be a severe price to pay, particularly where the map is concerned.

In other news...

* * * * * *

The Speaker was working against the implications of Harlan Cleary's story, real or imagined, as well as the clock. The court was scheduled to rule on the recount in less than two weeks and he was desperate for a timely Robinson victory. Should the recount be extended for a fraud investigation, the map was suddenly in great jeopardy.

There was no question that Eddie Cobb, or whoever was behind Harlan Cleary's crime, also understood the stakes and was pressing his advantage. The talk show strategy was likely to gain momentum, especially once Cleary was exposed. That shoe was due to drop at any time.

At best, the Speaker had a week. There *had* to be more to that little shit Cleary's story. Had the Speaker skipped an essential clue? Was there another angle that made sense other than Cobb? Either way, if and when whoever was pulling the strings exposed Cleary, the Speaker's fleeting advantage in the recount would be lost. And all else with it.

* * * * * * *

E-MAIL

To: Atlas, Tom Robinson, Barb Jenkins

From: The General

Sent: May 1 7:00 a.m. (CST)

Subject: Conversation with Speaker Kennedy

I received an impromptu call from Speaker Kennedy last evening. He began with a bit of a caution concerning his end of session strategy. Wanted us to be in the loop as we enter what he called "The Two-Minute Red Zone Drill" in a bastardized analogy to pro football. Said we either win together at the end of the regular session or face a very unpleasant and extended overtime.

He referenced the need to pass the budget and the remap. Didn't talk details, but wanted to ensure we have open lines of communication and, as he called it, the ability to instantly react and pivot. He specifically inquired about Barb as our point person.

He congratulated us on our response to the Super PAC campaign and apologized for pulling the plug on HB1. Said he has a plan, but is not in a position to elaborate.

He closed by asking permission to meet with Elaine Richards. Said he has a critical update on the recount but, given the complexities, can only share directly with counsel.

Sorry if I jumped the gun, but I told him to go ahead. This is the first conversation with the man where I felt he was trying to maneuver an outcome, and, despite all the talk about budgets, remaps, and recounts, that outcome was getting to Elaine Richards.

As to the session endgame, perhaps a conference call is in order relatively soon.

CHAPTER THIRTY-SEVEN

After almost forty years in politics, this was a first. David Kennedy had always honored his late wife Theresa's request to maintain absolute separation between politics and family life. He could work 24/7/365, but when he walked through the front door of their humble abode, his singular focus was to be husband, son, and brother. Over time, that role had expanded to father and grandfather.

Although for many years disgruntled by this decree, he had come to appreciate it for the blessing it was. Theresa's demand for absolute bifurcation had provided him comfort, solace and, on certain occasions, escape. Of course, that was in the days of rotary phones, before the advent of technology that enables anyone to be reached anytime.

He and Theresa Lyons had grown up together in the immediate neighborhood of their South Side bungalow. As was the custom in those days, they'd married young. Though David would ultimately grow to become the center of power and influence in Illinois politics, Theresa had always insisted they stay true to their local and Catholic roots.

It had been almost a decade since her death, but she remained the Speaker's fulcrum. Particularly these days, when divorcing himself from the demands of his political world became impossible, he literally and figuratively found his way back to 4718 South Harris Street. Today, after a period of soul searching, he was convinced his dear wife would approve of his decision to open their living room for his meeting with Elaine Richards.

Elaine Richards was immediately struck with the simplicity and modesty of the Speaker's accommodations. She'd expected more flamboyancy in the décor, more obvious statements that money and power were in play. This home was as humble as any she had known. Although the décor and its trappings were unmistakably Catholic, the antiques with their well-placed doilies were in excellent, understated taste.

The Speaker welcomed her at the door, politely took her jacket, and without ceremony offered her a seat on one of the living room's dated, oversized chairs. She sank into it, surprised at how comfortable it was.

"Thank you for coming on short notice," Kennedy said.

He offered her a cup of tea, which she accepted gratefully, adding to it a boost of honey.

"I know how hectic things are with the election challenge."

"Not at all," said Elaine courteously, while thinking, *Why am I here?*

"I also realize you are here without much in the way of an agenda, but I think the issues are such that no preparation will have been required."

"Please," Elaine said, "the floor is yours, Mr. Speaker." She was dying of impatience.

"To begin, I wish to hire you to represent me and the Democratic Party of Illinois in a legal matter related to the recount."

"Oh," said Elaine, nonplussed. "But, Mr. Speaker—"

"David," he said.

Elaine had to take a breath. "If that's the case…David," she said, "I'm afraid this meeting will be quite brief. I am not looking for clients, and my current client may not appreciate sharing my time and talents."

Disappointed, she moved to get up. It wasn't graceful, given the depth of the chair.

"Wait," said the Speaker. "Please."

Elaine sank back down with an equal lack of grace. Luckily, the Speaker didn't appear to notice.

"I understand. And I agree one hundred percent," he said. "But it is essential that our conversation take place under the umbrella of the attorney-client privilege. Why will be immediately apparent if you give me the chance to explain. At the conclusion, we can discuss how you wish to proceed. I give you my word that I will abide by your decision."

"Very well...David. I acknowledge this conversation will be held under the auspices of the attorney-client privilege—with the understanding that I will have no further obligation once it concludes."

"Agreed," said the Speaker.

"Then I'm all ears."

"As I am sure you are well aware, Elaine, I am keenly interested in the outcome of the recount. Without elaborating, the election of Tom Robinson has far-reaching political consequences for me and my party. To that end, I have been observing the various...developments on a daily basis.

"For the past few weeks, the matter now being referred to as Floodgate has become a bit of an obsession. I trust you have advised your client that there is a definite stench that threatens the victory you have worked so effectively and valiantly to protect."

Elaine went to respond, but the Speaker continued. "If you'll forgive me," he said, "in my business, almost nothing happens without a reason. So, from the very beginning, this 'random event' where a sprinkler system drenches the election ballots from three Chicago precincts that happen to provide Robinson's margin of victory on election night—well, let's just say this caught my attention."

"Interesting observation," said Elaine carefully.

"I would not have expected you to make such an observation, of course, given the pressures of so many recount hearings. But that, and a few other anomalies, are what caused me to do some digging. It is this digging that has unearthed significant voter fraud."

"*What?*" Elaine struggled for composure.

"Through a series of inquiries," said the Speaker, "I learned that one of my long-standing patronage workers at the State Board of Elections was approached with a rather...shall we say, innovative scheme."

Elaine waited anxiously.

"This worker was asked to remove approximately 900 ballots from three precincts and replace them with roughly 900 identical ballots. All of the ballots he was told to remove had to be votes cast for Tom Robinson. Curiously, all replacement ballots were also to be votes for Tom Robinson."

"Let me get this straight," Elaine said. "Someone you placed in a state job was asked to switch ballots—but not to change the outcome of the vote. I must be missing something."

"Took me a while, too," admitted the Speaker, "but consider this: What better way to suggest that Robinson was elected with benefit of illegal action than to plant replacement ballots that would prove to be illegal substitutes. The easiest conclusion would be to suspect the switch was made on election night sometime between the close of the polls and the reporting of the vote totals. All three of the precincts in question reported unusually late, so someone did their homework to make sure it all tied out."

"But," Elaine exclaimed, disbelieving, "all of those ballots were examined during the due diligence period. No one caught the switch."

"Exactly! Which is why I think Floodgate became necessary. The difference in the switched ballots was evidently so subtle that it was easily missed. Which is why the person I mentioned received very careful instructions as to which ballots needed to be placed under sprinklers and how to discharge those sprinklers to make certain they would be thoroughly soaked."

"This scenario is curious, to say the least," Elaine finally said, "but it also effectively ensures a Robinson victory given where the recount stands."

"Perhaps," cautioned the Speaker. "It's one thing to win the case, but another entirely to govern under the enormous public pressure that would develop in light of any investigation.

"Unless I'm mistaken, the gentleman I mentioned, and I use that term loosely, would quickly and easily be linked back to me. Once that happens, the press will pound relentlessly on Robinson for having benefitted from my team's voter fraud."

Elaine shook her head. "I understand," she said. But she didn't, not really. How could this happen?

"Winning the election, but then having to govern under a huge black cloud...that would not be in your client's interest, or in the interest of his party.

"Ah," she finished suddenly, "Now I see. My representing you in any legal proceedings would avoid any possible division of interest."

"Exactly," said the Speaker.

"I am certainly glad you brought this to my attention David," she said. "Needless to say, I'm beyond shocked. And, obviously, I need to discuss things with my client and the E Party leaders. Can I assume you'll make yourself available to fill in all the blanks—and that you have this completely locked down on your end?"

The Speaker nodded. "As soon as you're ready to move ahead, my general counsel will deliver an affidavit reciting all known facts. As to being completely locked down, this is politics. Sadly, whoever orchestrated this crime will be pulling the strings for the foreseeable future. Our only advantage lies in the fact that the perpetrator must not suspect we have uncovered the fraud.

"The court is scheduled to rule by May fifteenth," he said. "Tell me, Elaine, if you were the mastermind behind this situation, how long would you wait to make sure there was blood in the water?"

* * * * * *

Atlas had also scheduled an all-hands conference call, this one for later that evening. Following a brisk round of E Party geography, he immediately yielded the floor to Elaine.

"I'll cut to the chase," said Elaine in her typical no-nonsense manner. "My meeting with the Speaker began with his telling me he wished to engage my services." At the collective gasp, Elaine went on. "I know. Shocking. But all will be clear once we drill down to the substance of the meeting. The bottom line is that I had no choice but to temporarily agree to his request for lawyer-client privileged communication. Naturally, I am somewhat limited as to what I can reveal, but that should not be an impediment to our discussion."

"Any chance you can elaborate on the attorney-client point?" asked Barbara Jenkins.

"Simply put," said Elaine, "once an attorney is placed in an employment relationship with a client, even a potential client about to divulge sensitive facts, the attorney is immediately held to a confidential ethical constraint. In this case, the Speaker wanted to make certain that I would be limited to the extent I could repeat parts of the conversation."

"But how can you serve as his attorney and Tom's at the same time?" Barbara asked.

"Again, without belaboring the ethics of the situation, I can represent both if there is no conflict and both clients agree. In this case, I immediately put the Speaker on notice that representation was both doubtful and contingent. He had anticipated that response. His primary concern was protecting our immediate conversation.

"I learned very quickly why the Speaker was seeking confidentiality and I was, as I said, shocked. He laid out a scenario suggesting there has been tampering with a portion of the ballots sequestered in Floodgate."

"What kind of tampering?" Tom asked.

"Assuming the Speaker's source is accurate, ballots were substituted after the election—which of course is the good news. But the tampering was designed to make it appear as though the fraud occurred on the night of the election—a very elaborate and clever crime."

"So," the General said, "what you're saying, or what the Speaker is saying, is that Tom may have won the election fair and square, but someone has gone out of their way to make it look as though his victory came as the result of manipulated votes."

"Yes, that is exactly what the Speaker believes."

"I must be missing something," said K.C.

"I'm not surprised you're confused," agreed Elaine. "The fact is, there's a lot more to it, but again, I'm boxed in a bit here. I'll do my best.

"According to the Speaker, the mastermind of this situation has crafted the facts so that the evidence will lead to Kennedy's doorstep. The crime was carried out by a person known to be loyal to the Speaker, so the particulars surrounding both the original transgression and the subsequent sprinkler malfunction will circumstantially lead back to him."

"And you found this believable?" K.C. asked Elaine. "Let's face it. Illinois is not Candy Land and the Speaker did appear to change the course of the election over the last four days."

"I have had some doubt," Elaine admitted. "I mean, why make all the fuss about confidentiality if there is no culpability? For that very reason, I suggest we proceed cautiously."

"What exactly *are* you suggesting, Elaine?" Atlas asked.

"There are a few immediate concerns. The Speaker believes the recent flurry of calls for an investigation is the prelude to a systematic leaking of facts and sources. He suggests that we proceed expeditiously before it becomes known that we have jointly, as he put it, connected the dots.

"I believe he wants us to have sufficient information to independently test his theory. Since he has no standing in the recount, he needs us—my legal team in particular—to act as his proxy to examine the ballots in question. I think that's our next step."

"How does that vindicate the Speaker?" K.C. asked.

"Actually, it doesn't. If, as the Speaker believes, this trap was carefully set, he will have a difficult time extricating himself. In the meantime, he said that Tom and his entire administration will certainly be indelibly stained and mercilessly haunted by the media."

The General coughed. "Then it looks like it's in our best interest to help clear the Speaker's name," he said dryly.

"Yes," said Elaine. "But at the first indication that his story does not hold, we will have to do a one-eighty."

"Let's hope that doesn't happen," said Atlas. "We have a lot riding on that relationship."

"Starting with the recount," Elaine agreed.

"Any updates you can share before you go?"

"Not really," said Elaine. "I remain cautiously optimistic. Our analysis still has us comfortably within the margin of victory needed to sustain any additional last-minute surprises. The upcoming hearings before the Supreme Court will be tense. Clearly, the Floodgate ballots are the key. Hopefully, the Speaker has scripted the path to victory."

There was a moment of silence while everyone processed this summary of events.

"Sorry, everyone," Elaine finally said, "but I need to run."

Atlas asked the others to stay on the line. "Barb, you asked for follow-up time. What's the agenda?"

"Sorry, hang on, Atlas," said Tom. "Before we get there, I feel the need to comment on Elaine's report. None of this is sitting well. We've been on the job for four months and it seems as though nothing is coming together. We came in with great expectations and, at best, we're treading water. The bureaucracy's a mess, the budget's a sham, the education bill is bogged down, and now we learn there was fraud in the election. Never in a million years could I have imagined such bullshit."

"I don't think any of us did, Tom," said Atlas. "Still, that's why we started all this—why we're all here in the first place. To use Elaine's words, I am also cautiously optimistic that we can finally begin to move forward. Once the recount is behind us, that is."

K.C. sensed that Tom was close to the breaking point, even from a thousand miles away and over the wires.

"Not to be difficult," said K.C., "but I have to agree with Tom. I didn't see this coming either. I expected it to be difficult, but Tom has faced far too many obstacles thrown his way from unknown sources.

"On the other hand," she added, "I am thankful every day that Tom and Barb are at the helm. From my perspective, you two have done an outstanding job. Tom, the way you and Avery jumped in to save the education package was nothing short of miraculous. Barb, the skills you have shown in navigating the day-to-day business of the state gives me great hope."

"Agreed," Atlas said. "All the more reason to get this recount behind us and dust off the E Party playbook so we can begin to accomplish what we originally set out to do."

"Thanks, K.C.," said Barbara. "It helps. As Tom said, the enormity of the job manifests itself daily. Without the support of the team, we wouldn't have a chance. I suppose I could come down on the side of optimism as well, at least for the long haul."

With less than a month remaining on the General Assembly's schedule, Barb was just short of paranoid about the need to pass their first budget, the decennial remap of all state and federal legislative districts, and HB1. She had intended to use the call to reach some consensus on the end of session strategy, but after what just conspired, she simply assured them all that her agenda could wait.

No sooner had she disconnected, though, than she felt the sting of her conscience. The Super PAC onslaught had injected some life into Tom by awakening his competitive nature for a cause that truly inspired him. Yet the balance of the situation was wearing him down. She found herself using an ever-increasing delicacy concerning when and how to engage him in the day-to-day.

She dialed the phone. The governor needed help. Where better to come from than his friends?

CHAPTER THIRTY-EIGHT

The days surrounding the final recount hearings before the Illinois Supreme Court were a whirlwind of stress and strategy, and the center of the vortex was swirling around Elaine Richards. Her meeting with the Speaker had bumped the stakes considerably.

Elaine had never considered the possibility of vote fraud or conspiracy. Now she was suddenly confronted with having to avoid both defeat and a seriously flawed victory.

The timing was also cruel and unusual. With the benefit of years, she might find a needle in a haystack. With the benefit of months, she might have a fighting chance. But she was down to days and hours. It was no longer sufficient for Tom Robinson to win the recount. It was now incumbent upon her to find the righteous path—and do it in a fortnight.

"David, it's Elaine." She'd placed the call to his personal cell, a number known to less than a handful outside the family. It had been carefully prearranged for a time when he would be home and alone. "I have spoken with my client. Predicated on a few conditions, I am prepared to move ahead with the representation we discussed."

"Thank you, counselor," said Kennedy, equally formally. "Please proceed."

"First," said Elaine, "I reserve the right to withdraw if at any point the facts, as they become known, in any way deviate from those you outlined at our meeting."

"Yes, of course. I'd expect nothing less."

"And I want it in writing that I will then be released from my attorney-client bond of confidentiality. Furthermore, if the story changes even slightly, David, I will hang you by your balls."

The Speaker chuckled, but the matter was too serious for more than that.

"Done, and done," he said.

* * * * * * *

"Hey, Nat. It's Mark."

"Well, hello, stranger. I'm guessing you're busier than a one-armed paper hanger these days."

"Something like that," said Mark. "There's all the usual day-to-day stuff, of course, but now I've become the party's remap expert."

"The remap? Really? With the recount and all, remapping sort of slid off my horizon. I'll bet Kennedy and DiMaggio haven't lost sight of it, though."

"That's a safe bet. We're on it, too. Hoping to shake things up a bit. Like the states with balanced non-partisan modeling."

"In Illinois?" Nat snorted. "What are you smoking?"

"Stranger things have happened, my friend. We're the E Party, remember? In a few weeks, when Robinson's victory is finalized, the veto pen might come in very handy. But, actually, I was calling to congratulate you on this month's article."

"Thanks to you. Putting Barbara Jenkins and some of the E Party's lesser known legislative leaders front and center was just the ticket. From my interviews with them, you've got some untapped star power, too. Especially that Jenkins. She's come a very long way in a few months. So...I'm thinking I probably owe you a beer."

"Sold," Mark said. "Saturday. I've got Hawks playoff tickets."

* * * * * * *

Nancy Rae Mitchell's patchwork quilt upbringing had taught her the necessity of staying in control of situations, especially those situations that involved men. Something at which she had excelled for all these years. Right up until her recent episode with Tom Robinson, a fact that still caused a flutter in her stomach and a pain in her heart. How could she have let herself care so damn much for that man?

And then here comes Danny Ryan trailing right behind. A pigheaded political maniac who has somehow managed to get past her brain, her need to dominate, and her ability to manipulate, to the place that had been safely under lock and key. What had happened to her barriers to attachment and commitment?

Nancy Rae had not seen or spoken with Danny in over a week. Her emotional state had reached the status of a broken kaleidoscope where none of the shapes formed the patterns they were supposed to form.

It seemed like an eternity since Danny had returned home after his "confrontation" with the Speaker. That's what he'd called it. His confrontation. Danny had been a physical and emotional wreck. His rendition of the day's events had therefore been disjointed at best, nonsensical at worst.

Danny's bungled attempt to reconcile Harlan Cleary's tale immediately had the effect of confusing and upsetting Nancy Rae. Danny Ryan was either a criminal or a dupe—take your pick. Either one could send him off to a shared cell with any number of Illinois' prior governors.

To make matters worse, if that were possible, as Danny finally managed to speak coherently enough to outline the circumstantial evidence connecting the crime to the precincts in question, Nancy Rae had felt the distinct tightening of the noose around her own neck. These were the very precincts that were the principle object of her eleventh-hour campaign work. She personally had spent considerable time in each as a poll watcher on Election Day.

When it hit her that she, too, was being criminalized, she had lost her composure. She was ashamed at her behavior, but at the time her attack of harsh criticism and blame had felt completely justified. Danny, shocked at her long-winded vitriol, responded with a lifelong repository of Nancy Rae indiscretions and imperfections.

Nancy Rae had exploded from her Springfield apartment in a fit of rage. Each had spent the ensuing days in solitude, trying to make any sense of the horrible situation.

She'd found out that Danny had returned to Chicago, furloughed from work and confined to his South Side bungalow. Nancy Rae continued to creep around as if she were about to be sentenced, but was unable to avoid client duties as the session drew to a close. It was the exact wrong time and the exact wrong circumstances for great minds not to be thinking alike.

* * * * * * *

"David? Elaine Richards again. I'm calling because I have decided to ask the court to allow additional discovery. I'd like my team to re-examine the Floodgate ballots. Sadly, it doesn't help that I have absolutely no idea what we're looking for."

"Unfortunately," said the Speaker, "neither do I."

* * * * * * *

Chairman Eddie Cobb's nostrils were flaring from the scent of the kill. Perhaps an Alamo-style massacre? His character assassins were working their usual macabre witchcraft on talk show after talk show. Daily polling in Illinois had public sentiment quickly building to the critical mass required to exert pressure on the Supreme Court.

Judges read papers and judges buy gas. Judges buy groceries and judges have wives who have opinionated friends. From every angle, they would be hearing about the need to investigate the flawed ballots. Floodgate was now a top three tweet, and the volume was staggering. Given the current trajectory of the polling and the amount of Internet chatter Eddie Cobb was generating, within a week, ten days at most, the court would be compelled to launch a sweeping and extensive criminal investigation.

The clues would lead directly to Harlan Cleary's door. The endgame trap would be set.

* * * * * *

THE BACK BENCH
"If you let it slip, we catch it"
May 8

Today was the first in a series of scheduled hearings before the Illinois Supreme Court in the Matter of *Allen v. Robinson*.

The lawyers danced and pranced through a sequence of procedural motions, the great majority of which were either denied outright or "taken under advisement." In this case, my lawyer friends tell me that the "taken under advisement" motions are Hail Mary passes that will eventually get knocked down in the end zone.

One of those motions was a request by attorney Elaine Richards, Robinson's chief counsel, to re-examine the Floodgate ballots. Richards stressed that time was of the essence and that waiting until the end of the hearing schedule might prejudice her client. Based on questioning from the court, there appeared to be a wide range of opinion as to the need to grant additional discovery and the appropriate timing.

The balance of the day was given to scheduling. The court originally set ten days aside for final arguments. But that was long before the Floodgate ballots surfaced.

For the time being, the court has announced plans to stick with the original schedule, but has added two hours to each day in order to devote the three final days to Floodgate.

What is planned for those three final days is the subject of tremendous speculation. It's possible that the court could hear evidence and rule immediately, and also possible that it could decide to entertain motions and set a subsequent investigation and a separate set of hearings.

Given the amount of media noise surrounding Floodgate, a full-blown criminal investigation seems highly probable. Organizations with both Republican and Democratic ties have released polls indicating that the public expects a thorough vetting.

None of this may affect the outcome of the case, but it could have a dramatic effect on the Illinois General Assembly. They are within weeks of adjournment, and passing the budget and remap legislation could prove impossible without knowing the outcome of the recount.

If the scheduled adjournment date is blown, both the budget and remap legislation will then require a three-fifths vote in each chamber. And, trust me on this one, Speaker Kennedy does not want to allow the Republicans into the game on either vote, particularly the remap. On top of which, Allen could become governor. Wouldn't that scenario make for strange bedfellows?

In other news…

* * * * * * *

"Elaine? David Kennedy. I hope I'm not catching you at a bad time."

"Not at all, Mr. Speaker. What can I do for you?"

"Actually, I'm calling to pass along a bit of information. Expect your motion to be granted. Your time to re-examine the ballots will be limited to a few hours. Under the circumstances, that was the best I could do."

"Thank you," Elaine said. "I just hope this doesn't turn out to be a wild goose chase."

As he hit the end button on his cell, the Speaker was struck by the futility of the situation. For all his power and for all his strategic brilliance, he would not be in the room for one of the most crucial, pivotal moments in his entire career. If the Cleary story held, if there was the slightest traction in the media, all his plans would be in jeopardy. He was within weeks of cutting the deal that would cement his legacy. He would pass the map that would protect the party for the decade to come and he would hand the E Party and children of Illinois a major victory in the form of HB1.

Then again, he had just arranged for a veritable stranger to examine a vital set of documents, even though she had no idea what she was looking for. What if she failed? Or, worse yet, what if she didn't find the mystery clue, but Joseph Cole did?

CHAPTER THIRTY-NINE

E-MAIL

To: E Party Leadership Distribution
From: Barbara Jenkins
Sent: May 10 4:04 p.m. (CST)
Subject: End-of-session legislative strategy

I have been meeting with the Speaker and his staff to discuss our end-of-session legislative strategy. Our E Party legislative leaders have also been in attendance. From the Senate, Senator Martin is focusing on the budget, Senator Cullen is focusing on the remap, and Mona Benjamin remains our point person on HB1. From the House, it's Representative Kubik on the budget, Jillian Cassidy on the remap, and Perle Abernathy remains our point on the education package.

For the time being, we are planning for two scenarios: 1) Tom as governor with the recount concluded before the legislature's scheduled adjournment; and 2) Tom as governor with the recount in overtime due to the Floodgate ballots. There will be no planning in consideration of Allen as governor.

At our insistence, all three bills will remain in the mix. The Speaker wants to have separate scenarios with and without HB1, but we have made it eminently clear that this is a non-starter. Notwithstanding, I do not foresee an outcome that gets us both HB1 and our preferred map.

In preparation for our call this evening, here's a brief description of where we stand:

1.Budget – The Speaker insists that the budget stay as vanilla as possible, unless and until Tom's election is confirmed. Unfortunately, it's more of the same smoke and mirrors crap. He says that our reform initiatives are too controversial to consider until the court has ruled. Making matters worse, recent federal budget cuts are projected to create an additional shortfall of approximately $1 billion. Even with my advanced degrees in math, government budgeting remains a mystery. Nothing adds up. Cash flow doesn't match up with revenues and expenses. Attached is an overview of the key elements of the "vanilla" budget.

2.HB1 – Assuming Tom wins, the Speaker expects relatively easy passage, including all of the Getting to 21 bells and whistles. However, that also presupposes passage of the Speaker's remap. According to Kennedy, he can leverage votes for HB1 off his map. In private conversations, he concedes the intellectual appeal of our map, but says this is a political exercise, not an exercise in good government.

3.The map – I already tipped my hand above. Passing the Speaker's map allegedly provides the votes we need for HB1 and, if things break our way in the recount, will allow us to advance our budget reforms. Per the Speaker, if we want to pass the E Party remap, there is "not enough pork or jobs in the budget" to provide even half the votes we need. As he put it, neither he nor Liz DiMaggio, should it come to that, could ever make the sale to their members.

Regardless of how we prioritize, I have now learned two important pieces of legislative sausage making: "structured roll calls" and "immediate effective date" pressures.

As it turns out, votes on contentious legislation are usually passed with structured roll calls. Each caucus negotiates how many votes they will contribute towards passage. In that way, those members who are experiencing difficult elections in targeted districts can be spared having to take difficult votes.

According to the Speaker, it's not whether the issue is necessarily complicated, but whether an opponent in an election can negatively spin the vote. So, in the case of the budget, even if it is the best budget ever passed (LOL), there will always be elements to pick apart in attack style campaign ads. All rather disgusting. No wonder leadership in America is dead.

The Speaker assumes all E Party legislators in the House and Senate will vote yes for both the budget and HB1. Since no Republicans can be counted on, the Democrats provide the rest of the votes needed. That requires thirty-five Democrats in the House and sixteen in the Senate. And, of course, he needs to have map-drawing flexibility to obtain (as in "buy") the votes he needs.

The immediate effective date requirement primarily affects the budget. The budget must be in effect when the state's fiscal year starts on July 1. Prior to May 31, the legislature can pass legislation with immediate effective dates with only a majority vote. After that date, a three-fifths vote is necessary.

So, if we do not pass the budget in the next twenty-one days, it may take Republican votes to get there. According to the Speaker, if the budget does not pass in that timeframe and the recount has not been finalized, the Republicans will attack Tom Robinson relentlessly and viciously for his fiscal failures.

The remap has slightly different deadline vote pressures. It has the three-fifths vote concern outlined above, but in addition, if legislation creating redistricting is not passed by June 30, the entire process is delegated to a legislative super-committee. That puts the Speaker's formulas for protecting his incumbents entirely at risk. While it may benefit our ability to craft a fair map by our standards, it also means we lose Democratic support for the budget and HB1.

Whether it's the budget, HB1, or the remap, the greater risk of not passing any or all of these by May 31 is that the Republicans stall until they know if Robert Allen wins the recount. In that event, we arguably lose control of all three issues because he then owns the veto pen.

* * * * * * *

Joseph Cole felt a twinge of redemption when the court granted Elaine Richards's *Motion to Allow Additional Discovery* of the Floodgate ballots. He had lost a good measure of sleep the past few weeks contemplating what he had originally missed. Or was he simply being paranoid in the face of a humiliating defeat?

Suddenly and unexpectedly, he'd been granted a second and last chance. The entire case now hinged on the legitimacy of ballots from the three mystery precincts.

What was Richards about? She had been surprisingly vague with the court regarding the reasoning behind her motion. What did she suspect? Or was she simply seeking to prove the negative, to assuage herself that nothing stood in the way of her imminent victory?

* * * * * *

As she began to come to grips with her wildly swinging emotions, Nancy Rae reconsidered the conversation with Danny. Had she overreacted? Was storming out the sign of a deranged egocentric girlfriend with low self-esteem?

In effect, Danny had triggered a self-preservation defense mechanism that had served her well throughout her life up until now. *Run for cover at the first sign of danger.* And, even more important, *don't take the hit for anybody.*

Her foster parents, her father in particular, had made no bones about using their kids as shields. When the money went to support his vices, Nancy Rae had covered for him with the Department of Human Services. When he beat her and her siblings, Nancy Rae had covered for him with the authorities. She once spent time at a detention center after claiming her bruises were self-inflicted.

"Cover for me," he'd plead time and time again. "You're a minor with a clean record. I'll get you out fast. If they lock me up you'll all be out on the streets." To a frightened kid who knew no better, her father's appeal—and word—was gospel. The life she had wasn't heaven, but it was better than any likely alternative.

"It'll never happen again," her father had assured her when she left for the detention center. Months later, when he came at her, she finally understood he would never change.

Lesson learned: *Don't take the hit for anybody!* The problem was, Danny was not her father. Nor had he asked her to take a hit for him.

She had leapt to conclusions. She had *run for cover at the first sign of danger.*

She was no longer a frightened minor in a life going nowhere. In fact, until a week ago, she was as happy as she had ever been and on the cusp of realizing her dreams.

The only thing Danny had asked for was her support and help. He needed her. And she had abandoned him. It was time to turn back the clock.

* * * * * * *

"Good evening, everyone," said Atlas as he opened the conference call. "I know we have a very busy agenda, and I have to confess that I'm looking forward to sitting back and listening as our folks in Springfield walk us through the session endgame strategy. Which means my main purpose as moderator is to ask Barbara Jenkins to get us started. Barb?"

"Thanks, Atlas. I trust everyone has had an opportunity to review the materials I sent a few days ago."

"Barb, this is the General. I got your e-mail, but I could not find earlier correspondence on the legislature's schedule. Could you please take a moment to provide that additional update?"

"Sure. We have nineteen days left until scheduled adjournment on the thirty-first. The legislature is scheduled to be in session Tuesday through Friday of this week, adjourn for the weekend, and then run straight through for the final ten days."

"Didn't we set some timing standards in a previous legislature that could cause a problem?" the General asked.

"Yes. As you recall, during the E Party's first legislative session, we said we would vote on a budget only if it literally sat on members' desks for one week before passage. That was to prevent last-minute budget deal shenanigans. The rules we insisted on—Rule 5-2 in the Senate and Rule 38 in the House—are still in place. Technically, two weeks are needed, but we have discussed with the Speaker and the President an abbreviated process that will run identical budgets in each chamber and then have one of them cross back to the other house to be passed in one day. That gives us until May twenty-fourth to have the final budget deal negotiated. There is no issue if the vanilla budget in your packets is our choice because that plan is drafted and ready to go. Should we decide to press for some or all of our reforms, we have very little time to get there."

"I guess I applaud your creativity on the timing," said the General. "Sometimes you make decisions on the battlefield that you wouldn't make in the classroom. But let me ask you this—if we don't make the cutoff in the rules, do we go to overtime?"

"I guess we would," Barbara said slowly, "unless we vote to waive the seven-day sunshine rule."

"We can do that?" K.C. asked.

"Actually, I've learned you can do almost anything you want when it comes to bending the rules. You just need the votes. Not that that's what I'm advocating, but the option is available should we find ourselves up against the deadline."

"I'd hate to see us backed into that corner," K.C. countered. "I suggest we revisit any timing issues before we get there."

"I agree," said the General. "But I also want our troops on the ground to know we have their backs if that's what it comes to. Anyway, thanks for that bit of education, Barb. I will now attempt to parrot my friend Atlas and fade into the wallpaper for the balance of the call."

"I have a C-note that says my buddies Atlas and the General can't last more than ten minutes as wallflowers," Tom said.

"You're on," they said in unison.

Barb spent the next thirty minutes presenting her review of the strategy options.

You've outdone yourself, Barbara," Mark said. "As you can imagine, I am troubled by the suggestion that the Speaker solely controls the votes on the remap. It's not that I'm insistent upon the intrinsic balance and fairness of our model, but I'm wondering if we shouldn't also talk with Elizabeth DiMaggio to see what the Republicans have to offer. As long as Tom holds the veto pen, that should give us leverage to cut the best deal. Remember, once the new map is in place, we're stuck with it for ten years."

"I didn't grasp the importance of the map when you first spoke about it last fall," Tom interjected, "but I totally get it now. However, I'm inclined to be selfish. I may hold the governorship for only a few days—perhaps weeks. This could be our last best chance to pass HB1 inclusive of Getting to 21, so that's where I'm putting my marbles."

"I'm with Mark," K.C. said. "When it comes to the Republicans, we should at least see what they have to offer. If they understand the calculus of the map, they will prefer our model to whatever the Speaker has concocted. Based on the vote totals, we can always partner with them to trump the Speaker and pass our education bill."

"Let's remember our deal," Atlas said, breaking his self-imposed silence. "Tom is the governor in part because of the Speaker. In exchange, we promised him a wide berth on his map. Barbara, when will he reveal the final details on his plan?"

"Actually, he's waiting for us," Barbara answered. "As soon as we give him the go-ahead, he promises to get back to us with the structured roll call on each bill within one week. Circling back to where we started this conversation, that will leave us with roughly ten session days to finish our business. Any objection to granting him the time?"

"How about a bit of compromise?" asked K.C. after a moment. "Let's tell him he has only four days to get back. If we grant the week, we lose too many precious days. My intuition tells me he can get it done in twenty-four hours, if necessary. In the meantime, I can't see any harm in Mark and you reaching out to Senator DiMaggio to get a read on whether she wants to negotiate. Who knows, she may still think Allen can pull out the victory."

K.C.'s motion carried unanimously.

* * * * * * *

"Atlas, I thought I should call you back immediately," Tom began. "I need some clarification on HB1. We kind of got off on a remap tangent there, and HB1 was sent to the showers. I don't mean to whine, but that's not acceptable. You mentioned the deal you cut with the

Speaker on the election and the map, but I thought passing HB1 was also part of that deal."

"I hear you," said Atlas, "but I also don't see that HB1 will be taken out of the game. As far as I'm aware, it remains the party's top priority."

Tom let out an audible sigh. "I'm glad to hear you say that. At the same time, the harder we press on our version of the map, the more unlikely passage of HB1 becomes, at least for this session. We've been trying to pass an education bill for over two years now. There's always another excuse to kick the can down the road. Something else always seems to take precedence. Another quarter of a million kids have since dropped out of school statewide and the entire system remains an intractable mess."

"Again, Tom. I hope I'm not misreading our call, but you know as I do that this map stuff has to play out. I'm no maven when it comes to all this legislative wheeling and dealing, but in the Speaker's mind, the issues are joined. And, given the Super PAC mess we just dealt with, well, I'm not in a position to second guess. Perhaps you and Barbara should talk this through to make certain that HB1 remains front and center in all negotiations."

"You're right," Tom said, relaxing somewhat. "Sometimes I forget that I'm the governor."

CHAPTER FORTY

THE BACK BENCH
"If you let it slip, we catch it"
May 14

This morning's scheduled hearings in the election challenge have been cancelled in deference to additional discovery regarding the Floodgate ballots.

Since this discovery is not considered part of the statutory recount process, it is not open to the public. Further, in granting the motion, the court has prescribed very tight parameters. Only two hours have been allowed and the parties have been given very strict instructions on the scope of their investigation.

In what is being called a first-ever event, the court will be represented by the Chief Justice Woehrmann. With the case being too close to call and with the threat of additional hearings related to possible ballot tampering, there is no room for error regarding process.

Each party to the recount is limited to one attorney. *The Back Bench* has learned that Elaine Richards and Joseph Cole will be present for Governor Tom Robinson and candidate Robert Allen, respectively.

It would appear these particular two hours could decide the entire case.

In other news...

* * * * * * *

Chief Justice Woehrmann was stunned when, after barely scratching the surface of the ballots, attorney Elaine Richards, and then, almost simultaneously, attorney Joseph Cole, announced that they required no additional time. Perhaps they each realized the exercise was a wild goose chase. Perhaps they each realized that two hours would not be sufficient. Perhaps they each needed more time to prepare for the afternoon's hearing. Perhaps all of the above. Under the circumstances, however, it didn't make sense for two such esteemed and cutthroat pugilists to spend so little time on discovery. Chief Justice Woehrmann was mystified.

The thirty minutes Elaine Richards had used to review the ballots had proven almost twenty too many. Armed with details provided by the Speaker, the vote fraud was apparent after having handled only a half dozen pink documents. She'd spent another ten minutes or so searching for the second key piece of evidence, then decided any additional time would only be to Cole's advantage.

Joseph Cole, too, had found the missing link. It was the evidence he would need to seal the victory for Allen. Not unlike the lottery winner of a mega jackpot, it took every ounce of restraint to keep himself from crowing.

When Elaine Richards declared that she would need no additional time, Cole was elated, though chose not to show it. He packed his briefcase without hesitation and was out the door quickly, without troubling to feign polite small talk. It was not until he was alone on the elevator that he began an uncharacteristic round of exaggerated fist pumps. It wasn't until he was safely in his car and about to dial Senator DiMaggio that another thought crossed his mind, and put a slight damper on his celebration.

Why had Elaine Richards summarily called it quits? Had she found the clue as well? And what would she do if she had?

Cole put his phone back in its car holster and drove to his office to collect and organize his thoughts. He needed a concrete plan of attack before informing Elizabeth DiMaggio and Robert Allen.

Similarly, Counsel Richards used the unexpected gap in time to seek the solitude of her hotel room. Her case was suddenly in jeopardy. She was unprepared for the consequences that corroborating Harlan Cleary's claim of having substituted copycat ballots would produce.

She was equally unprepared for the consequences of not being able to corroborate the timing of Cleary's actions. Tom Robinson's victory depended upon her being able to show that the vote fraud occurred after the ballots had been counted and sequestered with the Board of Elections, not on election night.

Her hands were tied. If Harlan Cleary were brought forth to testify, not only would he face significant jail time, but the reputations of both the Speaker and the governor would be at stake. In all likelihood, Elaine's next assignment would be defending impeachment proceedings for one or both of them.

No, for the time being, Cleary was off limits.

* * * * * * *

The double-play combination of Cole to DiMaggio to Grusin had the Republicans ready to light their victory cigars. Joseph Cole would prepare a brief to present to the court within forty-eight hours. There was no getting around the fact that the Floodgate ballots were fraudulent. No matter what vote lead Robinson currently enjoyed, Allen would easily make up the difference once the fraudulent ballots were stricken.

When Scott Grusin called Eddie Cobb with the news, Cobb was effusive with his compliments to Grusin and his legal team for snatching victory from the jaws of defeat. Upon hanging up with Grusin, Cobb immediately called Javier Sanchez to set in motion their strategy for passing their version of the remap. It had previously been fully vetted with Grusin and DiMaggio, who both understood and agreed with the plan.

* * * * * * *

E-MAIL

To: E Party Leadership Distribution
From: Barbara Jenkins
Sent: May 15 9:56 a.m. (CST)
Subject: Conversation with DiMaggio

I also spoke with Senator DiMaggio earlier today to indicate our willingness to discuss the remap. She said her team was close to finalizing their model and asked if we can meet on Wednesday.

In turn, she inquired about our plans for the budget. I told her that we, too, were a few days away and that I would have our staff brief hers with the expectation that she and I would meet afterward.

I did not mention HB1, nor did she. She clearly has to know that it will be our elephant in the room (pun intended) at some point.

I spoke to the Speaker first thing this morning to lay out our parameters for moving ahead with the budget, HB1, and the map. As to the map, he did not flinch when I told him we needed an update in four days instead of the week he had requested.

* * * * * * *

"Mr. Speaker, this is Elaine Richards calling. Sorry I missed you. Please call back when you get this message. I need to bring you up to speed on events, and I have a rather urgent request for some additional information on our favorite topic. I also need to set time for us to meet to discuss strategy as soon as possible."

* * * * * * *

THE BACK BENCH
"If you let it slip, we catch it"
May 15

After over three months of hearings, motions and pleadings, the Illinois Supreme Court today heard closing arguments in *Allen v. Robinson*.

Most observers, particularly those who have been tracking the case from day one, are of the opinion that Tom Robinson's Election Day lead will hold.

Notwithstanding, the recount will immediately turn to consideration of the Floodgate ballots. The court's forensic experts will present their findings tomorrow on why certain ballots cured differently while drying following the sprinkler malfunction at the Board of Elections' storage facilities. The parties will have two days to review the findings. The court will then entertain all related motions and set a hearing schedule if necessary.

In other news...

* * * * * * *

E-MAIL

To: Barbara Jenkins
From: Elizabeth DiMaggio
Sent: May 16 12:17 p.m. (CST)
Subject: Follow-up

Following up on our recent discussion, I am prepared to work to pass meaningful budget legislation in a timely manner. However, I wish to table our discussions regarding redistricting. Thank you.

E-MAIL

To: E Party Leadership Distribution
From: Barbara Jenkins
Sent: May 16 1:01 p.m. (CST)
Subject: FW: Follow-Up

I received a rather cryptic e-mail from Senator DiMaggio today. See below.

Unless anyone objects, I will continue our budget negotiations, but assume that, as far as the Republicans are concerned, both HB1 and the remap are off the table. Mark and I will be meeting with the Speaker tomorrow to discuss his proposal.

For the Speaker, creating the legislative map for the decade to come was akin to a Dickens novel. It was the best of times and the worst of times.

The best of times because, to the extent the demographic and political data was maximized, he would be insuring the legacy of a Democrat-dominated legislature.

The worst of times because, with the pressures of preserving the party's control of seats to the exclusion of its sitting members, there were some longstanding friends whose seats could not be sustained. There were also risks taken in terms of designing new, open districts where the outcomes, although anticipated to yield Democratic victories, could never be assured.

The new map required delicate, one-on-one, member-by-member discussions and negotiations. Despite the rhetoric they fed their constituents, these members were all career politicians with commensurate power and perks. Even their salaries had advanced to the point where state legislators were better paid and pensioned than the significant majority of working stiffs.

All of their political futures were at stake. Unlike every other bill and resolution, it was the most personal and emotional of votes.

On top of which, this would be Speaker David Kennedy's last map. The legacy he had so conscientiously prepared for hung in the balance like a tightrope walker without a net.

* * * * * * *

"Javier, you heard anything about Kennedy's map?"

Javier shook his head at the other end of the phone. He'd never get used to Cobb's lack of social skills.

"Only bits and pieces. He's calling in the reps one by one, as he's always done. It's all cloaked in secrecy—also as usual. This year he doesn't even have Danny Ryan in the room. Just the Speaker and his chief-of-staff. He called me just before the process began to tell me he was grateful for my assistance. He said he'd call me if he needed help with the Hispanic Caucus. Nothing yet."

"And?" Cobb prodded.

"And…I've spoken with most members of the caucus who seem pleased with the districts that have been drawn for them. It's very curious that some of the caucus members for whom we had the most difficulty drawing protected districts appear to be the most satisfied. They refuse to divulge any specifics concerning the boundaries of their new districts, so I have no way of knowing what the Speaker is up to."

"Curious," Cobb said.

Javier could picture Eddie chewing on his cigar. Scratch that. He could *hear* him chewing on his cigar.

The Chairman went on. "No denying Kennedy is a brilliant tactician. Still, I can't imagine we overlooked anything. Are you all ready on your end?"

"Yes, all set," said Javier. "If your information about Floodgate is correct, and I trust it is, I can start selling our map as soon as the news hits."

"Grusin tells me Cole will present his brief the day after tomorrow at the latest. Good luck, Sanchez."

"Yeah," said Javier, seeing himself as Speaker of the House and smiling. "Thanks, Eddie."

* * * * * * *

Joseph Cole bounded up the courthouse stairs with amazing agility and energy. He and his team had just worked over forty straight hours, completing the vote fraud brief he was about to present to the Supreme Court. Nevertheless, the adrenaline was pumping and his sleep-deprived body was humming like a finely tuned Porsche. The brief was spectacular. All of the case law precedent was demonstrably in Allen's favor. The court had no choice but to disregard over two thousand votes for Robinson. It wasn't even close. Never before had Cole researched an issue that was so clearly in favor of the position he was advocating.

Court was called into session. Immediately Joseph Cole rose to address the judges.

Elaine Richards beat him to the punch.

"May we approach the bench, your Honor?" she said.

* * * * * *

THE BACK BENCH
"If you let it slip, we catch it"
May 17

EXTRA EXTRA EXTRA EXTRA EXTRA EXTRA

Just as the court was called into session today, counsel Elaine Richards asked if she could approach the bench and her request was granted. No one has the slightest inclination about what she said and yet the court summarily adjourned to chambers for a closed-door session with both Richards and her counterpart, Joseph Cole, in tow.

I am told that it is exceedingly rare for the entire Supreme Court to meet behind closed doors with counsel and, in this case, all the more rare to the extent that they have now been sequestered for almost five hours.

That's right. For the past five hours, the court has been meeting in executive session without any hint of the purpose or intent of the conference.

As you can imagine, the media throng is crawling all over itself in an attempt to manufacture a story, but not even a good sniff of a rumor has emerged.

In other news…

* * * * * * *

"Mr. Speaker, it's Elaine. I'm wondering if I might meet with you this evening. We've had a very good day."

"Of course. I hope it's not too inconvenient for you to come to my Springfield home. It's the one place I know we can have privacy and will not be interrupted."

"I'll see you at eight thirty, Mr. Speaker."

* * * * * * *

Funny thing about the interplay of adrenaline, sleep deprivation, and a gigantic whack over the head. Elaine Richards had popped Joseph Cole's ego-filled balloon without batting an eye. He was fortunate that he managed to function long enough to pour himself into a cab. Twenty minutes later he barely made it to his couch before collapsing. When he awoke ten hours later, there were over twenty frantic messages from Elizabeth DiMaggio and Robert Allen, all with the same question: What the hell had transpired in chambers?

CHAPTER FORTY-ONE

Nancy Rae Mitchell's calculating, strategizing, manipulating ways were getting her nowhere. She was used to the paradigm where all she had to do was ask for something to get it. The fact that she was stumped when confronted with one Harlan Cleary was unnerving. Disappointing.

It was pissing her off.

The man's particular lack of either brains or brawn presented a unique challenge. Under normal circumstances, Nancy Rae would rise to that challenge with a war cry. This time, she didn't have the time or energy. The only thing going for her was Harlan's devotion to the Speaker—and, to a lesser extent, Danny Ryan.

Accessing Harlan Cleary was not the problem. When he was not at work, he was holding down his regular spot at the Crossroads Tavern, one of Springfield's less desirable redneck hideaways in a metropolitan area teaming with less desirable redneck hideaways.

It was only a question of timing. Should she arrive relatively early before he had downed his first few rounds or relatively late when his tongue might have loosened but his mood might have soured? It was fifty-fifty. She went with early.

She was already in the parking lot when he showed up. She watched him amble into the decrepit joint, then waited an additional fifteen minutes before staging her entry. Aware of her ability to draw attention in any crowd, Nancy Rae had dressed down.

Fortunately, Harlan's favorite stool was on the end of the bar closest to the door. Nancy took the empty seat next to him, slipping onto the stool without fanfare and looking down at the bar as if to say, I'm here, but only a little bit. The tavern was sparsely populated at this hour and would remain so until the live entertainment began playing around ten o'clock, although it was beyond Nancy Rae's ability to comprehend who would want to spend their evenings in this dump.

Harlan Cleary shot Nancy Rae a look. He didn't even bother to disguise the rapid eye-blink of the full body scan he performed.

Jerk.

Nancy Rae's loose clothing, lack of exposed cleavage, and unmade-up face must have done the trick because his brief nod had the enthusiasm of a man who'd just opened a Christmas card from his banker.

Nancy Rae settled in on her rickety stool and offered up a weak smile.

When she made eye contact Cleary seemed to reconsider. Maybe he'd seen through her costume to her body's pluses. Or maybe he was just plain desperate. Either way, for some reason he offered to buy her a beer. Nancy Rae didn't like beer, but she had developed a mean thirst playing her role in this drama and the idea of ordering a chardonnay in this place was an oxymoron.

When the Bud Light arrived she took a sip and grimaced.

She turned to Harlan to thank him. Then she expressed best wishes from Danny Ryan.

Harlan had been raising his glass to her. His arm stopped in mid-air. His already close-set eyes drew together in a frown.

"Who are you?" he said suspiciously. "I don't want no trouble."

"No trouble here," she said, keeping her voice low. "My name is Nancy Rae Mitchell. I work for Danny. People call me the Black Pearl."

For a few minutes they sat in awkward silence as Nancy Rae let it sink in that she was there to do business and would wait for his signal to carry on. She pretended to sip her beer.

Sure enough, in the time it took for Harlan to finish his draft and order another, he'd made up his mind. "Then, what do you want?"

Nancy Rae took her time answering. "Well, here's the thing, Harlan. I need your help. Or should I say that Danny Ryan, and possibly the Speaker, need your help."

The mention of the magic words "Danny" and "Speaker" and "help" stopped Harlan in his tracks. He shifted on his stool, put down his mug, and stared into the grimy mirror over the bar. Slowly, a sly grin appeared on his face. "Anything for my boys," he said.

Nancy Rae leaned in a bit, making sure to keep a modicum of space between herself and any part of his slimy body.

She nodded. "Thank you, Harlan. I appreciate that. And I can see that you're a good guy. That's why I'm going to give it to you straight." She sighed dramatically. "Danny Ryan came to me because he feels you are the only person he can turn to."

Harlan preened.

Nancy Rae felt like gagging.

"But he's confused by the story you told the Speaker, Harlan. That's why he asked me to come talk to you. See if we might, um, go over your recollection of the events together."

Harlan turned to her, face suddenly contorted, his nose an inch away from her face. "What the fuck you saying there? You saying I didn't tell the truth?"

"No, no, of course not," Nancy Rae added quickly. "It's just that, to Danny's recollection, he hasn't spoken to you in over a year. He knows you have a memory like a steel trap." Harlan looked appeased for a second. Then he said, "That's bullshit."

"What's bullshit?"

"I do have a memory like a steel trap," said Cleary. "And as sure as shit did speak to Danny Ryan, and it wasn't no year ago neither."

"See, that's what I mean," said Nancy Rae. "This is exactly what I need to hear from you. To get to the *real* truth. To figure out, *together*, what really happened."

She watched as Harlan processed her words, praying that he wouldn't think too hard.

He was quiet, sipped his beer some more.

Time was running out.

"So, can you help me, Harlan?" Nancy Rae pushed. "Can you walk me through it so we can try to make sense of the situation?"

Harlan took a deep breath. "Look, I'll tell you this once and only once. Danny Ryan calls me and tells me he wants me to cooperate—*fully*, that was his word—with a guy named John Smith, who'll get in touch with me and give me my assignment. A few weeks later, this guy walks in, sits where you're sitting, introduces himself as John Smith, says we have a mutual friend in Chicago. Asks me to step outside to talk." Harlan gave Nancy Rae a sidelong look.

"I'm guessing you know the rest."

Nancy Rae sat back, reeling. Shit. Someone had gone to a lot of trouble to perpetrate this crime. "At least as much as I need to know," she managed. "And you're sure it was Danny Ryan?"

"Fuck, yeah," sneered Harlan. "I'd know that Mick voice anywhere. Besides, his fucking name popped up on my cell when he called. I sure as fuck can read."

Nancy Rae "um-hmmed" noncommittally. Time to take it up a notch. Putting her hand on his thigh, she leaned a bit closer.

Harlan's eyes got big.

"Your memory really is amazing, Harlan. It wouldn't surprise me if you remembered when you got this call from John Smith—er, Danny Ryan."

"Right around Thanksgiving," Harlan said smugly. "I was watching the Bears/Packers game. He shoulda known better than to call when the game's on."

Nancy Rae nodded as if she cared. "Let's just check the date here," she said, punching a few keys on her iPhone. "It says here that game was on November twenty-third and the Packers won in overtime. Would that be the game?"

"That's the one, alright. Fucking Bears had it won six times and gave it back seven. At least they covered the spread." Harlan had suddenly become a little more animated.

Nancy Rae leaned in again. She had to keep his attention.

"Harlan … if I share an … intimate secret with you, can you keep it in confidence?"

Harlan licked his lips. *Not that kind of secret, you jerk!* Her toes curled in revulsion.

"For Danny and the Speaker," she added quickly.

Harlan gave an odd sound between a snort and a puff of air. "Does a bear shit in the woods?"

"In this case," Nancy Rae said, "I sure hope so. Because the thing is, Harlan, on the day of the Bears-Packers game, Danny and I were in Mexico together. You are now the only person other than Danny who knows that. So I'm trusting you.

"Just as you're sure the call came to you during that game, that's how sure I am that Danny and I were fucking each other's brains out. And Harlan, no man has ever gotten out of my bed to make a phone call!"

She had no idea how to read the expression on Harlan's face. But it was quickly followed by a very expressive "holy fucking shit."

* * * * * *

It seemed unfathomable to Elaine Richards that it had only been twelve days since the Speaker had reached out to discuss voter fraud. In some ways, it felt as though a year had passed. In others, it could have been a day. Although she'd called ahead, when she looked at her phone she saw it was almost two hours past her estimated time of arrival and late in the evening. Time clearly had its own agenda these days. She ran a hand through her hair, regretting that she hadn't even taken a minute to put on some lipstick, and rang the doorbell.

"I'm so sorry, David—" she started.

"No, no," said the Speaker. "No need to apologize. I completely understand…in these circumstances…but come in, come in. Can I get you a cup of tea? And then there's someone I'd like you to meet."

"That would be perfect," said Elaine, suddenly uncomfortable. The Speaker trusted someone else enough to join them? She didn't like the sound of that.

As he moved about the kitchen, Elaine couldn't help watching Speaker David Kennedy with fascination. The Speaker was just a man after all, puttering around making tea like any other man, pulling down a mug, setting out some English digestives on a plate. She shook her head to clear it. "Thank you for making yourself available, sir."

"David."

Elaine couldn't help smiling. "David. I know it's late. Seems there is simply not enough time in a day."

Finally, the water had boiled, the Earl Gray tea had been poured, and they were moving into his home office. Elaine was dying to discover the identity of this other guest. Her mind furiously scrolled through the possibilities, but no one individual came to mind. "Elaine," said the Speaker as they turned the corner, "I'd like you to meet Erik Phillips."

Erik Phillips was already standing, holding a glass of what appeared to be wine. He set it down on the coffee table and crossed the room with his hand outstretched.

"Elaine, nice to meet you."

Elaine shook his hand firmly. "Pleasure," she said, not knowing if she meant it yet.

"Erik is my general counsel, Elaine," said the Speaker. "I thought it would be best if he came in person. That way he can ask any questions directly without my having to burden you at a later time."

Elaine's shoulders fell a notch. She must really be tired if she hadn't figured that one out.

"Of course," she said.

"So, Elaine," said the Speaker, "it's in your court."

Elaine swallowed quickly, burning her tongue on the hot tea and cursing to herself.

"Well, David, Erik, I think we had a rather positive outcome in the recount today. Given our unusual attorney-client arrangement, I felt it was imperative to meet before my court appearance tomorrow.

"As I'm sure you heard, Joseph Cole and I met in chambers with the judges today for an extended session." She looked directly at the Speaker. "Thank you for arranging for the judges to recognize me over Cole, by the way. That was a critical maneuver."

The Speaker inclined his head. "Actually, it was Erik here who should be thanked. I'm sure you can appreciate that someone in my position does not ever engage in ex parte communications with the court."

Of course. The faux pas was just one more indicator that Elaine was exhausted.

"Then, thank *you*, Mr. Phillips."

Elaine inclined her head. "Erik. Well, as I anticipated, Cole came loaded for bear. The ballot fraud was obvious, actually, painfully so—"

"Sorry to interrupt," said the Speaker, "but I'd really like to know more about that."

Elaine nodded, sneaking in another bite of her belated dinner of cookies. They were dry as heck, but each crumb was making her stomach a little less frantic. "Certainly. In retrospect, it was a fairly clumsy maneuver. Original ballots all have union bugs on them, which are fairly prominent. The counterfeit ballots have no union bugs. Otherwise, except for the fact that they turn color when wet, they are exact duplicates. Therefore, if we assume it was Chairman Cobb's people who produced the copies, they obviously did so in a right-to-work state."

"Excellent, counselor," said the Speaker, "go on."

"So, back to this morning. Cole solved the riddle easily, too. He'd arrived with a comprehensive brief and was prepared to move immediately to have the ballots stricken. Without exaggerating here, had he been recognized before me, who knows where this might have gone. If nothing else, the story would have been over the airwaves and Internet in the blink of an eye. We would have been forced to play an extended game of catch up."

"And during that time," the Speaker said quietly, "my entire political operation would be run through the shredder."

Elaine nodded. "Once in chambers, I advised the court that vote fraud had been discovered. It had to come from me, or Cole and his brief would have eventually dominated the session.

"I also immediately alerted the court to the fact that we have a source who has informed us that the fraud occurred in the weeks following the election—and that we had proof." Elaine looked at both men. "Honestly, for a minute I thought poor Joseph Cole was going to have a stroke.

"The judges bought our argument. My discovery motion still had at least one and a half hours of time remaining. Thanks again to you, Erik.

"Then we called the board of elections. They did a preliminary run that confirmed our suspicions."

"And, for that, Elaine," said the Speaker, "we shall be eternally grateful. Your insight has been brilliant. That one is all yours."

"Well, let's just say the bad guy's strategy had a major flaw—and we got lucky. Very, very lucky."

Elaine drove to her hotel with one hand on the wheel and the other gripping a slice of pizza she'd picked up on the way. Nothing, not the caloric content or even the tomato sauce landing on her white silk blouse, could keep her from groaning with bliss at her first bite. In her head, she went over the conclusion of her meeting with Erik Phillips and the Speaker.

To wrap up, she'd outlined where they stood. She had explained that when court convened in the morning she'd again move for expedited discovery, assuming it would be granted. Chief Justice Woehrmann, Cole, and she would proceed to the Board of Elections where the totals would be rerun in their presence. The totals could only confirm today's findings.

"After I make my motion," she'd told them, "Cole will file his brief. The court will set a hearing date for the next day. If nothing changes, at that hearing the court will rule in favor of Cole's brief—but also find that the fraud occurred *after* the ballots were cast and counted on Election Day. Then Tom Robinson Jr. will officially become governor of Illinois."

"And about our Mr. Cleary?" the Speaker had asked dryly.

Elaine had understood. This was the missing piece, the one that potentially affected the Speaker the most.

"The court will rule that the question of any criminal election fraud is not properly before them," she'd told him. "It is for the criminal justice system, whether state or federal, to determine if the facts support that a crime has been committed—that's if the local prosecutor wishes to bring charges."

Then she had suggested that even under the most expedited timetable and notwithstanding the outrage that would certainly be expressed by the Republicans, he would have sufficient time to plan for that contingency.

"Let's hope so," the Speaker had said quietly. "For now, I am eternally indebted to you, Ms. Richards."

"Elaine," she'd said, and the Speaker smiled.

* * * * * * *

Joseph Cole would have preferred to be anywhere but where he was. Even the briar patch would have been a step up. As it was, he was in the midst of a pack of thorny sore losers.

Robert Allen had spent the preceding days setting the stage for a grand victory. He'd begun the process of creating his transition team. Now he sat with his head in his hands.

Senator Elizabeth DiMaggio was scrambling to finalize her assault on the remap and the budget, not to mention her ultimate ascension to the presidency of the Senate. Her usually taut nerves were strung tighter than a drum. You could see it in the deep circles under, and the haunted expression in her eyes.

Although his victory might have been more elusive, Scott Grusin's dreams of a day when, under the leadership of a Republican governor, Illinois might be in play for a presidential election, had now taken on the decided fogginess of the Scottish moors.

CHAPTER FORTY-TWO

THE BACK BENCH
"If you let it slip, we catch it"
May 20

EXTRA EXTRA EXTRA EXTRA EXTRA EXTRA

Joseph Cole, attorney for Robert Allen in the recount case, dropped an atomic bomb today when he filed a brief with the Illinois Supreme Court today alleging massive vote fraud leading to Tom Robinson's victory total.

According to Cole's brief, the now infamous Floodgate ballots were all fraudulent and all represented votes cast for Robinson. Exhibit A to the brief contains a replica of an authentic ballot showing a union bug printer's label in the lower left corner, whereas Exhibit B contains a replica of a Floodgate ballot but without the union bug.

Unless Robinson's counsel can refute either the facts or legal precedent cited therein, this case has taken an abrupt U-turn.

In response to Cole's brief, attorney Elaine Richards requested additional expedited discovery. It is unclear what the purpose might be other than to somehow discredit the facts presented in Cole's brief.

And around we go.

In other news…

* * * * * * *

An invigorated Speaker Kennedy entered the capitol building. He was on a mission. The preeminent rule of politics, to pass a bill as soon as you have the votes and before any slip away, had to be addressed. Things could change before you could say "voter fraud." If ever there was a session in which timing was everything, this was it.

Elaine Richards—brilliant woman—was not only about to win the recount for Robinson, she had achieved the most favorable outcome possible. He now had a two-to-three day head start on the court's ultimate resolution and eleven days till the end of the session.

At last the map was within his grasp.

His first call had been to Danny Ryan to lift his house arrest status. Danny, who had sounded wounded and depressed, had heaved a great sigh upon hearing the news. "Thank God," was all he'd said. Then he'd driven through the night in order to join the Speaker by morning.

The Speaker checked his pocket watch. Ryan would be here any moment and in time for their meeting with Barbara Jenkins and Mark Stone to finalize the details for the map.

The Speaker offered a heartier than usual greeting to the guard as he bypassed the metal detector. His meetings with members to date had gone exceedingly well. Whatever changes Jenkins and Stone might demand, he felt he could sell the final product. At some point relatively soon, he would be compelled to deal with Javier Sanchez. Either way, based on his discussions to date, he was certain he could hold the Hispanic Caucus.

* * * * * * *

E-MAIL

To: E Party Leadership Distribution
From: Mark Stone
Sent: May 21 6:00 p.m. (CST)
Subject: Map negotiations

Our map team met with Danny Ryan earlier today to review the Speaker's draft proposal. Ryan claims the map is drawn to protect approximately 50 Democratic seats and roughly 25 Republican seats in the House and 26/12 in the Senate. Taking him at his word, this would leave 43 competitive seats in the House and 21 in the Senate.

As you are aware, our model was drawn to be more top-down democratic and created an estimated 60 competitive seats in the House and 32 in the Senate. No matter what data is used to draw the map, the Chicago-centric districts are going to be won by Democrats and certain suburban and downstate districts will always lean Republican.

Assuming we agree with Ryan's representations, the question will be how many competitive seats we can insist on while still allowing the Speaker to structure his roll call. The same goes for President Welk in the Senate.

Other than bargaining for the maximum number of competitive seats in each chamber, I assume we let the Speaker decide how he wants to structure the balance.

Bottom line: We're very close!

E-MAIL

To: E Party Leadership Distribution
From: Barbara Jenkins
Sent: May 21 10:11 p.m. (CST)
Subject: DiMaggio update

FYI: I received a call from Senator DiMaggio today. Apparently, she wants to schedule a chat about year-end issues, including the map. She must have received a jolt of reality from Joseph Cole!

* * * * * * *

THE BACK BENCH
"If you let it slip, we catch it"
May 24

EXTRA EXTRA EXTRA EXTRA EXTRA EXTRA

Tom Robinson Jr. proclaimed governor!!!

The lengthy, contentious, and, of late, suspenseful recount has ended. The Illinois Supreme Court issued its final ruling today in the matter of *Allen v. Robinson.*

In the weeds of the Order, we learn that the final margin of victory was ninety-nine votes. A landslide by any other name.

The court also gave lengthy attention to Floodgate. They threw Joseph Cole and Robert Allen a ceremonial bone by acknowledging that all of the fraudulent ballots would be subject to disqualification.

However, it was demonstrated by clear and convincing evidence that the fraud occurred after Election Day and after the Board of Election's canvas.

Apparently, the vote totals for Tom Robinson from both election night and the Floodgate ballots remained unchanged. However, it was discovered that the vote totals from the precincts in question were different for all other candidates on the ballot. Whoever perpetrated the fraud was either very sloppy or was convinced that the recount would strictly be limited to the governor's race.

In the press conference following the court's ruling, a triumphant Tom Robinson Jr. credited his counsel, Elaine Richards, with having saved the day.

In other news…

* * * * * * *

Hell hath no fury like a Texas party chairman scorned.

Chairman Eddie Cobb's initial reaction to the Allen case ruling was to inflict his version of Hurricane Katrina on his office. This was followed by a series of phone calls to his senior staff to castigate and berate them for any manner of wrongdoing.

Still frothing, the next call was to Representative Javier Sanchez, on whom Cobb unleashed a torrent of foul rage unlike one Javier had ever received.

Cobb began by heaping blame for all the E Party's successes over the past two years at Javier's door and didn't stop until he'd threatened him with all sorts of individual and career-related harm if he did not "cooperate to the fullest" and help him "bring down" the Speaker.

Javier congratulated himself on his restraint even as the smoke trailed out from his ears. At long last, once Eddie had disconnected, Javier simply went back to strategizing his plan B: support of the Speaker and the passing of the map.

Abandoning Chairman Eddie Cobb was the easiest thing he'd ever done.

* * * * * * *

Nancy Rae was lamenting the approach of summer and the session's impending adjournment. A few short weeks ago she and Danny had been talking about endless summer days and nights together, about plotting their escape from the bonds of politics. Now, he was back in the bosom of the Speaker's endgame and she was at a loss as to how to approach him. He'd been back in Springfield for almost a week and still had not called. Was it her move?

* * * * * * *

E-MAIL

To: E Party Leadership Distribution
From: Barbara Jenkins
Sent: May 25 7:56 p.m. (CST)
Subject: Meeting with delegation

Mark and I had a very spirited meeting today with our entire legislative delegation. We have much to be proud of. Although they challenged us on many points, they are fully engaged and the meeting concluded with general agreement moving forward.

In addition to Mark's presentation on the remap, our legislative leaders on both the budget and HB1 presented detailed updates.

With respect to the map, the discussion of election law and demographic modeling was somewhat akin to a deer in headlights. The sense of the group is to trust Mark and his cartographers on details, while pressuring for a map with the maximum possible number of open/contestable seats.

The budget discussion caught us off guard, though. Our members are willing to vote only for a budget that addresses our fiscal priorities. They are not interested in the Speaker's vanilla, wait-til-next-year approach.

Representative Kubik, Senator Martin, and I have been given a set of negotiating parameters on a series of spending targets. If we make sufficient progress, we will have our votes for a structured roll call. The caucus is also willing to vote to waive the posting requirements and other transparency safeguards if the right deal can be negotiated.

Otherwise, our group is content with the consequences of an overtime budget battle. Kinda like the old days. Reminds me of what got us here in the first place.

E-MAIL

To: E Party Leadership Distribution
From: Barbara Jenkins
Sent: May 26 10:10 a.m. (CST)
Subject: DiMaggio meeting

We had a surprisingly productive meeting, although DiMaggio remains totally guarded with respect to the map. My sense is that she is leery of what deals we have already cut with the Speaker and that her role may be solely as spoiler.

On the budget, she recommended cuts that are aligned with many of the proposals we have in our shopping cart, which makes me wonder if we can get more aggressive with a three-way structured roll call. I plan to call a leader's meeting to discuss options. Tom will attend and lead. By the way, we have blown through our sunshine deadlines on the budget.

As for HB1, my suspicion is that it will be unshackled now that the recount has been decided. Although Senator DiMaggio remains opposed, I think Tom's meeting with Allen will help.

E-MAIL

To: Barbara Jenkins
From: Danny Ryan
Sent: May 27 3:13 p.m. (CST)
Subject: End of session

The Speaker asked me to advise you that he has obtained the votes necessary to move the most recent legislative package, specifically including the E Party's proposed changes to the map and budget. However, as to the budget, he insists that Republican votes be included in the structured roll call.

* * * * * * *

Representative Sanchez was becoming…how could he put it?…unsettled. The Speaker had been meeting one-on-one with members for over a week to discuss the map and end-of-session voting. As a member of the Speaker's leadership team, Javier had expected some courtesy regarding strategy. The Speaker had asked him to assist on remap modeling early on, but not of late. He'd give it one more day. No reason to rock that boat quite yet.

* * * * * *

THE BACK BENCH
"If you let it slip, we catch it"
May 28

Robert Allen appeared at the capitol yesterday for a meeting with Governor Robinson. Details of their meeting remain unknown. At the ensuing press conference, the two indicated that the heated recount was behind them. Allen pledged his support for the Governor's pet project, the education bill.

With Allen's support, there is speculation that passage of HB1 is all but assured. Although Allen has been a businessman his entire life and never held elected office, even in defeat he remains the symbolic figurehead of the Republican Party and his support still carries weight.

At the other end of the spectrum sits Senator Elizabeth DiMaggio, the defacto party leader. She may be reluctant to hand Governor Robinson a victory. As the prominence and power of the E Party expands, that of the Republicans continues to wane.

The Republicans need victories that arguably come at the expense of the E Party, the Democrats, or both. Preventing passage of HB1 fits that description.

In other news…

* * * * * * *

Even a blind pig can stumble across an acorn, thought Senator Elizabeth DiMaggio as she perused *The Back Bench*. Carson had, for once, read her mind. She desperately needed a victory. Fortunately, Barbara Jenkins had opened the door.

During the many years of Democratic dominance, David Kennedy would never, ever, ever have considered the budget cuts and programmatic changes Elizabeth had discussed with Jenkins.

However, the combination of E Party votes and Republican votes could pass any legislation. Getting Kennedy and Welk to call bills featuring her conservative fingerprints had previously been unthinkable, but that's where Jenkins and the E Party would carry the burden.

Pass a conservative budget and steal the map. The price: let Robinson have his precious HB1.

The hourglass was running down on the session, though. Was there sufficient time to pull it off? Or, better yet, was there a benefit to derailing the entire process and forcing the session to overtime?

Probably not. For once, DiMaggio had Kennedy in her sights. She would so enjoy pulling that trigger. While sugarplum fairies danced in Senator DiMaggio's head on the west side of the Capitol, Speaker David Kennedy was envisioning a rather nice Christmas in May for himself and his party.

This particular session, with all of its Shakespearean twists, turns, and drama was wrapping up just as he would have scripted—with a nice bow on top. His one-on-ones had produced the votes he needed for his map, even with the E Party's changes. A few Democratic members of the legislature would not appreciate the last-minute changes, but he could always smooth things over with promises of sufficient campaign funding and staff support to allay any new fears.

As for the budget, he could afford to leave Barbara Jenkins, the E Party, and even Elizabeth DiMaggio a few crumbs. While he could never publically concede their points without incurring the wrath of his most important constituencies, particularly the unions, the changes they were insisting upon were prudent and fiscally sound.

At the end of the day, Speaker Kennedy had the ability to sell them. It wasn't as if the liberal factions of the party had anywhere else to go. At least not yet.

* * * * * * *

<u>E-MAIL</u>
To: Atlas, General
From: Barbara Jenkins
Sent: May 28 12:00 p.m. (CST)
Subject: Tom?

Tom was a no-show at today's budget negotiations with the legislative leaders. He called me just before the meeting was to start and begged off. His exact quote was: "You can handle it. In fact, it's better in your hands." He hasn't returned any of my calls.

On the positive side, bringing Republicans to the table has softened the Speaker on some key issues. I don't want to jinx the process, but I think we're close to a very favorable end-of-session legislative package.

CHAPTER FORTY-THREE

When Representative Javier Sanchez finally saw the Speaker's map and saw that his district had been eliminated—*eliminated!*—his political life flashed in front of him. The Speaker made some pathetic noise that this was the best map for the party; that he would clear a place on the statewide ballot for Javier to run for comptroller or treasurer during the following general election cycle. Yada, yada, yada. He even suggested that, in the alternative, the mayor had agreed to offer Javier an aldermanic seat created for him in the City of Chicago's remap. Javier easily read between the lines: "Hasta la vista, baby!"

The first thing he did was call Eddie Cobb and unleash a torrent of Hispanic expletives.

"Whoa, there, cowboy," Cobb said at Javier's foul-mouthed introduction. "You're beginning to sound like me.

"So, our illustrious Speaker solves his map problems by pushing you out. You think he's on to us?"

Javier had given into a dire need to vent his anger and frustration when he'd called the chairman. He regretted it already. Still, who else was as conniving, as connected ... as without compunction?

"With Kennedy, you never know," Javier told him, running out of steam. "And you'll never find out."

"Don't be so quick there, Javier," said Eddie. "Maybe, just maybe, there's a way."

Javier's heart rate picked up again. He could sense the Joker's evil wheels turning.

"I heard from Scott Grusin that the E Party has made overtures to Elizabeth DiMaggio concerning the map. At the time she hadn't responded—said she didn't know where you stood or whether you could deliver the Democratic votes they'll need to override Kennedy. She said you hadn't responded either. Frankly, I thought you decided to cut a deal with Kennedy. Wouldn't have blamed you if you had."

"No deals," said Javier, uncomfortable with this revelation to Cobb. "But I did want to see what he was offering before talking to her."

"Sure, sure, I get it," said Eddie. "But, now that you know what he's offering, I need to know where you stand, Javier, and I need to know now."

* * * * * * *

Javier turned to the one person who knew him best in this arena: Nancy Rae Mitchell. Her guidance was always unwaveringly unbiased and accurate.

Nancy Rae was surprised that Javier had lost his district, but thought the Speaker's offer was intriguing. Running statewide was a great opportunity and many representatives had abandoned Springfield for aldermanic positions. In terms of issues, it amounted to trading education and transportation for street cleaning and trash pickup. So what? He'd avoid the schlep to Springfield, be paid better as an alderman, and have a second pension plan.

Javier thought about what Nancy Rae said. Her counsel was sound, but she didn't know enough about the backdrop. He couldn't tell her that Eddie Cobb had no interest in the future prospects of a Chicago alderman or state comptroller, or that living at home year-round would conflict with his sex life with Carla Hilton. Javier already knew he'd made his deal with the devil and that there was no turning back.

What really surprised Nancy Rae was that Javier had called to beg—yes, *beg*—for her to find out from Danny what was "really" going on. Amazingly, Javier's outreach to her, although filled with mixed news for him, had solved Nancy Rae's dilemma. He had supplied her with the perfect excuse. Interceding on Javier's behalf had given her a face-saving reason to call Danny Ryan.

Her hands shook as she pulled up his number and pushed "send."

* * * * * *

E-MAIL

To: Barbara, K.C., General
From: Atlas
Sent: May 28 9:52 p.m. (MST)
Subject: Tom

I spoke with Tom. I am uncomfortable with his tone. I've been here before with him a few times. Not sure what's going on, so I'm flying to Chicago to meet with him. He told me he didn't attend the budget meeting because he didn't want to get in Barbara's way. He is very concerned that HB1 will not pass.

* * * * * *

THE BACK BENCH
"If you let it slip, we catch it"
May 29

In a session already strange for its lack of action, we are heading into the last days without so much as a good rumor of the endgame. Remap dominated sessions are notorious for tension and last-minute angling over favorable line drawing, but the members appear remarkably calm.

It's known that the Speaker held one-on-one sessions with Democrats to discuss map options and Barbara Jenkins has held a few extended caucus meetings with the E Party. As for the Republicans, their time seems to be devoted to wound-licking over the Allen case.

In other news...

* * * * * * *

E-MAIL

To: E Party Leadership Distribution
From: Barbara Jenkins
Sent: May 29 10:16 a.m. (CST)
Subject: End-of-session deal

I met with the Speaker and Senator DiMaggio this morning to finalize the end-of-session deal. Later, I met with our entire caucus to review all its elements.

The budget has been sufficiently revised to include cuts and program changes proposed by us and the Republicans. I'm not sure why the Speaker was so quick to acquiesce, but then again, he is exceedingly pleased with the map.

As you are aware, Senator DiMaggio was furious that we cut a deal with the Speaker over the map, but she well knows that she was very late to the game.

HB1 will pass, with Getting to 21 fully intact. Tom almost fell off his chair when I told him.

The last two puzzle pieces were the order in which the bills would be passed by the legislature, and the number of votes per caucus to get to the required majority vote.

As to the structured roll calls, our caucus is "all in on each bill." As you can imagine, there will be no Republican votes on the map. Conversely, the Republicans will supply the bulk of the remaining votes needed to pass the budget.

As for HB1, to hear the Speaker and Senator DiMaggio talk, I wouldn't be surprised if we come close to a unanimous vote in the senate. Quite remarkable given the long and winding road it has taken to get to this point.

As for sequencing, I learned a few more Governing 101 lessons, Illinois style. To ensure that all three measures are passed and that Tom signs all three, there will be language added to each measure that says none of them become law unless all become law.

All of this has been well scripted for the final two days of session with committee hearings and floor action pre-scheduled.

This has all been quite fascinating. Keep your fingers crossed and keep the champagne on ice!

* * * * * * *

THE BACK BENCH
"If you let it slip, we catch it"
May 30

In an amazing and rare sequence of press conferences, the Democrats, Republicans, and E Partiers announced their intentions to advance a budget, an education package, and remap legislation.

Each press conference was a veritable love fest, and it appears as though each measure will pass with structured roll calls.

The Republicans seem exceedingly pleased to have finally imposed some conservative, fiscal, and monetary principles on the budget. The Democrats seem exceedingly pleased with the map, although they concede that in neither the House nor the Senate will they have a clear shot at regaining majority status.

Finally, the E Party seems exceedingly pleased that their crown jewel education plan will finally become law.

In other news…

THE BACK BENCH
"If you let it slip, we catch it"
May 31

As advertised, the budget and HB1 passed in both Houses yesterday and now sit on the governor's desk awaiting his signature.

The Back Bench has learned that a major signing ceremony is planned for early next week and that HB1 will become the first piece of legislation ever signed by Governor Tom Robinson. It has all the makings of a media circus, but he and the E Party have earned it.

The last day of session will be devoted to the map. Evidently, Barbara Jenkins negotiated for the Republicans to be allowed all the floor time they need in debate to lament the process used in designing the map. Of course, they will then be voted into ten years of political exile!

In other news...

CHAPTER FORTY-FOUR

THE BACK BENCH
"If you let it slip, we catch it"
May 31

EXTRA EXTRA EXTRA EXTRA EXTRA EXTRA

Unbelievable!!

The Illinois remap failed to receive the required number of votes in the Illinois House this afternoon.

Representative Javier Sanchez gave an impassioned speech on the floor, decrying the failure of the map to protect the interests of Latino voters across the state. It was later revealed that Representative Sanchez was not given a district under the map and had managed to pull all the Hispanic votes.

This is the last scheduled session day and if the map fails, so too will the budget and HB1.

After today, a three-fifths vote is required to pass the budget. That will never happen without Republican support. Does the phrase "when hell freezes over" ring a bell? Or, in this case, when elephants fly!

The Speaker was reportedly meeting with the Hispanic Caucus as *The Back Bench* went to press. We will issue updates as they occur and will tweet and blog every rumor fit to print and then some.

There are fewer than seven hours left, but don't count out the Speaker. Ever!

In other news…

* * * * * *

As soon as the Hispanics had played their little game in the House, the Speaker immediately sprang into action. Although unanticipated, this was not the first time legislators had banded together to exert eleventh-hour leverage over the process and it would not be the last.

Such uproar was usually over the budget. Whether the Black Caucus, the Hispanic Caucus, the downstate caucus, the suburban caucus, or the Conference of Women Legislators, there was invariably some last-minute funding crisis demanding attention. The grievance would be aired. The Speaker would meet with the group in concern. The train would be put back on the tracks.

Accordingly, the Speaker called the entire Hispanic Caucus, Senate members included, to his office, with the lone exception of Representative Javier Sanchez. Along with the Senate president, he sat and listened patiently to expressions of outrage at the treatment of Representative Sanchez.

Just as patiently, the Speaker responded.

He reminded them that the map they needed to vote for provided each member of the caucus, other than Representative Sanchez, with a new district that consisted of at least 60-plus percent Democratic voters. Their re-elections were all but guaranteed.

"Yes," he told them, "it is true that Representative Sanchez's current district was cannibalized to make your new districts stronger. I could draw a district for Representative Sanchez, but each of you would then have new districts with significantly fewer than sixty percent Democratic voters. Your Latino majorities would become pluralities. I strongly suggest that each of you avoid that risk."

At this point, he asked Danny Ryan to distribute to each Representative a handout of their projected new district with an overlay of the district they would have if the alternative accommodating

Sanchez were favored. Each handout also included a demographic breakout to back up his statements. He knew that self-preservation would win the day, but he also understood that the Sanchez-imposed guilt complex needed attending to. Most important, there was no way Javier Sanchez had told them about the options the Speaker had put on the table.

"Further," he said, "I selected Representative Sanchez to suffer this fate because he is, in my opinion, a rising star in the party with an excellent chance of becoming the first successful statewide Latino candidate. He has been offered my full support in the next general election. Alternatively, the mayor will carve an aldermanic seat for him when the city completes its own remap."

The body language in the room shifted from hostile to neutral, and the Speaker drew a breath, satisfied that he had thwarted the uprising. Master of the situation that he was, he immediately asked for a show of support for the map and had Danny call roll to ensure there was no room for error.

Prior to meeting with the Hispanic Caucus, the Speaker had called Barbara Jenkins to assure her the situation was under control. Following this meeting, his first call was again to Barbara. She was a gifted rookie, but had never experienced the roller coaster effect of last-minute gamesmanship and he needed her to keep the E Party Caucus in check.

* * * * * *

Javier Sanchez and Eddie Cobb were anything but rookies. Last-minute gamesmanship was their strength. The Speaker would pass the remap bill in the House, but it might still be vulnerable in the Senate. They needed to create doubt and they were ready.

As the House went into session, Javier and Carla sprang into action. Over the span of two hours, they met separately with each of the members of the Hispanic Caucus from the Senate. Javier showed each the outline of a new district totally different from the Speaker's. He explained that he could protect all of the Hispanics, including himself, but at the expense of the Blacks.

Carla Hilton was there at the back end of the one-two punch to explain her views concerning the constitutionality of the Speaker's map. She knew the Supreme Court would never overturn it, but the Senators did not. Especially in the heat of the moment. She and Javier also chose her outfit wisely, assuming correctly that a pair of perky nipples peeking out from a provocative blouse would help distract the mostly male senators from the issue and be just the touch the situation called for.

They left their meetings knowing that each Senator was still likely to vote for the Speaker's map. They also knew they had created sufficient doubt and weakened the Senators' resolve. There was a viable alternative for their consideration being offered by a trusted friend. And Carla Hilton was smoking hot.

* * * * * *

THE BACK BENCH
"If you let it slip, we catch it"
May 31

EXTRA EXTRA EXTRA EXTRA EXTRA EXTRA

The House has been called back into session at 7 p.m. to reconsider the vote on the remap. The Senate is scheduled to reconvene at 9 p.m. It is safe to assume the Speaker has redirected the thinking of his Latino renegades.

One additional note of interest is that Representative Sanchez and Senator DiMaggio have called a press conference for 8 p.m. to unveil an alternative map design. Not sure what's up, but this unusual political alliance will definitely draw an audience.

In other news…

* * * * * * *

"They're too late," the Speaker assured Barbara Jenkins. "The votes are locked down. I will personally be on the floor of the Senate to handle any situation that arises. Besides, if we get too close to midnight, we can always stop the clock."

Funny, Barbara thought. I've worked with the man for months and he rarely ever smiles. Then, in the most heated of moments, he develops a sense of humor.

Only the Speaker's comment was anything but humorous. If need be, as had actually been done in the past, they would pretend to suspend the laws of nature by literally stopping the clock at 11:59 p.m.

* * * * * * *

THE BACK BENCH
"If you let it slip, we catch it"
June 1

Unbelievable. Simply *unbelievable!*

For those of you who crashed before the late-night monologues last night, you missed the performance of a lifetime. To set the stage:

4:40 p.m. The legislation that has been crafted by Speaker Kennedy to maximize the number of Democratic seats in the legislature for the decade to follow comes upshort in the House because the Hispanic Caucus boycotts. The Latinos are showing solidarity to Representative Sanchez, who apparently has no seat in this game of musical chairs.

5:30 p.m. The Speaker meets with the entire Hispanic Caucus, both House and Senate members. The Speaker apparently works his usual magic because the House is called back into session as soon as the meeting breaks.

7:00 p.m. The House convenes to consider SB603, the remap legislation. This time, all Hispanic Democratic members (other than Representative Sanchez, who votes present) vote yes. The bill passes and it immediately goes to the Senate.

8:00 p.m. A joint press conference is called by Senator DiMaggio and Representative Sanchez. At the press conference, they unveil an alternative remap proposal. They also boldly proclaim that they have the votes to pass their version if Senate President Welk will let it be heard in the Senate. Under intense questioning by the press, including yours truly, Representative Sanchez staunchly defends his mutinous actions. The centerpiece of his argument is that Kennedy has sold out the Democrats to the E Party. In particular, he calls out Kennedy for using his influence to elect Tom Robinson. He also suggests Kennedy has conspired with the Supreme Court to ensure Robinson's victory. True or not, it played well on the Twitter meter.

9:00 p.m. The Senate convenes to vote on SB603. For the first time anyone can remember, the Speaker is present in the Senate Chamber to observe the vote and is seen actively engaged in discussion with various Democratic Senators, particularly the amigos.

9:30 p.m. In the middle of the debate, Represent-ative Sanchez enters the Senate Chambers. He approaches Senator Ortiz, Head of the Senate Latino Caucus, and, following a short conversation, the Senator requests a brief recess so that the Hispanic senators can caucus on a matter of "extreme urgency." This is a highly irregular request, but they are granted fifteen minutes.

9:45 p.m. After fifteen minutes, the Hispanic senators have not returned and the chair asks the sergeant-at-arms to locate them. The sergeant returns empty handed and the chamber erupts in confusion.

10:30 p.m. As the chair is pounding his gavel to request order, Senator DiMaggio rises to ask for a quorum call and, upon its passage, moves that the Senate be called into session. There are forty-seven Senators present, more than enough to transact business. She does this knowing that the remap bill cannot pass without the votes of the missing Senators. She asks the president to call her version of the remap. Request denied.

12:30 a.m. The Hispanic senators do not return until 12:30 a.m., long after the deadline for passage of the bill by simple majority vote. Knowing this, Senator DiMaggio asks the chair to confirm that it is 12:30 a.m. on June 1. The news channel video is running. The chair has no alternative but to concede her point. At that moment, every soul in the capitol with a pulse is either in the gallery or the hallways contiguous to the Senate chamber.

12:40 a.m. Senator Ortiz enters the chamber and seeks leave of the chair to address the body. He then drops the bombshell! Senator Ortiz announces that he has been advised by Representative Sanchez that he has obtained evidence proving the Speaker was directly involved in the Floodgate fraud.

Need I explain the ensuing pandemonium. And since words cannot do it justice, video of the entire scene can be found on *The Back Bench* blog.

So, boys and girls, the Illinois Legislature has failed to pass a map. Since they were linked at the hip, this means both the budget and HB1 are also in limbo. Incredibly, the Speaker has been accused of being an accomplice to a felony. If true, we could be heading for an impeachment.

Unbelievable. Simply *unbelievable!!!!*

CHAPTER FORTY-FIVE

THE BACK BENCH
"If you let it slip, we catch it"
June 4

Unlike any time since this reporter has been covering Illinois politics, state government is totally paralyzed. There are just over three weeks before the state's budget must be in place on July 1. It is impossible to see how that happens.

Speaker Kennedy has yet to respond to the accusations of his criminal activities related to Floodgate. Representative Sanchez has allegedly met with the attorney general to share whatever evidence he possesses. Even if Sanchez is not able to sway the Democratic A.G., the political damage has been done. The Speaker carries the burden of clearing his name. In the interim, the General Assembly is rudderless.

Many are looking to Governor Robinson to demonstrate leadership. However, he has essentially been painted with the same brush. The Republicans are shouting accusations from every rooftop, demanding investigations and resignations.

Reliable sources indicate that the governor has granted an interview to Kathryn Collins, host of the nationally syndicated Emmy-winning talk show. Robinson appeared on her show to announce his candidacy for governor and again after the election to talk about his hopes and plans for his administration.

Both appearances were home runs for Robinson. Having him again take the stage with Collins makes sense, particularly from a public relations perspective. Hopefully, he can effectively use it as a platform to lay the groundwork for the legislature to regroup and begin working toward solutions that will avoid a fiscal calamity.

In other news…

* * * * * * *

Collins: We are joined today by the governor of Illinois, Tom Robinson. Tom was recently declared the winner of a highly publicized and protracted election recount. He is also the de facto standard bearer of the E Party, perhaps at this point the most successful third political party in American history. Tom, welcome back.

Robinson: Thank you, Kathryn. It is always a pleasure to be on your show.

Collins: So, how does it feel to finally have your victory from last November upheld by the Illinois Supreme Court?

Robinson: In some ways it's as if the weight of the world has been lifted, but at the same time it's as if the weight never left and has only intensified.

Collins: How so?

Robinson: Obviously, to finally be declared the winner of the election is a great thrill. The case was touch-and-go and really too close to call until the very end. I owe a deep debt to my chief counsel, Elaine Richards, and her entire team of attorneys and staff.

However, as you may be aware, there were some very controversial aspects of the case, and it would appear that there may be a criminal vote fraud investigation. Accusations of the vote fraud have recently spilled over to the state's legislature, and very important legislation now hangs in the balance.

So, in some ways, the recount remains an albatross.

Collins: I know you have asked that questions related to any possible criminal investigation be avoided, but I'm wondering if you can expand on the albatross, as you call it.

Robinson: Well, let's hope I don't get struck by lightning. Anyway, as most people know, the Illinois Speaker of the House, David Kennedy, is one of the country's most dominant political figures. I may be governor, but, at least historically, not much happens in Illinois government without his blessing.

As the Illinois Legislature headed into the last evening of its spring session, three pieces of essential legislation still hung in the balance— the budget, the decennial legislative redistricting required by the constitution, and an education reform bill that was the centerpiece of my campaign for governor.

Just before scheduled adjournment, as the legislature was about to vote to pass the final piece, a somewhat unknown legislator accused the Speaker of playing a role in the vote fraud from the recount case. The accusation was timed perfectly to derail the final vote, and because of that, all three pieces failed.

Collins: How can something like that happen and what are the next steps?

Robinson: To say the least, the past five months have been quite an education. It has been said that no one should watch sausage or legislation being made. Suffice it to say that, after the lessons of the past few months, that metaphor is an understatement.

To get these three critical pieces of legislation to pass, my chief-of-staff, Lieutenant Governor Barbara Jenkins, worked with both the Democrats and Republicans to weave a very complex web of votes. Bottom line is that they were all linked in the end, so it was either all pass or all fail.

As it stands today, the state of Illinois has no budget, no legislative remap, and no education reform.

As far as moving ahead, the constitution of Illinois now requires a three-fifths vote to pass the budget, and there is a legislative formula for how the legislative remap process moves forward. The education bill becomes the hostage for purposes of negotiations.

Collins: Sounds like quite a mess. How do you see this playing out?

Robinson: As of a week ago, the budget requires a sixty percent vote to pass. That means nothing passes unless Democrats and Republicans join the E Party in voting on these issues. From what I've learned these past months, politics trumps good government.

Collins: Can you give me an example?

Robinson: Take our education reform initiative. It was developed by some of the best minds in the industry and enjoys amazing support from teachers and other education professionals. My pet project, Getting to 21, has a chance to transform the lives of millions of our most vulnerable children. And yet, it languishes in the Illinois Legislature from a series of political game playing.

The most recent episode was the attack campaign launched by people hiding behind the façade of Super PACs. It was all about politics and stopping the vote in the Senate. Like everything in our political world these days, it was negative, negative, negative. When does it stop? When do we start protecting and educating our children?

Collins: I certainly share your concerns about the sorry state of American politics. Sentiments I am sure the audience shares as well.

Robinson: It gets worse. If there is no budget by June 30, by law the state is not authorized to spend any funds in its fiscal year beginning July 1. There are certain essential services that are protected, but most workers stop getting paid and things start to shut down. It's not like the federal government where there's often a series of resolutions to fund government in the absence of a budget.

Collins: You do not sound hopeful.

Robinson: Actually, I'm not. I ran for office to advance many causes, especially education reform to help our kids. But the system is daunting and has worn on me, mentally and physically. I grew up with Jack Kennedy's "ask not what your country can do for you" speech, but all I've seen so far is the opposite. The great majority of the people I meet with want to know what government and Tom Robinson can do for them.

So, Kathryn, since I originally declared my candidacy on your program, I'd like to take this moment to say that I am resigning as governor.

Collins: Governor, did I just understand you correctly. You're … quitting?

Robinson: You know, Kathryn, I hate that word quitting. It was just a few months ago that I pledged to do everything in my power to serve the people of Illinois. It's just that, well, it's not in me, and I have come to realize that the people of Illinois deserve a leader with the potential to make a difference. Our Lieutenant Governor, Barbara Jenkins, is that person. So, I don't think of it as quitting. More like getting out of the way.

Collins: Governor, I'm shocked! So many people saw your honesty and your party's ideas as a way to finally make a difference, to get government working again. What will they think now?

Robinson: Kathryn, I knew my baseball career was over when two things happened. First, I couldn't hit the curve anymore, and soon after that, I couldn't hit the fastball. Unfortunately, from day one, I haven't been able to handle either the curves or the fastballs that come across the governor's desk. I'm just not built for politics, at least not the way the game is played in Illinois.

I'm not planning on riding off into the sunset, though. During the past four months, the time I most enjoyed was the two weeks I spent in Chicago with Avery Watkins defending our education platform. As repulsive as the Super PAC media campaign was to the cause of helping our kids, it helped me rediscover my passion. Avery and I will be forming a coalition to take the cause of Getting to 21 nationwide. Life's simply too short to spend four years being a square peg trying to fit into a round hole.

The other good news is that I have the utmost faith in the leadership of the E Party, especially Barb Jenkins who will succeed to the position of governor. Now that the uncertainty of the election is over, I'd like to think my getting out of the way will actually accelerate the pace by which Barb and the entire E Party leadership can put the state of Illinois on a path to greatness.

Collins: I assume the E Party leadership, as you call it, has their succession strategy all mapped out.

Robinson: Actually, no. The significant majority are hearing about my decision for the first time on your program. Or else they're getting bombarded by e-mails and tweets as we speak. I left the signed letter of resignation on my desk earlier, just before leaving for our interview. Effective July 1, Illinois will have a new governor.

CPSIA information can be obtained
at www.ICGtesting.com
Printed in the USA
FSOW02n0925150816
23662FS